BRUSH WITH THE LAW

THE TRUE STORY OF LAW SCHOOL TODAY
AT HARVARD AND STANFORD

Jaime Marquart
Robert Ebert Byrnes

RENAISSANCE BOOKS
Los Angeles

Library of Congress Cataloging-in-Publication Data
Marquart, Jaime
    Brush with the law : the true story of law school today at Harvard and
Stanford / Jaime Marquart, Robert Byrnes.
        p. cm.
    ISBN 1-58063-178-9
    1. Marquart, Jaime. 2. Byrnes, Robert (Robert Ebert). 3. Harvard Law School—
Students. 4. Stanford University. School of Law—Students. 5. Law students—
Massachusetts—Cambridge—Biography. 6. Law students—California—Stanford—
Biography. I. Byrnes, Robert (Robert Ebert). II. Title.
KF373.M293 A3 2001
340'.071'17444—dc21   2001019993

10 9 8 7 6 5 4 3 2 1

Design by Geoff Bock and Tanya Maiboroda

Published by Renaissance Books

Distributed by St. Martin's Press

Manufactured in the United States of America

First edition

dedicated to
our brothers, the smartest guys we know

INTRODUCTION

This book is divided into ten chronological parts. The chapters within those ten parts alternate between Jaime's story and Byrnes's story. At all times we are doing the same things—arriving at law school, taking our first exams—but at different law schools, one in Massachusetts, the other in California. Eventually, we meet.

All the events are real; some have been moved in time to conceal identities and organize the story. Dialogue is reconstructed from memory. Apart from Harvard Law School and Stanford Law School, the names of most places have been changed. With a few exceptions, the characters are composites. For example, no one person did all of the things Lucy Faar, Brian Green, or The Barrister did, but someone at one of our law schools did each thing they did. There's no law firm called Young & Mathers, but there's one just like it. The drug recipe is completely bogus. But all the verbs—smoked, spent, bet, screwed, flipped, ditched, flew, died, crashed, married—are true to their original actions. Which is to say everything in here really happened.

I would caution you to be somewhat circumspect about what you write, whether or not it's true. You may find yourselves to be very clever, but the value of your degrees—and that of every one else's—may be affected by what you write.

—an e-mail sent to www.brushwiththelaw.com from a Yale Law School graduate (name withheld)

PART 1 | **WHO WE ARE**

CHAPTER 1 | **MY OWN PRISON**

Dumb people do go to Harvard Law School.

Not just cheaters, crybabies, or hypercompetitive assholes, all of which are also in abundance at Harvard Law School. I mean dumb. Dense. Dinks. By the time I had the sense to understand that, and the courage to accept everything that went along with it, it was basically too late for me. I was already in the summer between my second and third year of law school, and getting ready to do a lot of dumb things myself. I was about to fall behind. Up to that point, I had always been ahead. Technically, you could say I started out behind—poor, undereducated, naive. But by the time it mattered, somewhere around first grade, I was leagues ahead. And stayed ahead. I got nary a B all the way through grade school and junior high. Then came high school and more of the same. When I was fifteen, I took the SAT, mainly to see what all the fuss was about. My score was 1110. Not great, but good enough for college. So a year later, when I was sixteen, I started college. I got all A's in college and started law school when I was twenty-one. A couple years after that, I looked up and there I was: twenty-three; in the summer before my final year at Harvard Law School; a $100,000-a-year job offer in hand; and a world-class fuck-up, two years in the making. Just as all the former fuck-ups were getting it together and starting their careers, I was treading air. Fittingly, it was then that I met Robert Byrnes, himself a former fuck-up on the rise and one of only two people I can honestly say understands my current situation, which is this:

Deep in my third and final year of law school, I am at a Foxwoods $100 blackjack table. It is 2:00 A.M. on a Friday. Anyone who was capable of leaving got out of here by 11:00. I didn't sit down until midnight. A Maker's Mark rests in my right hand. A stack of black and purple chips, which only hours before was a financial aid check, is in my left hand. Over either shoulder stands an extraordinarily plain woman who passes for gorgeous at family gatherings and at Harvard. Each watches and shares in the tension. The stack is now composed of twenty black chips and one purple chip, or $2,500. Not bad. Not bad, were it not for the fact that the financial aid check I cashed three hours earlier was written for $5,000. Twenty-five hundred bean—a full year's tuition my last year of college, my T-Bird's Blue Book in 1995, just before I shipped off to law school—all blown in two hours' time.

I've seen this situation enough times to know what will happen next. I'm not leaving the table until I've recouped my losses or lost it all. Or, I could win. It happens 48.5 percent of the time if you're on the up and up, or about 50.5 percent of the time if you are not. I am not.

Counting cards in blackjack is a lot like being a lawyer. You make money by exploiting the rules of a system. Technically, it's not cheating. That said, the whole system would crumble if everybody played it that way. But they don't and you do, so they lose and you win, and the flaws in the system persist. In theory.

In reality, it hardly matters. When you're only talking about a few hundred hands of blackjack, you just have to be lucky. And lately, I've been playing with scared money. Still, I approach my situation as any compulsive gambler would, hopefully. I'm just one good hand away from breaking even. Even so, there's nothing like gambling away the next couple months' worth of rent and food to make you wonder what the hell you're doing. As I push the rest of my stack into the circle in front of me and the pit boss phones upstairs for approval, I wonder aloud to myself and those around me, *How did I get here?*

Well, first things first. *Where* the hell am I? That I can answer. I am a third-year student in my last semester at Harvard Law School. I am losing large at Foxwoods' high-stakes blackjack table. Most of my classmates are getting ready for exams, which start in two weeks. I don't remember, off the top of my head, what classes I'm taking; I couldn't pick half of my professors out of a police lineup.

My situation is as dreary as it seems, but this blackjack hand has little to do with it. There's that law firm job waiting for me after I graduate. The financial aid check I'm about to blow can be replaced by another five grand, from my law firm, meant to help me study for the bar exam. I'll probably gamble that away, too, but I'll just cash advance more. Win or lose, I'll be OK. But one thing is certain, and pardon the tired old phrase: it is a long way from Eagle Lake, Texas, to where I sit now. I reflect on the distance I've traveled, remembering the essay that got me into Harvard Law School in the first place.

HARVARD LAW SCHOOL PERSONAL STATEMENT

Eagle Lake is a small Texas town with hardly a lake or an eagle. Surrounded by rice fields and old oil patches, its people work and live hard. My own beginnings are not unique in that world. I'd like, however, to share with you a bit of my experience there (far beyond all the objective measurements of entry, you ask to glimpse the man). My journey and becoming were rich in turmoil, chance, and unsolicited kindness, elements that can go a long way in creating good stories and personal strength.

I grew up in a single-parent household with one older brother. Possessing little education, my mother worked two, sometimes three jobs. Her efforts yielded never enough. I learned early not to ask for things I could do without (or could provide myself). Throughout a series of unsuccessful romances, my mother could not keep her emotional tides at bay and shared her pain with my brother and me. Lord knows I do not blame her, but worrying about the bills and our personal safety was a little more than most thirteen-year-olds could take. More than anything I hated the lack of control and daily unpredictability.

Today I marvel at the fine line that separates perseverance from surrender and wonder how close I was to giving up. Instead, I grew strong and learned early the joy that external order can bring to an unsure existence. Public school, with its rules and regulated peace, offered that order. Academically I thrived, but economic necessity required my early contribution. After part-time jobs mowing lawns and flopping burgers, I landed a job with a local farmer who also happened to run the town pharmacy (I call him a "farmercist"). I worked in the pharmacy during the school year and on the farm during breaks. Working the rice field from sun up to sun down, close to the earth and alone, I grew more sure of my thoughts and dreams.

At the age of sixteen I was unexpectedly given the opportunity to move on. Encouraged by teachers to take my last two years of high school at the Texas Academy of Mathematics and Science (TAMS) and supported by a scholarship from the farmercist's friend, I enrolled at the University of North Texas. At TAMS, I gained college credits while I completed high school. Much of the friction in my environment was absent and I learned and grew as never before. I truly believe my success there was a gift of those early struggles. It just seemed so easy compared to what I had to worry about at home. I had the time of my life, graduating first in my class and being voted Most Likely to Succeed. The rest of my college career has been as smooth. Supported still by the scholarship of those in Eagle Lake and my own year-round employment, I will graduate from the University of Texas at Austin in May with highest honors.

Daily and deep down inside I revel in these small successive steps toward building a fulfilling life and look forward always to the continuing journey. I return often to Eagle Lake to see my mother, family, and friends. Their lives seem better, calmer, even happy; the town still quiet and unchanging. I've been luckier than most and appreciate what I learned there, the value of hard work, the wide variety of personal and emotional choices available to any one individual, and the inner effort and faith required to endure and succeed. All this I carry as I move on.

Jaime Marquart 1/2/95

As the pit boss gets the OK from upstairs, I am awakened by two excited feminine taps on my shoulder. The pit boss nods to the dealer. The game will continue. Having consoled myself with the promise of certain financial freedom and congratulated myself for my risk-perverse spontaneity, I take the hand with ease.

Reality intervenes again. I am holding a queen and a five. Fifteen. Blackjack's second-worst hand. The dealer is showing a ten.

I am reminded of why blackjack is a losing proposition. The essence of the House's edge can be summarized in one statement: When you both bust, they win, and you have to go first. Because the dealer has a ten showing, the chances are good that he will have a total of seventeen or higher, and he won't have to take another card. If that's the case, I lose with fifteen. So I have to hit. But, if I take another card, the chances are that I will bust. Then, only then, I might find out the dealer really had a five under his ten all along, that he would have busted, and that I could have won by standing on fifteen. But by then he will have already taken my money.

Either way, I'll probably lose—a fitting outcome given the events of the last three days. For all the drama around me, I don't particularly care if I win or lose. But it wasn't always like this.

The day I was accepted into Harvard Law School was the day I decided to go to Harvard Law School. By the time that big packet with return address Cambridge, Massachusetts, found its way to my door, I'd already arranged for housing and had a roommate at the University of Texas Law School in Austin. I was raised with my hands in the earth, not one hundred miles from the forty acres that make up UT. I'd never lived outside of Texas and saw no reason to leave. I only applied to Harvard on a whim, more or less out of curiosity. And I didn't even have enough money to visit Harvard before deciding whether to go. But a packet that big could only mean one thing. Only one thing to do, too. It was like my brother said, "You get into Harvard, you go."

I would go to Harvard, site unseen, almost by reflex, on faith. I would be leaving behind Elise, the only girl I'd ever loved, a decision that would have been impossible had it not already been made for me. A few days after I'd said good-bye to Elise and headed to Harvard, she was on a plane to Spain for a year abroad. Spain and Harvard or Spain and Texas. It made little difference.

Elise and I knew distance might take some toll, but who could blame either of us for being confident about our prospects. From the time I was

seventeen, I had been in love with Elise. She was there from the beginning, at the creation of me. Elise taught me not to scoff as I had at those
who speak of "becoming one." We had. And as I watched her drift into the
distance, I finally understood everything that meant. I could never separate
my feelings from hers, my self-image from her image of me. The only way
to understand that sort of simultaneous fear and hope is to experience it.
I hope you have.

Back then, I ignored fear and focused on hope. Harvard Law School
lasts three years—three long, solitary, rigorous years, from everything I'd
heard. But that wasn't how I looked at it, as I leapt blindly into a foreign
world with Elise jetting thousands of miles toward another continent. Fortunately, law school broke down neatly into smaller chunks.

Most of the action is in the first year of law school, especially the first
semester. The goal during the first semester of law school is the same as
mine and Elise's had been all along: to last. For the first couple of months,
lasting would mean fitting in socially, holding up under Harvard's humil-
iation-driven teaching methods, and keeping up with intense reading
requirements. For me, it would also mean sparsely allocated phone calls
and daily e-mails to Spain until the end of the semester, my first chance to
see Elise. Ultimately, lasting would mean getting a passing grade on each
of my final exams at the end of the semester. Those final exams would be
my only measure of success or failure; at Harvard Law School, there are no
midterms, no homework grades, and no extra credit.

After a brief respite with Elise in January would come one more
semester of the same. For those in the top 5 to 10 percent of the class, the
goal would then be a U.S. Supreme Court clerkship or teaching law further
down the line. That would require getting onto *Law Review* (Harvard's
highbrow legal periodical) at the end of the first year, getting good grades
the rest of the way out, and making nice with an egomaniacal and well-
connected professor or two. Like most of my classmates, I never entertained those notions. Instead, my focus after that first year would shift to
working for the first time in a law firm, where Elise and I would be together
again for an entire summer, probably somewhere in Texas. After that, I
figured the worst would be behind me. Elise would be back in the States
during my last two years. The only remaining challenges would be with-
standing more of the same in class, writing a thesis, and getting a job,
preferably one wherever Elise was. And then, the rest of our lives.

I knew that three years in law school would bring its challenges, but I had faith that the Bigger Things would always survive any man-made obstacles. From the beginning, I had been taught that strange mixture of reverence, fear, and comfort the Bigger Things offer. Religion continues to occupy a mighty role in the day-to-day lives of Eagle Lake's 3,551. If you're not from around those parts, you may not completely get what I'm saying. I'm not talking about just saying you believe, or going to church on Christmas Eve and Easter, or christening your babies. None of that Pascal's wager, what-could-it-hurt-to-believe bullshit, either. I grew up among high-octane, ten-gallon-hat *believers*. In my world, it was natural to hear voices and see spirits. Whether you were crazy or enlightened depended on who the voice was and what it was telling you. For 99 percent of us, the voice was Christ. And the message: You are most likely going to Hell. I was one of the 99 percent, full of all the piousness and the pain. Like every other institution I've entered into, I took religion seriously. I mean, if you're faking it, the omniscient Creator is probably onto you. So, I figured, why fake it?

And it didn't hurt that Satan himself paid me a visit. Sometime in the summer, when I was three, I sat on the kitchen counter helping my mom wash the dishes. I was the dryer. The phone rang. I answered, my favorite thing to do back then:

"Hewo . . ." I must have said.

"Jai-meeee!" growled the otherworldly voice on the other end of the line. "This is the Devil. I'm coming to get you tonight."

For a perpetual inferno, back in the days before cellular phones and fiber optics, Hell had pretty good reception. You might have thought the call had come from the other room. I dropped the phone and began to scream. Then I cried. Then I screamed some more. My mother took me into her arms and rocked me, asking what was the matter. My eight-year-old brother rushed in from the other room, panic-stricken himself. He didn't ask what was the matter.

I couldn't sleep in my own bed for months. Despite my family's attempts to convince me that it was actually my brother Jeff doing his best Satan impersonation on the other line, they couldn't fool me. I knew what he sounded like, and that was no Jeff. That was no *human*. They hadn't heard the voice. Eventually I was able to sleep in my own bed again, but for a year or so after that I prayed for forgiveness every time I colored outside the lines or left a skid mark in my Fruit of the Looms. I was a serious little boy.

As I grew older, fear and guilt gave way to calm and perspective. With education, my faith had undergone many evolutions. I was not the Bible-thumping, hellfire-and-brimstone Baptist my mother raised. But my spirituality remained one of the most quotable sources of my success. To borrow a phrase from my law school entrance essay, which I admittedly lifted from Tim O'Brien, all this I carried as I moved on.

And why law school to begin with? I can finally answer that honestly. I did well in college, didn't like the jobs (translated, the money) available to me at the time, and thought law school was a great chance to put off any important career decisions for three years. Best of all, I'd make a hell of a lot more money when I got out. All of this proved to be true. In an IPO-happy, dynamic dot-com world, law school and the law remain holdouts to the static and predictable. No Bill Gates wealth possible; but no Bill Gates risk either. Just guaranteed, $200-an-hour freedom. Modest comforts, maybe, but modest comforts had been elusive in my life. First, though, you have to get in.

You apply to law school on the basis of your college grades, your score on the Law School Admission Test (LSAT), and, to a lesser extent, recommendations and a "personal statement" (you just read mine). As far as these basics go, Harvard is the same as all the rest. But when it comes to actually getting in, Harvard is unlike almost any other. Of the 100,000 people a year who take the LSAT, 8,000 apply to Harvard. Only 800 get in. Among those 800, the median college grade point average is 3.8 (lower than an A, higher than an A–). The average LSAT score is at the 97th percentile (which means you did better than all but 3 percent of the people who took the test). Of the 800 who get in, 550 go. The 250 who get into Harvard but don't go there go to Stanford or Yale. Or they don't go at all.

All of this makes it really hard to believe that dumb people go to Harvard. Well, they do. There are only a few different ways to get into Harvard, but there are a lot more ways to be dumb.

For those who do make it to Harvard—good year or bad year, recession or boom—there's always an armful of law firms clamoring to pay Harvard *students* $20,000 during the summers between years in law school for the privilege of buying them fancy meals and throwing them extravagant parties, kissing their asses on a daily basis, and shielding them from the job's grindingly mechanical realities. It's called being a "summer associate." Why do law firms do this? So they can pay you $150,000 a year when you graduate and become a law firm "associate." It sounds like a ridiculous amount of money, but for the law firms, it's a lock. They pay you $150,000, but you bill 2,200 hours (about 45 a week, working a lot more), with the law firm billing those hours to their clients at $200 a pop. So they shell out the hundred-and-a-half grand to you, but make about $300,000 on the margin—or more, if you work more, and a lot of people do.

Just like getting into law school, all of this happens without the law firms ever considering whether you know anything about the law. In fact, if you graduated from Harvard, chances are you don't know anything about the law. But chances also are you're pretty goddamned good at faking it and figuring it out later. The firms know this, but they don't give a crap. Their customers want Harvard. It's a proxy for being a good lawyer, which is something that usually doesn't matter and basically doesn't even exist in day-to-day law practice. Being a big-firm lawyer is like playing tic-tac-toe; hard to lose and hard to win against a competent opponent. Harvard is the comfort of competence, a minimal competence: the ability to avoid bone-headed blunders and play to the expected draw.

So that's my take on why people go to Harvard, or most law schools, for that matter. A Harvard law degree is a blank check written on every developed market in the world, the ultimate get-out-of-jail-free card, the soft fallback, the master-key door opener. You can shelve all of that Save-the-World sentiment for your entrance essays, campaign speeches, and TV interviews. People go to Harvard for the same reason Willie Sutton robbed banks—because that's where the money is. At least that's why I went.

But that doesn't have a thing to do with how I went from the hopeful twenty-year-old in my personal statement to the bitter twenty-four-year-old sitting at Foxwoods who just bet a student loan on a hand of blackjack. *How did I get here?* I'm still not sure, but I know the answer has everything to do with going off to law school.

CHAPTER 2 | **WHY, LAW SCHOOL**

Where I am now—California, married, bike messenger, lawyer, coauthor of this book—has everything to do with going off to law school. I'd do it again.

Why go to law school in the first place? A lot of reasons, for me:

1. Got in.
2. Needed a change.
3. Nothing better to do.
4. California.
5. Live off loans.
6. Bought the myth.
7. Told hometown, "I'm going to law school."
8. College girlfriend said, "Go."
9. Chain of fate: A happened so B happened, then C and D and, therefore, law school happened.

I kept saying I'd go to law school. Answering *law school* dispatched that annoying question: *what do you want to do when you grow up?* For a time, I wanted to be a magician, the only thing I'd done well or with any care, apart from my driving test, before the age of seventeen. I made money performing at birthday parties. And in competitions I'd placed well enough that the local newspaper headlined, with some hyperbole: *Young Durham Magician Wins National Acclaim*. Despite this validation, adults never regarded my long-range magician aspirations as anything but fantasy.

Law school, though, had a plausibility and a scholarly sheen that seemed to please the hometown power elite. So I repeatedly announced that I would be the first in my family to go to law school and, by implication, to college.

My parents weren't the ones bugging me about my future. They didn't set many rules, in fact. When I was five, they did drag me to church. I thought it was bunk and never went again—my decision. I liked my parents and had a pretty happy time growing up, so this isn't going to be one of those stories about childhood phantoms making for a screwed-up adult. If I'd told my parents that when I grew up I wanted to be a bike messenger, they would have replied, "If that's what you like." They would have meant it, too. Like I said, though, they never really asked.

Others asked. We lived in a college town. Most of my friends' parents were professors. My high school didn't much care about you unless you were aiming to go to Harvard or Stanford or Brown or Dartmouth, the only out-of-town colleges I could name as a kid. Teachers and friends' parents asked. And I told them: law school, not quite clear on the point that college and law school are separate things. Knowing nothing of personal statements or the LSAT, I figured that when the time came you just got in the car, headed south on Interstate 95, and signed up for Harvard Law School. Keep in mind that all my early law school information came from a movie.

When I was eight, my parents took me to see *The Paper Chase*. I wasn't the sort of kid who tinkered and took things apart. Content to be dazzled by myths, machines, and movies, I walked out of *The Paper Chase* with the feeling that law school was a secular temple, an ascetic ordeal that promised a close brush with transcendence if you worked your ass off and survived. The hard work and survival part didn't appeal to me. We're all looking for Big Truth, though. And to me, law school, not church, seemed the place to find it. So whenever older people asked, I resorted to *The Paper Chase* answer, *"Law school."* When I was fourteen, the local newspaper reporter asked what I might do if my career as a professional magician fizzled (and it did; I was about to stop winning "national acclaim"). I told her: *law school*. Not that I meant it. It was just a better answer than the vapid truth: *I don't know; nothing*. I was all for finding truth and meaning, but not at all keen on having a job, which I gathered was what happened after law school. Still, I kept saying I'd go, sometimes symbolically. When I was sixteen, my grandfather died. He had asked that his grandchildren give tokens of themselves to be buried with him. I stole two noncirculating copies of the *Yale Law Journal* from the University of New Hampshire library and submitted them to be interred with my grandfather, an attempted channeling of my promising future at a time when I was in fact an extreme fuck-up, wobbling near expulsion from high school.

I'd flunked a lot of classes, so many that I was declared "academically ineligible" for the baseball team, though I just kept playing, and no one bothered to yank me off the field on account of grades. It wasn't until I was accused (accurately) of adding bogus entries to the Latin teacher's grade book that things took a bad turn. During baseball practice, I saw the principal strolling my way, and I knew why even before he said, "Coach, may I borrow your second baseman." *Borrow* was a euphemism for *boot out of school*.

It turned out there were plenty of crummy high schools for people like me. At my second high school, for reasons I'll come to later, I was a stunningly *good*, and impeccably behaved, student. So a few years after the hometown guidance counselors had nudged me to "consider noncollege options," I was in college, which is just about life's happiest and easiest stretch; so much so that I stayed around for a fifth year. I finished college, and by law school's twin admission pillars I was mediocre yet viable at the ultra-swank schools: 3.8 GPA and the 96th percentile on the LSAT, both about average at places like Stanford and Harvard.

I was going to law school—just not yet.

The day after college graduation, I slipped back into the hometown to beat a filing deadline for political candidates. My first post-college "job": running for New Hampshire state representative. The leap into politics wasn't entirely on the level. That running for office was so blazingly ambitious and commendably mainstream concealed my true objective, which was the same as stoner friends who followed the Grateful Dead that summer: slacking and job avoiding. I campaigned door-to-door on a bike, put in a woeful televised debate performance, had bumper stickers, mailing lists, yard signs, and sloganeering sweatshirts ("Hard Headed & Soft Hearted").

The year was 1988. Michael Dukakis was running for president. We both lost by spacious margins.

After the election I split Durham, New Hampshire, more or less for good. An hour south, I found my all-time favorite job avoider: two years at the John F. Kennedy School of Government. Getting a soft master's degree there was a license to do nothing, remain unbound to a profession, and answer the *what are you doing* question with the assertion, technically true, that you "go to Harvard." As graduate school wound down, law school or a dreary job seemed the only option. Then one afternoon, in Harvard Square, I saw a bike messenger. He was going faster than the traffic, his messenger bag bent around a junkie-thin, agile body. If you stumble upon romantic destiny twice in a lifetime—job, love—all that remains of a day is deep sleep and sweet dreams. I'd found job destiny. The next morning, I became a bike messenger.

The taking things from here to there, fast and full of risk, made sense, happened outdoors, and involved constant motion. There's no subtext to being a bike messenger; no such thing as ass-kissing or face-time; no office in which to politic. Riding, I had no regrets, no future plans, just a persistent physical tingle and the uncomplicated assurance that the job had been done correctly so long as the package got there, fast. I existed happily in the present. As I whipped through Boston, though, a slice of my future did glide in front of me. On a State House delivery dash, I glimpsed the recently elected Massachusetts governor, Bill Weld. I couldn't have known that one day, and soon, he would turn to me and say, about being a bike messenger, "Probably the best job you'll ever have."

He was right. Life apart from biking was also on a fast course. Helen and I had met in graduate school. *Helen.* My first instinct is to attempt a Joycean catalogue—exactly how and where we met, the ice cream and music we shared, the astonishing succession of coincidental feelings. But we've all had a Helen. The best way I've heard it put is: she was there at the creation of me. Which means true Genesis didn't happen until well into my twenties. That late creation was a reconciliation of opposites, simple enough in theory. To some people I was forever the lazy high school burnout. To others I was the bookish young man who got A's at tony universities. Only to Helen was I both. Helen and I celebrated my integration with ceaseless sex; several hundred times during our year together, and just once substandard— a lone, clumsy morning romp, we both agreed.

So when Helen took a teaching job at Yale and moved to New Haven, I went with her despite having to quit as a bike messenger. We adopted a shelter cat, Zoë. When Helen applied for a teaching job at Stanford, I applied to Stanford Law School. My application essay was a rambling bike messenger story set around a post-delivery elevator ride with (yet another Massachusetts governor) the recently deposed Michael Dukakis. The essay suggested that going *down* in the elevator symbolized our broader fates. He had fallen from presidential nominee to just another lawyer; I'd made the social plummet from plucky young political candidate to bike messenger. Law school, the essay proposed, would send me back into ascent. Helen read it and said:

"It's pretty obvious you adore being a bike messenger and have nothing but contempt for the suit-wearing office dwellers. Don't worry. I won't go to California without you."

Helen had a point. Stanford Law School wait-listed me.

It didn't matter. Weird fate intervened when Helen was visiting her family in Chicago. Alone in her apartment one December afternoon in 1991, I picked up the ringing telephone. That phone call was the trip wire to every important thing that has happened to me since. It was a call for Helen, her graduate school professor confirming he'd recommended Helen for the Stanford teaching job. Had I been anywhere but Helen's place that afternoon, I might still be at Helen's place; probably never would have gone to law school, certainly not where I went; definitely never would have taken, or even known about, the job that fell upon me by pure chance. The caller had also been my graduate school professor. Though we barely knew each other, the conversation branched off his original topic. He mentioned that Bill Weld needed a speechwriter. Maybe I'd be interested?

I saw the speechwriting job as a chance for a lot of life to be thrown my way. Helen returned from Chicago and I headed back to Boston. Then there was the slow fade between us, rich in details but too common to bother documenting. Not long after I resettled back in Boston, Helen and I vanished from each other's tangible lives.

Narrowly elected governor in 1990, Bill Weld stood "to the right of Attila the Hun" on crime and to the left of Bill Clinton on affirmative action. He was a gun lover who frequented Dead concerts. He picked polar and unpopular enemies like Jesse Helms and Mike Dukakis. The challenge for a Weld speechwriter was writing the occasional phrase that maintained his "thoughtful" yet "quirky" reputation. During my job interview he asked:

"You drink?"

Unable to decide which way to take my answer, I defaulted to the truth.

"Good!" Weld said. "Don't want any teetotalers in this administration."

I came to the job tattooed, pierced, in favor of gay rights and abortion, against taxes and wary of statist authority. That fit with Weld's own iconoclasm: Republican frugality without the Rotarian cant. We differed only over his punitive shittiness toward welfare recipients and fairly extreme environmentalist bent. Back then, I didn't give a toss what became of the Earth; might as well pave it over and make one big city.

With the speechwriting job came the usual advantages of being in the orbit of a sort-of-famous person. My compatriot was Niccola Renton. Niccola and I were on the younger end of those who attended Weld's morning staff meetings. A lot of guys around Boston will tell you their best fuck ever was the first time with Niccola. Their worst, however, was the second; and there rarely was a third time. Although we were just Weld's entourage, not the main event, Niccola and I acquired our own entourage. Our positions filled us with a blithe arrogance that made me and Niccola irresistible to those with crap jobs and crimped lives.

I had a good job. I could write a fifteen-minute speech in half an hour, which meant my day was generally wrapped before noon. Occasionally, emergency struck. One afternoon as I played darts at Drumlin's Pub in Cambridge, Weld's secretary phoned and summoned me back to the State House. Weld needed a speech for the next morning, to be delivered at the First Circuit Judicial Conference. Topic: the law.

"Teddy Kennedy's speech to the judges sounded like Cicero," Weld told me. "So make mine a corker." As I was leaving his office he added: "By the way, Byrnes, the people's governor is sitting in the bleachers at Fenway tonight."

I went to the ball game, and then into the night with Niccola. We began at her Beacon Hill townhouse, sipping a grainy mushroom tea as I composed the next day's speech in my mind. Then we headed out and claimed our Boston prerogative—queue cutting, saved tables, secret rooms. The last stop was a Harvard Square bar that allowed us a special dispensation to smoke pot on their premises. Niccola and I drifted separately. I played darts. She started a conversation with two youngish women and their male friend. Although we were formally regarded as a couple, Niccola and I didn't observe monogamous confines. On her way out, Niccola said to me:

"My work is done. Those two girls are quite curious to meet you. And I'm taking the boy home with me. Edgar. He's the pretty one's brother. Sweet little thing. But kind of tense. He could use a screw."

So that night I fell in with two members of Weld's most admiring constituency—not soccer moms, but their daughters. These two Radcliffe sophomores weren't alone in finding the red-haired governor "strangely sexy" and transferring their idolatry onto me. Rather than go back to my tiny apartment, we headed into the State House, drank Jack Daniels, rolled naked about the oval "cabinet meeting" table, and then looked up to see a uniformed cleaning woman standing in the governor's office doorway. She asked what the hell we were doing there at 4:00 A.M. I stood and said, to the cleaning woman, then, minutes later, to her supervisor, then, more minutes later, to a state trooper—*It's me, Robert Byrnes*—preposterous words only as effective as the twisted faith to speak them. It worked. The state trooper put an end to the interruptions. We resumed. Although the Radcliffe sophomores wanted to have a full sleepover in the executive chambers, I did know a bad idea when I heard one. The scene was already getting dodgy before the cleaning woman showed up. Sitting at Weld's desk, my new friends had started reviewing pending legislation, to be signed or vetoed the next day. Having crossed so many ultimate rule boundaries in my younger days, I'd developed a prudent quitter's instinct. It was time to clear out of the State House and go to my apartment, three to a futon. I waited for my new friends to fall asleep before sneaking out to catch an hour of rest on the State House lawn, Boston Common side, then heading for a bike ride at sunrise, and then to my office to write Weld's Judicial Conference speech on a mercifully broad topic: the law.

This speech was more demanding than the usual ribbon-cutting exhortation. The audience would be predominantly judges and lawyers, all of whom thought themselves smart, many of whom actually were. I plopped in a weighty John Rawls reference; then scrawled a few straw man slashes at law school radicals throughout a fatuous and barely long-enough speech on the importance of justice being administered fairly and speedily. Weld read it on the way there, crossing out a Bob Dylan passage about white-collar criminals that worked better in song than oratory. The speech was now too short. Weld asked his driver to pull over halfway to the Judicial Conference, on jammed Newbury Street, where we finished writing the speech. A bike messenger carved around our car. Weld turned to me and said what he said about it being the best job. "They have...an obvious freedom," he added.

We made it to the Judicial Conference on time and Weld spoke. The after-speech chatter and handshaking gave no indication that these learned jurists heard the speech for the piece of slapdash crap it was. Then, I dropped into worry. Bouncing toward us: Stephen Breyer, at the time a First Circuit judge. Weld was occupied. His advance man didn't know Breyer from Montgomery Burns. So I intercepted and greeted Breyer.

"What a splendid speech," Breyer said. "I loved the Rawls."

On the ride back to the State House, Weld turned to me and said, with the same twinkle that endeared him to Massachusetts voters:

"We skated on that one."

Working for Weld was all scam and skating. I did hear from Helen one last time. She clipped and mailed me a copy of a *Boston Globe* article that said I was writing some "visionary" speech. She attached a note: "here's wishing you vision." I never responded.

Vision and clarity were confined to a morning bike ride at the Charles River's edge. Being a bike messenger had addicted me to riding—a healthy, cleansing addiction, fixing damage done the nights before. I'd be out my door as the sun was rising and roll back up Beacon Hill at a quarter-to-nine; shower; cross the street; wind through the State House's disjointed labyrinth and breeze past the security detail, into the governor's office for the 9:00 A.M. staff meeting. Sometimes a punch of coke, en route, would snap me into a functional way. Weld ran a loose, hands-off operation. For everyone at the morning meeting, even those without formal policy-making roles, there was an open invitation to weigh in on any issue. I never did, not a single time.

I was always somewhere else, past or future—recalling the night before, envisioning the next night, the next place, after Boston and after politics. I'd get Helen flickers, but before they caught fire there Niccola would be with the next adventure. Distraction crowded out regret. When there's a lot of action, there's no need to preserve, revive, or grab on to something lasting.

By my third year, though, when Weld won reelection with a thumping 70 percent of the vote, the action was going stale. On that suspenseless election day in 1994, I sent off a second application to Stanford Law School, this time with a vague but optimistic essay[1] that gave the appearance I had one foot in the door, out of the bike messenger gutter. The essay made no mention of law school. I had my reasons for applying. Those reasons just didn't have much to do with law school. Laying out the truth would have gotten me rejected. The truth: I was bored, and my speeches were becoming bad, like the Judicial Conference one, and sometimes fatally bad, like the health care speech that not only failed to capture the controversies around managed care, but read as if I didn't know there was such a thing as managed care. Or, to bring it back to that entirely representative day in the life . . . It is a funny story, I suppose, to have been dragooned from a bar by the governor of the Commonwealth. But after it happens many, many times, it goes generic.

The same goes for drugs. When you wake up and barf into the *Globe* sports section, just trying to start your day like the next guy, there you are. You are the next guy.

And the zany sex always degraded into conventional recrimination. Having exhausted the passion between ourselves, Niccola and I became arrangers and administrators of others' passions. A corrosive pattern emerged, typified by those two Radcliffe sophomores who wanted to sleep in the corner office. One did become my girlfriend, whatever the hell that meant. And Niccola gave in to Edgar's push to "make a commitment." Soon, however, they no longer found us irresistible. I was chastised for not "sending flowers" on Valentine's Day. Edgar "intervened" when he judged Niccola's eating to be disordered. Edgar also confided to me his opposing fears: that the incendiary energy between him and Niccola might not last forever, but that if things did stay so sleeplessly hot it might imperil his chances of being admitted to Harvard Law School. Either Niccola and I had been misunderstood or we had become rescue fantasies. Whichever, we cut them loose, "broke up," and I think they truly missed us, because they called and cried, and we stopped taking the calls or maybe just drifted away, without bothering to say why; hard to say, hard to care or remember.

---

1. It's on pages 99 and 100.

I'd had enough—of everyone having fucked everyone else to the point that whatever old-world preciousness remains in romance was wilted dead in Boston.

Before I left Boston there was one failed grab at the glimmer of something lasting. Dawn. She worked around the governor's office; not, as I thought, as an intern; but she was making money, paying her way through college. If I told you I might have married her, right there, on faith, you wouldn't believe me. So I'll just say she made me want to have a kiss and a conversation. She was a nose-pierced, biker-jacketed cross between my high school music heroes, Patti Smith and Chrissie Hynde. There's not a great deal to say, because Dawn and I barely spoke. I was enchanted just gazing at her, which I did, a lot, manufacturing chances to linger near and watch her exist as she clipped, copied, and distributed newspaper articles about the Weld administration. Looks-driven attraction is accorded a certain shallowness. But I don't think so. Though this was a time of serial lust and disposable people, Dawn inspired me toward preservation and permanence. She snapped me into the present tense, as only biking did, and as Helen had, too, for a time. Dawn gave off a stoic energy—she was reserved but not cold—and seemed somehow destined to give me the shove that would set me straight for good. She was poised, quietly at ease; one of those people fortunate to have known herself instinctively at a young age.

Once, I did introduce Dawn to Niccola, to lay the foundation that I was both sexually viable and straight. A flawed strategy, it went nowhere.

"So what are your career plans?" Niccola asked Dawn. "Maybe cash in on all the connections you've made?" It was about the dullest and most tight-ass thing I ever heard Niccola say. I often neglected to notice the ways in which she was utterly not my type—blonde, suburban-rich, ambitious.

Dawn said something in response. I don't remember what, nor does either Dawn or Niccola. It may have been a simple "No." Dawn was spare with words.

And for me, no kiss, no more conversation. Dawn's work-study soon ended. She headed back for a last round of finals at Harvard and stopped turning up at the State House.

It was time for me to go, too. I told Weld. His farewell words: "Have a long, strange trip."

The departure from Boston to law school really came by increments. I told Niccola:

"I'm leaving Boston."

"Why?"

A few weeks later I told her:

"You know why."

And she did, so she said:

"To where?"

"Far away," I said, thinking that took care of it.

"What are you gonna do?"

And because I had to "do something" for the same reasons most people do, I needed an answer, but I hadn't thought it out, and nothing fresh or unfamiliar occurred to me, so I reverted to my standard answer.

This time, though, I meant it.

WELD-CELLUCCI WORDSMITH
IS CYCLING OFF TO LAW SCHOOL

Gov. Weld and Lt. Gov. Cellucci are losing the services of one of their more iconoclastic phrasemakers come the end of this week. Robert Byrnes, a bicycle messenger turned gubernatorial speechwriter, is headed off to Stanford Law School. Byrnes, 31, recently persuaded Weld to utter what became his most bizarre Weldism of the year—when he declared at budget-signing time that Cellucci was "itching to slide down the Batpole and put on his government-cutting cape." His $47,000 post remains unspoken for, although word is Weld wants someone with Washington chops to replace Byrnes.

The Boston Globe 8/27/95

PART 2 | **GOING TO LAW SCHOOL**

CHAPTER 3 | **HAPPY TO BE THERE**

Call it appropriate, prophetic, or absurd, but the first thing I remember about arriving at Harvard was its facade. Coming from Any Old Place, America, I was a little too enchanted with the red-brick-as-far-as-the-eye-could-see, the black iron gates, the Weld Boat House, the picturesque banks of the Charles River, and, of course, Harvard Yard. Walking through the Yard for the first time, I figured out why I got into Harvard, despite an LSAT score (165, 93rd percentile) that was three points below Harvard's average and a "vocational" degree from a state school. Harvard chose me for the same reason God created man.

Despite my teacher's warnings about using logic to explain the Almighty, I spent way too much time in Sunday School wondering why God bothered to create us. I always figured He did it for one reason. It's lonely at the top. Even God needs a reference point, and mankind gave measure to His greatness. A rich kid I knew from Sunday School, Jonathan Thatcher III, operated under the same principle when he invited me over to use his swimming pool and tennis court. Thatcher III was no longer capable of enjoying all of his possessions on his own, but he re-experienced their coolness when he saw me playing with them.

Like a deity, or a rich kid with too many toys to appreciate all of them, Harvard nursed its spectral loneliness by including in its class a few ever-so-slightly inferior people, like me, who would look up at its true inhabitants and experience its (and their) greatness. These inferior types weren't necessarily supposed to belong, at least not in the beginning. And when they finally did feel like they belonged, they might have a good laugh at the fear and reverence with which they first greeted the place. But they would never be able to stroll through Harvard Yard or dust off the Latin sheepskin on the wall of their office without pausing to smile. And that gave measure to Harvard's greatness.

Or maybe my type wasn't ever supposed to belong. I wasn't sure, and I didn't care. I was happy to be there. And they knew it. As I stepped out of Harvard Yard and onto the law school campus, I remember thinking that nothing could kill my buzz. Then I saw Gropius.

Contrary to its name, the Gropius Complex is not a disease of the mind. Yet it always engenders the same *state* of mind in its visitors. Visitors to Langdell Hall (the immaculate World's Biggest Law Library) or Austin Hall (Harvard Law's gothic, timeless lecture hall) inevitably feel a sense of awe and reverence, a connection to Harvard's past. Visitors to the Gropius Complex feel functional. Nothing more, nothing less. While Austin and Langdell are renowned for their adornments—carved stonework, mahogany, patinaed copper trimmings—the Gropius Complex is defined by what it lacks. The Gropius Complex has nothing it does not absolutely need. It is also the place where most of Harvard Law's first-year students, the One Ls, live.

The Gropius Complex was designed sometime around 1950 by a famous architect named Walter Gropius. I think his passion was function over form. Or form follows function. Whatever. The Gropius buildings are composed of nothing more than four walls joined to themselves and a flat roof, all at perfect right angles. In fact, there are no acute or obtuse angles inside or outside any of its residence halls, which are in a square configuration. Any columns exist solely for the support of the structure and consist of perfect steel and cement cylinders, unadorned.

Gropius Room, Plan 1 (Basic): 120 feet square, consisting of one bed, 21 feet square, one desk, 10 feet square, one closet, 14 feet square. Remaining living space, 75 feet square. Bathroom, down

the hall or up the stairs and down the hall (depending on sex).
No sink. One trash can.

In fifteen minutes I was unpacked in my Gropius room. Natalie Merchant's *Tigerlily* was spinning on the ROM; *Beavis and Butthead* reruns were on the tube. I plugged in my phone, not expecting a dial tone. It was there. A piece of the familiar was touch tones away. I hung up. Elise and I had imposed a strict schedule of phone calls between Massachusetts and Spain, and we were three days away from the first call. In a couple of years, an influx of 10-10 companies would come on the scene, making possible pennies-a-minute international phone calls. But in 1995, a ten-minute phone call to Spain was more than ten bucks, if there even is such a thing as a ten-minute phone call between two lovers separated by thousands of miles of ocean. I put the phone down. My first class, Introduction to Legal Studies, would begin tomorrow.

CHAPTER 4 | GOING TO CALIFORNIA

Near the end of my Boston speechwriter days, I crossed paths with Alan Dershowitz. He asked me: why law school? I told Dershowitz I was going to law school for the rigor and the solitude. The idea was to dry out, slow down, and convert to the ascetic law school way. Mr. Hart could barely manage both law school and a sex life in *The Paper Chase*. It was "work, work, work" according to Scott Turow in *One L*. Given a true choice, I would have opted for three years on a full-service yoga ranch. I didn't have that choice. I needed to find my jobless retreat and solitude in a place where federally subsidized student loans bankrolled me. Law school would do. With his stentorian boom, Dershowitz told me:

"THAT IS THE WORST REASON I HAVE EVER HEARD FOR GOING TO LAW SCHOOL."

When I got to Stanford, I did try to exist spare and light. I lived alone, in a dorm room. I had no television, no car—only a bike—no governor to part the seas, no VIP room at the DMV, and just a Walkman, no stereo. Most of my stuff (music, books) was back in Boston, with Niccola. I imposed a draconian spending rule: one twenty-dollar bill per week.

The music situation was instantly intolerable. That set me in motion. I rode my bike from the Leland Memorial Hall dorm, at the center of Stanford's campus, down El Camino Real to Fry's Electronics, where I bought a low-end stereo and two CDs. On the way back to Leland, I picked up a jug of Jack Daniel's, a Boston holdover. So much of it had been stocked in the private bathroom adjacent to the governor's office that all the bottles I'd lifted during my three years in public service went unnoticed. The Massachusetts State House had been both my personal cut-rate liquor mart and palatial nocturnal retreat. Now, Leland Hall was my home. The only amenity in Leland rooms was a sink.

The stereo wires connected, Pink Floyd and Natalie Merchant set on perpetual repeat, I unpacked the one delicate possession I'd brought to law school, a glass Graffix bong. I'd also flown from Boston with a good ounce of very good pot after Blaine McKisco, who worked in Weld's legal office, calmed my fears of doing federal time for carrying drugs interstate. It turns out the long, mandatory, federal sentences for small drug amounts that are nonetheless considered "dealing quantities" are for crack and acid, not weed.

Law school's defining elements, therefore, during the first two weeks, before classes began: being endlessly baked, listening to the same 150 minutes of music, throwing back Jack Daniels to sleep, waking up at noon, and going for a bike ride. After the rides, I propped myself toward the sun and read Richard Powers's *Galatea 2.2*, a book about lost pasts. In the lonelier passages, Niccola and I spent hours on the phone as I avoided the orienting get-togethers for Stanford's new One Ls.

I had stepped neither fully out of my prior life, nor at all into the new one. Away from Boston, there was nothing to grab on to. California loomed with a natural bigness, more menacing than protective. I believed the Pacific actually *looked* larger than the Atlantic. Early attempts to find harmony with nature were a failure. I misplayed the weather every day, loading up with too many heavy clothes, before learning September's morning clouds would always dissolve by noon. Nor did bike rides give the satisfaction they had in Boston. Palo Alto proper is a flat suburban grid with too many cars for a smooth freedom ride; not enough cars or city density to make it the bike messenger's close-call grit ride. Drab, commercial El Camino Real bisected Palo Alto and the Stanford campus. There were mountains to Stanford's west. I bought a map at the campus bike shop, and it appeared that something called Skyline Boulevard ran the full spine of their ridge. Down the mountains' other side was the Pacific. It sort of looks like this:

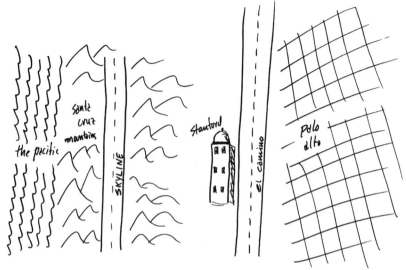

Every time I rode toward Skyline, though, the mountains stayed impossibly far and fixed on the horizon. The futility only deepened my awe of these elusive, permanent hills.

Food was another unforeseen challenge. My tight money policy had landed me in a dorm on a surprisingly rural campus. Although Stanford is "in" Palo Alto, it is a separate enclave, with its own zip code. Stanford is gigantic; about one acre per student. Despite this vastness, law students have no college-style dining hall. A handwritten flyer in the Leland foyer suggested a possible food source:

Join Breakers Eating Club
See Tim Apparel, 2L
(Leland Rm. 119)

I roamed the dorm in search of Tim Apparel, lost, like when Spinal Tap couldn't find the stage, and repeatedly passed the same door with a raised-lettered, thick-and-creamy-colored card affixed to it—

MR. A. BURLEY MAHNMEETS

STANFORD LAW SCHOOL

CLASS OF 1998

Seemed like a serious person. This guy already had personal billboards printed up, and I was hunting for food.

After a few more loops around the dorm, I found Room 119. I knocked, and Tim Apparel appeared at his door. His room sent out an odor that was as unfamiliar as it was distinct, though not at all fetid. At thirty-one, I thought I had taken in the full olfactory register, but this was a first-time smell. The next thing I noticed was that Tim Apparel wore an armless Stanford Cycling Team windbreaker. His arms were slim, not skinny, and each had the protruding bicep vein that zealous bikers develop.

I gave what I thought was a compact summary of my eating, money, and transportation situation. Throughout, Tim Apparel offered neither an obligatory nod nor a courtesy chuckle. So I came to the point:

"Breakers . . . this eating club. The flyer said to see you."

"Fifty-something bucks a month. You take a cooking or hashing shift."

"Hashing?"

"Cleanup: grill scraping, mopping. It's basically a co-op. Come by at dinner tonight. Six."

"Right."

"Ahhhh, actually, if you want to swing by around four I'm riding down to the bike shop."

I'd always ridden alone, but I agreed to meet him. Then I asked:

"What do you know about that A. Burley Mahnmeets?"

"The guy with the business card taped to his door? He's a Brit. Big pompous fuck. I call him The Barrister. Met him once. Came by about Breakers, too. Said he was hoping it would be 'more the Princeton sort of eating club.' Told me he's closed himself up in his room working on some major opus about American civil procedure. Then he bored me with a bunch of questions about *Law Review.*"

"What is the deal with *Law Review?*"

"You join. Beginning of second year. Not a grades thing. They put you through a bunch of shit. Editing. Fact-checking. But they don't reject anyone. The Barrister's taking the hard route, though. Trying to publish his way on as a One L."

Tim Apparel closed his door. My attention refocused away from him, I heard "Comfortably Numb" playing on a tinny stereo. My room was directly across from his.

At four, I knocked on Tim Apparel's door.

"Open."

The weird smell wafted to me again. The sight line this time also allowed a deeper view into Tim Apparel's room. He had a first-generation Pentium computer, the casing removed and its innards exposed. Tim Apparel also had bicycles—more than one, but hard to tell exactly how many as the various parts were disconnected from their recognizable forms. He sat at his desk, on the Internet, drinking an amber liquid with ice and smoking, pot I assumed, out of a blackened glass pipe.

Tim Apparel popped up, grabbed a bike that was still in one piece, and rode into the hallway, down the stairs, out the door, and down another set of stairs. I followed.

The ride to the bike shop was short and fast, faster than when I rode alone. Tim Apparel showed me his purchase.

"Chris King headset. Fucking thing of beauty."

Despite having lived around them as a bike messenger, I had never contemplated bikes as anything but a unitary thing: *bike.* Tim Apparel had a finer sense for the fact that bikes, like everything else, are made up of lots of little things.

"You should probably get a bike," Tim Apparel said.

"I've got one."

"That's shit. You need a road bike to do the hills here, to hit Skyline."

I did feel partly initiated for having already discovered Skyline, if only on a map.

"I'm just a poor student, scraping by on loans."

Tim Apparel expressed the merest wince, a signal that his tolerance for the hackneyed—*poor student, scraping by*—was low. Over time, I learned he would prefer that his companions be either original or silent. The Barrister had already run afoul.

"Actually, you could use two—mountain and road."

"And pay tuition with my X-Games and Tour de France winnings?"

"You came to law school with credit cards—for emergencies?"

Tim Apparel and I were late for dinner at Breakers, the eating club. The ride back from the bike shop was less brisk than the ride there. Tim Apparel rolled my new mountain bike alongside him, and I did the same with the new road bike. The aluminum Gary Fisher Mt. Tam was $1,495, plus 8.25 percent California sales tax. The steel, celeste-green Bianchi Veloce cost $1,200. Shoes, one pair mountain and one road, were $200 each. Pumps (one mountain, one road, and one dual-purpose standing pump), tubes, tire levers, tube patches, helmet (bike messengers don't wear helmets), fifteen-watt halogen headlight for night riding, pulsing red taillight to avoid tickets from Stanford cops, all-purpose repair tool, fingerless gloves, body-mounted hydration system, two accessory pouches, Oakley glasses with dark, clear, and yellow lenses... all totaled out to $3,993.57. Tim Apparel persuaded the bike shop to throw in two plastic water bottles, no charge. Titanium water bottle cages, three of them, were another $55 each. The revised total: $4,163.11.

Before attending a single law school class, I had violated my new beginning's first two commandments: solitude and frugality. Sensing unease, Tim Apparel said:

"Think of it as two weeks' summer associate salary."

"Law firms sound heinous."

"Check out Young & Mathers. L.A. firm. New place. Started a few years ago by a bunch of Cravath rebels. Word is they pay the most money and have the fewest rules. No dress code. Even bought a guy a tricked-out mountain bike as a signing bonus last year."

Tim Apparel had given me financial peace of mind, so I volunteered the next friendship offering:

"Get baked after dinner?"

"I'm sort of laying off weed right now."

After dinner, I joined Breakers Eating Club, paying $232 for the semester—less than a day's pay as a summer associate. I signed up to cook Sunday breakfast.

Back at Leland, I geared up for a ride on the new road bike. The skinny tires were precarious. The special shoes felt as if they had been cemented to the pedals. Biking, this biking, was alien. The ride down car-clogged El Camino and back to Leland left me doubting the bolt to a faraway law school before it had really begun. I did a bong hit, finished the Jack Daniel's, had a wank, pissed in my sink to avoid the hallway, and went to an early, sleepless sleep. Wild thoughts blazed; my eyes stayed closed. I called Niccola, to run by her the idea of returning to my speechwriting job, which still hadn't been filled. No answer. Wilder still: I came to the edge of another phone call, to Helen—a confession, an apology, a plea to return to the past. I didn't do it. But as I drifted away that night, the future was unknown, unknowable. My only future-vision borrowed from the past. *Maybe Helen took that teaching job at Stanford, and she's here, actually here, but I know she's still in New Haven, settled, and I'm here, California, to stay, and tomorrow, first day of school, classes, law school, new place, new people . . .*

PART 3 | **LAW SCHOOL BEGINS**

CHAPTER 5 | O'TOULE

The first taste of the law for Harvard One Ls is the Introduction to Legal Studies course. During the first nine days of that course, we learned everything you need to know about legal research and writing. For nine days One Ls learned how to find the answer to any legal problem and how to write a memo about it. Following those nine days were about eight hundred days of learning how to "reason legally" and a bunch of philosophical bullshit. But for nine days, it was all about the law.

Turns out, nine days is enough to learn everything you need to know to start work in a law firm. That's why every top law school spends most of its time on the history and purpose behind the law. The day-to-day practice of the law is too simple to justify three years of schooling. A lawyer rarely knows the answer to a legal question off the top of his head. Lawyers aren't paid because they know the answer; they are paid because they know how to find it. Most lawyers would admit as much. They just wouldn't want you to know it takes only nine days to learn how to do it.

I got my first assignment as a Harvard Law student from my Introduction to Legal Studies teaching assistant, Greg. Greg was not a professor. He was a Two L assigned to introduce our small group of ten to the law.

He opened our first session with a pep talk—nothing too confounding, just your typical I-worried-my-ass-off-and-I-made-it-through-so-you-will-too sentiment. Then he handed out our assignment and sent us home. It was a legal problem involving a broken promise:

INTRODUCTION TO LEGAL STUDIES—PROBLEM 1

A young professional, Bob, perfectly happy with his current job at Company A, decided to apply for a few new job opportunities to see if he could enhance his career. A manager from one of the companies he applied to, Company B, offered Bob a job. The next day Company A offered to give Bob a promotion and higher pay, as well as a $10,000 bonus if he'd stay. Company B's offer was still more lucrative, however. So Bob decided to quit his job at Company A. A few days later, Bob's old position at Company A was filled. A few days after that, Bob went to report to Company B. When Bob arrived, the manager at Company B who had offered the job to Bob gave him some bad news. Bob's job at Company B was no longer available. Distraught, Bob comes to you and asks what legal remedies he might have against Company B or Company A.

In short, Bob was screwed. Our task was to find out what Bob could do about it. Greg made it clear that we weren't supposed to do any research on the problem.

"Don't y'all go and hit the library as soon as class ends," Greg said in a familiar Southern drawl. "Just use your basic instincts about justice and common sense to figure out a solution to Bob's problem. As for the law, we'll cross that bridge when we come to it."

This didn't seem so bad. Just use my common sense. Simple enough. If it was one thing I had plenty of, it was common sense. I approached our second session feeling confident that, for now at least, I was in the game. As everyone settled in, Greg opened with a few more obligatory words of encouragement:

"By now I guess a lot of you have started your assignments for your other classes. Don't worry if they seem impossible to grasp. I remember that first Contracts case. Damned thing took me two hours to read. Two pages, two hours! But 'fore you know it, same case'll take you ten minutes. Take it from someone who's been there. It's never as bad as you think."

I know Greg was well-meaning, but I look back on inspirational talks like his and can't help but think that the talker unwittingly did more to reinforce our fears about law school than law school itself. I mean, when someone tells you, "It's all going to be all right" ten times a day, even if you *are* having a good time and you *don't* think it's that bad, you'll always be wondering if you've somehow missed the turmoil. And if you look around long enough, you're going to find it. I hadn't read that first Contracts case yet. But after Greg's talk, I was going to look for the nearest tall building if it took me a minute longer than Greg's two hours to finish it.

Next, Greg went through the sign-in sheet.

"Is there someone here by the name of Mr. Kankoos? He missed our first session, and I don't see his name on today's sign-up list. Does anyone know if he's still planning to attend?"

There were chuckles from a couple of guys. Then one of them, who wore a Texas A&M Aggies cap, piped up:

"It's just Kankoos. No mister. He's enrolled. I think he's a little under the weather right now."

More chuckles.

"What is he, a rock star? Well, tell Kankoos to give me a call, provided, of course, he is well enough to do it. OK, why don't we go ahead and start without Kankoos. Let's talk about Bob's little dilemma."

Edgar, my neighbor in the Gropius dorm, spoke first. Edgar was the first person I met at Harvard Law School. A twenty-four-year-old Harvard graduate, Edgar had spent two years between college and law school in management consulting. He was a good enough guy, but a jumpy son of a bitch. Edgar had already been through four years of Harvard, but he seemed at times more in awe of the place than I was. He was third-generation Harvard, and Harvard was the only law school for him. In fact, Edgar went into consulting only because he got wait-listed at Harvard Law School the first time he applied. And even though our little ten-person group session looked more like a highbrow AA meeting than Professor Kingsfield's Contracts class, it held all of the romantic import for Edgar. He edged forward in his chair, coated his throat with a hard swallow, and spoke: "It seems as if Company B made a promise to Bob, and it seems that Bob was hurt when he relied on that promise. The law should protect people who are in Bob's situation, because we want to encourage people in Company B's situation to keep their promises. It seems as if they had a contract."

"What makes you think they have a contract, Edgar?" Greg asked.

"Well, it seems that each party had agreed to the same terms: that Bob would report to work at Company B for a certain salary and benefits."

"That's good, Edgar. But how do we know they had a contract? Do they have anything in writing? Isn't a contract usually in writing?"

As Edgar was coughing out his fifth "it seems" in as many sentences, an intellectual-looking man in his mid- to late twenties with Benjamin Franklinesque, wire-rimmed glasses that were way too small for his head took the floor.

"Allow me to help." He spoke with second-natured eloquence and forced civility. "Bob may have a binding oral contract, provided that there was a bona fide offer and a subsequent acceptance, and provided, as well, that the terms were sufficiently definite for the court to enforce. But, of course, the contract would have to be in writing under the Statute of Frauds, assuming, *arguendo*, it could not be completed within one year. If no term were specified, this creates another predicament with respect to Bob's oral contract claim vis-à-vis his employment. Because the typical employment relationship is 'at will' in the eyes of the law, Bob has no damages sounding in contract, using the typical expectation measure of damages. The appropriate legal theory under which Bob would pursue a claim is promissory estoppel, the elements of which are a promise, the intent by the promisor that the promisee rely on the promise to his detriment, actual reliance by the promisee . . . "

He went on like that for what seemed to be a half hour, prattling off words and phrases I had never heard before. He spoke with the canned polish of Brokaw or Rather, but he was more possessed than poised. His voice filled the room's walls like a Pentecostal preacher at revival, and he seemed at times to be speaking in tongues. As far as I was concerned, he might as well have been. Where did he get this statute of frauds? It seemed a bit of an overstatement to call what Company B did fraud. And what the hell was promissory stoppel? Employment at will? Expectation measure of damages? I consoled myself: clearly, this guy is full of shit. But Greg was impressed:

"That's right . . . uh . . . I'm sorry, I didn't get your name?"

"O'Toule. Thomas O'Toule, Harvard '95."

You only hear people from Harvard introduce themselves that way. "Jack Wanker, ITT '93" just doesn't have the same ring to it.

"That's right, Thomas. Promissory estoppel is the applicable legal theory."

Greg went on to explain a few basic legal concepts that made it difficult for Bob to win on a contract claim. He then explained the legal theory of promissory estoppel. I wrote down everything I could, hearing almost none of it, understanding even less.

"OK, that's enough for today. See you tomorrow."

Greg ended our session, none too soon. I had been ambushed. I sat there in a daze, looking around to see if I could sense the same in anyone else. The faces around me were expressionless, the kinds of faces made for poker halls and board rooms. Even Edgar was contained. If they were as mystified as I by O'Toule, they weren't about to let me or anyone else know it. Quickly, I closed my jaw, relaxed my eyes, and tried my best to appear as everyone else did. Inside, I felt tired. Beaten, in fact.

As the room emptied, I sat contemplating my next move. Should I go to the library and figure this all out? I assumed that would take days. Should I ask Greg what the hell O'Toule was talking about? I could, but I was reminded of a little wisdom my grandfather often imparted: "Boy, it's better to shut up and be thought a fool than to open your trap and prove it."

Finally, I knew what to do. I would just go up to Mr. O'Toule and ask. I caught up with him down the hall, where a small crowd of people surrounded him, doing what could only be construed as giving congratulations on his triumph. After the crowd had dissipated, I introduced myself, in my most learned tone: "Hello, Thomas. I obviously already know your name. Mine is Jaime Marquart. I gathered from your discussion on promissory stoppel and the Fraud Statute that you had previously studied the subjects. I was wondering if you could be so kind as to, uh, point me to your sources."

"Oh, Texas, I presume? How quaint."

I'm not sure if he was correctly guessing my accent or my college. But I was sure he was patronizing me, so I dispensed with the pleasantries and stilted tone, which obviously weren't working.

"I just wanted to know where you got all of that stuff in there."

"What 'stuff,' exactly, are you talking about?"

"Uh, you know what I mean—"

"I am sure I do not."

"You know, promissory stoppel, the Fraud Statute—"

He laughed. "It is promissory es-toppel. Look, we are at Harvard Law School."

"I was just wondering if you could tell me where you read all of that...stuff. I'm giving you an opportunity to help me out. You never know, I might return the favor someday."

By now, I was regretting having approached Mr. O'Toule in the first place. Whether it was genuine or not, I was beginning to see the utility in my classmates' deadpan reaction to O'Toule's performance. I was just about to say forget it, when Mr. O'Toule said:

"Thank you for the opportunity, but I have to decline. I am late for my study group session. Good day to you!"

"Good day!"

Good day? What the hell had gotten into me? At UT, I'd found myself in a foreign social setting here and there, but I was always true to myself. I never nodded like I knew when I didn't, and I was always fine with that. Now, after one slightly intimidating experience, I was coming off like Gomer Pyle trying to pass for William F. Buckley. Feeling behind, it was time to get ahead, or at least as far ahead as O'Toule seemed to be. I changed my course and headed for the library. On the way, I felt a tap on my shoulder. It was Greg. Great.

"Don't worry about Mr. O'Toule. There's hundreds of his kind around here."

"What kind is that?" I asked.

"I've searched long and hard for a word to describe it. Sort of a mystery. So far all I've come up with is 'asshole.'" I was interested, if not relieved. Greg continued, "You want to know how he knew all of that stuff, don't you?"

Again, I was no longer sure this conversation was helping. Apparently, Greg had seen in me the fear I had not been able to detect in any of my classmates. Had he sensed the same in them? Either way, I was too exhausted to argue. I had to know.

"Yeah."

"One word. *Gilbert's*. It's a legal outline. You can buy it at the Coop. It costs about seventeen bucks and has everything he just said right inside. When Thomas found out he got into Harvard Law School, he picked up the *Gilbert's* outlines for your first-year courses. Trust me. I know this because I've walked in your shoes. And also because I saw Mr. O'Toule reading *Gilbert's* for Contracts in the library last night. The first fifty pages have everything he just said in class, written at the sixth-grade level for anyone to understand."

"You kiddin' me?"

I let out a breath, half laugh, half sigh.

"I wish I was. Have you read the introductory statement to your Contracts class?"

I had.

"You know where it says that the law is an amorphous body of rules descended from centuries of legal scholarship?"

"Yeah, I remember. Something about the living and breathing, constantly evolving common law which cannot be contained by even the largest of libraries."

"Well, that's not entirely true. About 95 percent of it fits in the first fifty pages of *Gilbert's*."

"No shit?"

"No shit. But don't bother picking the *Gilbert's* up for now. Try to learn it on your own. The first year of law school is like learning a new language. The best way to pick it up is complete immersion from the beginning. It'll all start to make sense soon enough . . ."

I didn't hear the rest of what Greg said. I was too relieved by the notion that O'Toule was full of crap. Still, I couldn't entirely shake the anxiety he had induced. I had never met anyone like Mr. O'Toule. What benefit could he possibly have gained from intimidating the rest of us? Why wasn't he honest about his sources? One thing I knew for sure, O'Toule definitely was an asshole. But an asshole unlike any other I'd met. Like Greg, I struggled to find a more exact name for him. What kind of person is happy only when others are sad; confident only when others are insecure; and feels intelligent only when others are made to feel stupid? For now I was content in the belief, albeit shaky, that he was just another asshole.

With that, I abandoned the library. I got back to my room at 3:30 in the afternoon. I took out my Contracts casebook and began to read the first case that everyone was talking about, the same one Greg had mentioned. At 6:30, I was done. I had taken an hour longer than Greg.

I substituted the nearest tall building for a pathetic phone call. I was still one day away from my first budgeted Elise conversation. And 6:30 P.M.

in Cambridge meant half past midnight in Bilbao, Spain. I grabbed the phone and dialed. After about fifteen long beeps, I hung up. Elise always answered when I called, no matter what time of night. I spent the next half hour going over all of the possibilities of where and what she might be doing. Those possibilities are surprisingly more limited at half past midnight than at 6:30 P.M. I had already been tempted twice to violate our calling schedule. I had broken down once. My phone had not rung.

CHAPTER 6 | **STARTING TO COME TO ME**

Torts, 11:15 a.m., Monday, September 12, 1995, Spaeth Room, Stanford Law School

I had been through high school, college, and graduate school, and never taken a class where I didn't have the slightest idea what it was about. Torts. The name was unrevealing. Torts? Whatever a tort was I didn't know, so I stayed quiet and observed.

Stanford divides its classes of 180 students into six "sections" of thirty. I reached some preliminary conclusions about my section. First, I was on the older side, but not the oldest. The Plumber was at least forty and had in fact been in the full blossom of a plumbing career when he decided to flip an application into a law school that maintained its campus at a suburban Baltimore mall. He got in and even received a personal phone call from the dean telling The Plumber he would be the first person in the history of Shitbag Law School to have scored a perfect 180 on the LSAT. Before Torts began I heard The Plumber explain:

"Then this girl says to me, 'Why don't you apply to someplace with a fancier name.' I figure I got nothing to lose. So two weeks ago I'm snaking out crapper pipes. Now I'm at Stanford Law School. Life!"

Second quick impression: at least three of the women in my section had distinctive energy. Lucy Faar was quiet and covertly sexual. Tabitha Mullen was a nifty blonde-Goth hybrid. Celia Shackles radiated pure intelligence. Tabitha and Lucy sat with one vacant seat between them. Although full rows remained empty, Davis Mund chose the middle seat, between Lucy and Tabitha. Ignoring him, Tabitha and Lucy kept talking.

Davis Mund was around my age, from South Dakota, and didn't conceal that he expected to become president of the United States. He had gone to the University of South Dakota; then to Oxford on a Rhodes or Marshall Scholarship; done some inch-above-internship job in Washington; gone to Harvard Business School; and now, finally, landed at Stanford Law School, his last plausible act of education.

One afternoon before classes started, he woke me with a confident— *snap-snap-snap*—knock.

"Rob Byrnes? Like to introduce myself. Davis Mund. I understand you worked for Governor William Weld."

Davis explained that he was "cut from the same Libertarian-Republican cloth as Governor Weld" and laid out his own path:

"Congress first, probably the House. Then governor. After that maybe back to D.C., the Senate. We'll see what happens from there. All of it's a leap into the unknown for me. Sounds as if you've been where the rubber hits the road, though. Any advice?"

"Stay in school. Don't do drugs."

"Well, I didn't even *almost* inhale at Oxford."

The Clinton joke had already gone unfunny back then. Politics isn't about originality, though, and Davis Mund understood this. Stating the obvious is a politician's affidavit of normalcy. Departures from normalcy are best cleared up early on. Davis Mund had stopped by my room to clear something up. He told me:

"One area that might be a problem...I've got a penchant for Asian women. Afraid that might not go over with Republican muckity-mucks."

"Turn a burden into a virtue. Like Phil Gramm. Major right-wing hard ass. A very important unelected Republican once told me, 'Gramm's got bigot insurance 'cause his wife's a slant.'"

Davis Mund wore a momentary dunce cap, to let the bad air of epithet settle. Then he said, "You mean he married an Asian-American woman?"

"Right."

"That's quite a relief."

As Professor Jo Howard walked in, I nodded hello to Davis Mund and watched Lucy and Tabitha end their chat. Celia Shackles sat apart and alone. She spoke to no one. Her demeanor said: stay away. The seats adjacent to Celia remained vacant. Bobby Boylan entered a few steps behind Professor Howard. I'd seen Bobby around Leland, where he had already accumulated a bundle of friends. Bobby veered toward, then away from Celia Shackles's region. He swept by Lucy and Tabitha, said something only to them, caused Lucy to smile, and then sat next to me.

"Hey," Bobby said, leaning so close to me I could see the outer rim of his contact lenses.

I thought it might be truer to my own objectives to move and sit alone, like Celia Shackles. On this, my last first day of school, I recalled my first: kindergarten, when Nixon was president. I'd arrived ten minutes late and saw that the class was already divided into conversational units. Though I wanted to belong, be a part of things, I was suspicious of instantaneous familiarity. I had a sturdy patience for a five-year-old and chose to wait for my friendships to evolve organically, slowly. Twenty-six years after walking into kindergarten late, I started law school with the same ambivalence and hopefulness, wanting to sit apart, yet also yearning to be a part of things.

As Professor Howard squared her note stack and the chatter faded, Bobby angled himself toward me:

"Come get a beer with us after class."

I nodded yes to Bobby, my resolve to stay separate weakened by the chance to meet what I took to be the rest of "us," Lucy Faar and Tabitha Mullen. The professor snapped her papers a final time. The overture was over. Law school begins:

"All right, let's get started. I'm Jo Howard and this is Torts, Stanford Law School, section 1-A. If you're a medical student, this is the wrong class, wrong building, wrong school [group chuckle]. . . . Contrary to what you might think, or hope, this is not a culinary course about making certain tasty confections [chuckle, chuckle]. . . . It is, however, a course about [fingers poised to type] what I happen to believe is the most exciting and dynamic area of the law: [rattle of laptops, notes being taken] . . . torts, the law of accidental injuries."

Professors in Criminal Law, Civil Procedure, and Contracts expressed the same mechanical chauvinism about their fields during the first week of classes.

"Now," Howard said, "I imagine you've all had the opportunity to purchase the casebook we'll be using, *Tort Law and* . . . "

I'd had the opportunity. But the night before classes began, over dinner at Breakers, Tim Apparel told me this about casebooks:

"Fifty bucks a pop. I don't buy them. They're useless. Worse than useless. They confuse the fuck out of you. You can get everything you need from old student outlines. Basically does away with having to go to class. Which frees up a lot of time for biking. Too much beauty here to piss your time away indoors."

"Where do you get these outlines?"

"Web site. You have Howard for Torts? I had her for Torts last year. I'll just give you my outline. Same script for fifteen years. *'Most dynamic area of the law'* my bunghole . . . "

"What exactly *is* an outline?"

"Ever take notes in high school and college?"

"Sometimes."

"Typed-up notes; that's an outline."

"You ditched all your classes first year?" I asked.

"No. I went to class compulsively. But now you can live by my hindsight."

Without the advantage of having read either the first-day case or Tim Apparel's outline, I couldn't appreciate Celia Shackles's rescuing a stumped Torts class when she said:

". . . while there is no colorable claim sounding in tort, for want of negligence, as to *this* defendant, one might, for instance, look to the automobile manufacturer for installing defective brakes. Too, there is a viable claim against the physician who prescribed what was arguably a soporific."

A Strunk and White zealot, Celia spoke in full paragraphs, said "presently" rather than "soon," and never split her infinitives or used contractions. She had been talking about *Hammontree versus Jenner*, a standard first-day torts assignment in which a guy named Jenner had driven his car into Maxine Hammontree as she worked in a bicycle shop. Hammontree (plaintiff) sued Jenner (defendant) to recover the costs of her medical expenses and compensate her for "pain and suffering." Hammontree lost, not because it turned out she was just fine, but because Jenner had done nothing wrong by tort law. Jenner was an epileptic. He had taken his epilepsy pills the day of the accident. For the first time in many years, however, he had a seizure, and so he plowed through the bike shop and into Hammontree.

Professor Howard explained that a tort lawsuit is the familiar day-to-day of people suing people—for crashing into them, polluting their water, even mailing them a loved one's corpse. To win a tort suit, the defendant has to have been at least negligent—has to have somehow fucked-up or used bad judgment and not been a "reasonable person." Jenner hadn't been negligent. On the other end of the spectrum is O. J., not at all reasonable. His second trial was a tort suit for killing and meaning to—an intentional tort, also a crime. Crimes are way beyond negligent. Crimes are crimes and land you in jail because you *meant* to cause whatever harm you caused. In the middle, between O. J. and Jenner, is classic negligence, doing harm without meaning to, but still not altogether blamelessly: fiddling with the car radio and rear-ending the guy in front of you. Then there's a tort.

Professor Howard pressed the class to think of other possible sources of negligence in the Hammontree case.

"Perhaps Mr. Jenner's physician for prescribing the pills—possibly the wrong pills for this affliction," Davis Mund said, repackaging part of Celia's earlier point.

"Anyone else?" Howard asked.

"California," Bobby said.

"How so?" Howard asked.

"For letting that clown Jenner have a driver's license." [Big laughter.]

Bobby's was the last word for the day. Guessing that he had forgotten our plan to get a beer, I made my own plan to wander alone until our next class, Criminal Law, at 2:30. As I left Torts, though, Bobby gripped my shoulder.

"Hey, Byrnes, you coming? The others are meeting us there."

Bobby and I walked together, away from the Law School, toward Stanford's campus pub, deceptively called the Coffee House. I'd had enough of being alone. I preferred this simple companionship to whacking off and blowing bong hits in Leland. We got a pitcher of Sierra Nevada and took it to sit in the sun. Before long, words were directed our way. Not Lucy, not Tabitha. It was a guy's voice. I squinted my eyes open. Davis Mund. Next to him, The Plumber.

Bobby produced two bottles of Napa Zinfandel from his fake courier bag. He held the floor for a long time, first propounding the utility of his "bag" ("literally my whole life is in this thing"), and then explaining that Zinfandel had acquired an undeserved reputation as "the acid-washed jeans of wine."

"*White* Zinfandel—that's the inferior stuff. Red Zinfandel is in fact the only wine that is indigenous to California. Did you know that? It is the equal to any Bordeaux. This bottle'd run you sixty bucks in a restaurant. But I have an arrangement with the distributor."

Bobby kept talking:

"I'm doing a joint degree. Already finished my first year over at the Business School. What a blast. Got a lifetime of poon last year. Not doing bad out of the blocks this year, either."

"Really," Davis Mund said. His eyes said more: *tell me how*. Bobby wasn't sharing his methods or looking to the past with greater specificity. He had a vision.

"This place isn't Harvard Law School—all dark and serious and miserable. There are five hundred fifty of those dorks. Only a hundred and seventy of us. We're just as smart but more rare. Which means we can have a rockin' time in law school."

"And still end up in the same place when it's all over," The Plumber said.

"Three years of pass-fail and sunshine," Bobby said.

"You can't take *everything* pass-fail," Davis Mund said.

"Absofuckinglutely; the whole first semester anyway," Bobby said. "Then any five classes after that. Got it right here in my bag."

Bobby was carrying the student handbook, which explained Stanford Law School's pass-fail policy.

"You with me?" Bobby exhorted. "It should be mandatory pass-fail, anyway. For everyone."

"Like Yale," The Plumber said.

"They kick back full-time at Yale," Bobby said. "And you know what they do instead of studying?"

We didn't know.

"They fuck like porn stars. Look at the people who went there— Gary Hart, Bill Clinton, Clarence Thomas, Anita Hill. Notice a pattern? Yale Law School has produced most of the modern figures in American sex scandal history."

Davis Mund turned serious, affronted. "Some people come to law school to learn the law, not screw around."

"Why not do both?" Bobby said.

"Why not reward excellence? A mandatory pass-fail system benefits only those who are below average. It makes *everyone* average. And average won't cut it for a Supreme Court clerkship."

"Supreme Court clerk? Not a chance. Might as well be crowned King Dork," Bobby said.

Bobby was right, to a point. He had no chance of becoming a Supreme Court clerk. Nor did I. Bobby's embedded premise, widely and conveniently believed, was that Supreme Court clerks, for all their academic accomplishment, were otherwise stunted, socially inept, or as Bobby had it, dorks. There was the additional suspicion that they were not even particularly smart, just hard workers, grinds.

"I think I'll just take my crappiest class pass-fail," I said.

The Plumber agreed. Davis Mund looked gravely at his beer glass and said, "At your peril, gents. For my part I'm going for the brass ring. Taking classes pass-fail reeks of early surrender to me. And it certainly isn't how things work in the real world."

"No need to be a fat old man before you absolutely have to," Bobby said.

"But I *want* to be a fat old man," Davis said.

Bobby signaled a topic change by producing from his "bag" the Law School Face Book—photos, colleges, hometowns. Occasionally a name had a checkmark next to it. Bobby explained:

"Means they're do-able."

Davis Mund cringed. Bobby ignored him this time and began flipping through the Face Book. He sported a deeper level of information about everyone. *This guy's father bought his way in . . . this other fella right here is brilliant . . . she's a babe, but she's got a boyfriend in L.A. . . . and Francine Lewis, what a sweet piece of ass . . . this guy, he'd kill to clerk for Scalia . . . she's a surgeon . . . and here's Byrnesie . . .* Bobby stopped talking, then said:

"Good picture. Word is you were quite the cocksman back in Boston. If I were you I'd check out that tasty foursome over there."

Bobby gestured to a table of four other One Ls, also drinking between-class beers. I had noticed them—two male, two female, fast friends a few days into school.

"My guess is those four are up for adventure," Bobby vouched.

He left the dangling impression that his guess was something more. Another time, I'd take it up with him and find out how he had tapped into my past. For now, though, we all slouched back into silence. Bobby, The Plumber, and I turned our faces back toward the sun. Davis Mund read his Criminal Law book. A third beer pitcher drained, the wineglasses flecked with sediment, Bobby announced it was time for our next class, Criminal Law. I expected him to suggest that we blow it off and make a trip over the hills, to the beach at Half Moon Bay, or up to San Francisco—an early act of take-life-pass-fail defiance. He didn't. We all got up to leave. I arrived back at the Law School as the afternoon buzz was turning to a throb.

Criminal Law, 2:30 p.m., a classroom, much bigger than the Torts classroom

There had been no assigned reading for the first day of Criminal Law. I sat in the last row. It was like those introductory first-days in high school, where the full extent of your obligation is to show up, sit back, page through the syllabus, and listen to the teacher. The drunkenness turned sweet again. The world was demanding exquisitely little of me. The syllabus laid out all the semester's assignments, about twelve pages of case-book reading per class, three class meetings per week. I snapped my Walkman on. The tape in it, labeled Fall 1991, sparked bike messenger and Helen memories . . . Tribe, a Boston band . . . *I saw the film/said that's the life for me/forsake the mundane/for some instability/so sue me* . . . while at the same time I heard the professor introducing criminal law . . . *the justifications for punishment: retribution, rehabilitation, incapacitation, denunciation, deterrence*. The class became animated. Over the music, I heard consensus skepticism about the efficacy of deterrence: *I agree with Celia. No criminal expects to be caught . . . Much less prosecuted and convicted . . . Jail is a weak deterrent for the addict who wants—I'd posit needs—drugs . . . Yes, I was liking law school.*

I ended my first day of law school classes with a bike ride down El Camino, dinner at Breakers, and, back in Leland, a visit to Tim Apparel's door.

"I was wondering if you had any spare liquor."

Tim Apparel walked out of sight. His room was still giving off that smell I couldn't place. He returned with an unopened handle-grip Jim Beam and said:

"I'm in a clean living phase. You can keep it."

Back in my room, I made a drunken yet careful search of the Stanford Directory. Helen didn't appear to be at Stanford, not as faculty, student, or staff.

The next day I had Contracts. The professor, a shaky novice, had recently graduated from Harvard Law School, and it showed—both the *recently* and the *Harvard*. Students were addressed as Ms. and Mister. Name placards indicated assigned seats. This Contracts professor kicked his Contracts class off just as Professor Kingsfield had in *The Paper Chase*, with *Hawkins v. McGee*, the so-called Hairy Hand Case. A patient had gone to a doctor to have the burned skin on his hand replaced with a skin graft. The doctor used skin from the patient's chest.

"There is no dispute that, following the operation, the hand became covered with thick, matted hair," the Contracts professor said, lifting his adjectives directly from the movie. "Plaintiff brought suit on two grounds: negligence and breach of contract. Regarding the contract claim, what result? Mr. Byrnes?"

Me. Not a beat of panic. I knew the answer.

"The doctor promised a healthy hand but delivered a hairy hand."

"And what does the court indicate as the measure of damages?"

"The damages would be the difference between the repaired hand that was promised and the hairy hand."

"Precisely. Damages in contract are designed to put the party against whom a breach has been committed in the same position in which she would have been had the contract been performed, *sans* breach."

To this day I haven't read the case. But I had seen *The Paper Chase* at least a dozen times. My answers were the same ones that left Professor Kingsfield wanting in the movie and sent Mr. Hart, the student who answered, to the bathroom for a puke. Hart's movie answers worked for me, though.

"And what, Mr. Byrnes, was the amount of money damages awarded?"

There was nothing in *The Paper Chase* about the amount of money damages. The scene just cut to Hart bolting for the toilet.

"Ahhhhhhhhhhhhhhhhhhhhhhhhhhhhhhhhhhhhhhhhhhhhhhhhh..."

I gave the impression of searching my casebook for a minor detail that had slipped my mind, though I had no casebook and, in any event, the Hairy Hand Case wasn't in the casebook. It was on a separate handout that I also didn't have. The name placard in front of me concealed the ruse. I stalled long enough for hands to shoot up.

"Mr. Mund," the professor said.

"Three thousand dollars, although defendant did except to the damage award as being excessive."

"Precisely. Well done Messrs. Byrnes and Mund."

I never went to Contracts again. Because the professor had never before taught Contracts, or anything else apparently, there was no student outline. So I would have to rely on a generic, store-bought Contracts outline, *Emmanuel*, which exposed me to the risk that this professor would have a fresh take on Contracts. Bobby Boylan did continue going to Contracts and he periodically told me there had been no surprises that could put me in a hole come final exam time:

"He blows. Worst professor—worst teacher—I've ever had. And he's always peeking at *Emmanuel's* himself."

I had found my crappiest class, the one I would take pass-fail: Contracts.

Civil Procedure was slightly less crappy. The professor seemed well-enough versed, but in the dreariest of subjects. The course is all about the procedural mechanics of lawsuits—how and where to file them, how and when to get a lawsuit dismissed. There's a reason *Ally McBeal* doesn't do a civil procedure episode. It would be too dull. Civil Procedure is all recipe, no food. Civil Procedure also lacks the law-bigger-than-ourselves overtones of the other first-year classes. It is an overt, worldly creation, its tenets not given in mythical times on stone tablets, but rather in a dry rulebook, compiled relatively recently, *The Federal Rules of Civil Procedure*. The underlying stories in civil procedure cases lack the quirkiness of torts accidents, the culture-shaping force of constitutional law, or the high stakes of crimes. The climaxes are without human or emotional dimension. A civil procedure litigant might be instructed to bring her suit in Missouri rather than Delaware, for example. Like Contracts, Civil Procedure met during prime biking hours, so I ditched going to it, too, in favor of a student outline that revealed the crux of the course.

As with Torts, the Civil Procedure outline was almost word-for-word faithful. The professor began the course with the same anecdote, every year: some congressman who is said to have remarked, "You write the substantive law, I'll write the procedural law, and I'll screw you every time." After the professor said "screw," she made a self-satisfied wiggle, as if she had shocked the class into a reverence for Civil Procedure. I saw Lucy turn to Tabitha, mouthing a word:

"what*ever*."

I bailed from Civil Procedure after a week, though I did drift in from time to time, to confirm the outline I would rely on to take the exam was still accurate. It always was.

Criminal Law also presented a biking conflict, meeting as it did during the sunny part of the day. It was tempting to attend. A Criminal Law casebook is full of people on the edge of important choices, facing hard consequences if they are caught and convicted. The prospect of going to jail or being executed commands attention in a way that being compelled to bring suit in an alternate jurisdiction doesn't. But there's less unfamiliar law to learn than in the other classes. Because interest in criminal law is so widespread, most people, including nonlawyers, have a sense for the black-letter basics. (With the time I'd invested watching *Barnaby Jones* and *The Rockford Files*, I could make a passable distinction between murder and manslaughter, for example.) This was never more true than when I was enrolled in Criminal Law, during the fall of 1995, as the O. J. criminal trial was winding down. In the end, a jury might have its own strange reasons for convicting or acquitting. You don't have to go to law

school, though, to know that throat slashing, bludgeoning, mugging, rap-
ing, shooting, dealing, and embezzling aren't allowed.

"Crim Law is tit-easy," Bobby told me, and I had no reason not to
believe him.

Criminal *procedure* is where the important, sometimes counterintuitive, action is. It's a branch of constitutional law, though, and doesn't turn
up in the typical one-semester first-year Criminal Law class. Criminal
procedure is about how excluded evidence can cause an obviously guilty
person to go free, a (not costless) protection against unjust prosecution.
O. J.'s a murderer and a jackass, but his getting off was a good thing. Keeps
the cops honest.

For One Ls, the class is Criminal Law. Latin puffery does obscure its
simplicity. A crime requires both a *mens rea* and an *actus reas*. Translated:
to send someone to prison for committing a crime they have to have done
something (committed a criminal act, the *actus reas*) and meant to have
done it (had a "criminal mind," the *mens rea*). There is a bit of nuance here
and there, as well as some undoing of popular myth. All crimes are subject
to defenses, such as: insanity (almost always a loser), impossibility (you
can't murder a person who's already dead), and self-defense. Self-defense
is mostly self-evident, but there is an important and limiting requirement. Self-defense has to be proportional to the threat. So it's not true that
you can blow away anyone who breaks into your house at night. Taking a
shotgun to an unarmed, nocturnal intruder could get you a murder or
manslaughter rap. When I read this in a downloaded Criminal Law outline, I called my brother, a gun owner since the L.A. riots, and told him
that the unfettered right to play executioner in your own home is dangerous urban legend. There's no death penalty for boosting a TV.

The first week of classes ended. On Sunday I cooked brunch at Breakers.
Making a meal for fifty is three hours of constant motion punctuated by
attempts at precision (everything hot, uncongealed, served simultaneously) and incredible leaps of faith regarding ingredient portions (brick-
sized butter slabs, fists of spice). It was all thrill to me. Done cooking, and
before going back to Leland, I snuck a look from the kitchen in the same
way a playwright in the stage wings watches for signs of audience delight.

Tim Apparel was there in his Stanford Cycling Team jersey, eating mightily after a mountain ride, and with fresh leg cuts from a crash.

Back at Leland, I passed the A. Burley Mahnmeets door again. Still no sighting of The Barrister himself, only artifacts of his existence. Outside The Barrister's door was a nesting of soiled pots, quaint miniatures of the ones I'd just cooked with. What appeared to be Ramen noodle detritus remained in every one. In my room, I ordered up an Internet search. *Sorry. No results found for "A. Burley Mahnmeets."* Then another search. One result for "Tim Apparel"—www.timapparel.com. On the Tim Apparel Web site was a single image, a photo taken through a slightly open Leland door, of a shirtless and lumpy man, wearing only shorts. Beneath the photo was a caption: **The Barrister . . . Exposed!**

The first semester took its form. I'd go regularly to Torts. Otherwise, I would stick with Tim Apparel's advice: outlines. Contracts I would take pass-fail. In the other classes, I'd chance a grade. And so what if I did badly? Stanford reports that 99 percent of its graduates have jobs within six months of graduation at a median salary of around a hundred grand a year. All I had to do was avoid being one of the two or three biggest dolts in my class. I'd never concerned myself with distant futures, except to make the repeatedly uninformed claim that I would go to law school. Now, there I was, in law school.

In the words of Dean Kathleen M. Sullivan, who left a professorship at Harvard Law School to join the Stanford Law School faculty: **Who could resist a world-class law school in paradise?**[2]

Who could resist? Not me. The irresistible was coming straight at me.

---

2. From the Stanford Law School Web site.

PART 4 | **SEPTEMBER AND OCTOBER**

CHAPTER 7 | UNSOPHISTICATED PARTIES

"Mr. Marquart! Is Mr. Marquart here?"

With Professor Norris there was no avoiding eye contact, appearing deeply involved in notetaking, or any other scheme to prevent being called on. It was as impersonal as being drafted. Everyone in the class (there were about 150 of us) had assigned seats. Norris had a chart with each student's picture, name, and college on it. Before each class began, Norris assigned numbers to each picture on the chart and had his computer randomly pull fifteen numbers. You might go through the entire semester and not be called on. You might be called on three days in a row. You never knew, and that was the point. That day, I was one of the fifteen.

"Uh, yes, sir."

"Mr. Marquart, could you please state the facts of *Williams v. Walker-Thomas Furniture.*"

I thought back to the assignment the night before and my decision to stay up late to finish it. That night, fear of Norris's interrogation tactics didn't factor into my decision to read the assignment. For the first time since I got to Harvard, I had found something I could relate to. The assignment was all about the laws of duress and unconscionability, two doctrines that help people who feel like they were screwed get out of a contract.

Duress can take many forms. Of course, there is the typical gun-to-your-head duress that voids a contract right from the get-go. But duress is pressure of any improper kind. Duress often involves economic pressure—the kind of pressure that wars and natural disasters create. Batteries cost ten bucks during a blackout. Canoes go for more than a Cadillac in a flood. The battery and canoe buyers are under duress.

A certain amount of pressure is just a part of life. For example, the higher price of canoes in a flood is what entices all of the canoe suppliers five states away to haul their extra supply into a flooded region. Americans tend to applaud the salesman who makes enough dough to retire in one hurricane at the same time they relate to the guy who blows half his savings on an aluminum boat and an outboard motor. The question is, when is the pressure so bad that we say the buyer was practically *forced* into the purchase and ought to be allowed out of it?

For me, that question was personal. It highlighted a conflict between the person I was and the person I was to become. My beginnings were meager, but I'd always had warm feelings toward capitalism. Starting out on the bottom rung, a freely moving economic ladder was all I could count on. Still, most of my empathies fell with the duressed parties that day in Contracts. A $500, 28-APR secured MasterCard looks like a good deal to a single mother with two kids, three jobs, and no disposable income. Or at least it looked good to my mom.

Mostly, the courts hesitate to void a contract because of money pressures. But that doesn't mean they never help the Little Guy. It just means they find a different way to do it. That's where the second subject of our assignment came in—unconscionability.

When the terms of a contract are so unreasonably in one party's favor, the courts will deem it unconscionable. One of the major themes in unconscionability doctrine is protecting the unsophisticated party. In a market full of Homer Simpson buyers and Monty Burns sellers, unconscionability levels the playing field. The case Norris had asked me to recite the facts of, *Williams v. Walker-Thomas Furniture*, was that kind of case.

"Uh . . . yes, sir. Walker-Thomas Furniture Company was in the business of selling furniture and electronics in a poor neighborhood of Washington, D.C."

"Anything notable, Mr. Marquart, about the manner in which these sales were consummated?"

"Yes, sir. Installment contracts."

"Go on . . . "

"Most of Walker-Thomas's customers couldn't pay cash, so they had to sign an agreement to make monthly payments. Walker-Thomas used an installment contract that actually only leased the item to a customer for a series of monthly 'rental' payments until the entire item was paid for."

"Get to the point, Mr. Marquart. Why does that *matter?*"

"Well, Walker-Thomas owned the item until the last monthly payment was made, and they could repossess it if a customer missed even a single payment."

"My conscience is not yet shocked, Mr. Marquart. Doesn't the bank own my home until I clear the mortgage?"

"The installment agreement had a tiny-print clause saying that every payment made under a lease of one item would be applied pro rata to every other so-called lease the customer had with Walker-Thomas. So customers who bought several items never paid off *any* of them until *all* of them were paid off. Walker-Thomas could repossess *all* of the items if the customer defaulted on only one of them."

I came up for air and choked down a few hard swallows to re-wet my throat.

"Keep going, Mr. Marquart. Tell us about Ms. Williams."

"She bought a stereo set from Walker-Thomas for $514.95. Ms. Williams had also bought some other items from Walker-Thomas. Not too long after she bought the stereo, she missed a payment. Walker-Thomas tried to repossess every single item she had ever bought, even though she was only a few hundred dollars short of paying for all of them. They moved to—"

"How did the lower court rule, Mr. Marquart?"

"They . . . uh . . . just a minute . . . the trial court ruled that Walker-Thomas's contract was enforceable and that they were entitled to repossess all of the items. They rejected Ms. Williams's argument that the contract was unconscionable."

"So Ms. Williams lost?"

"Yes."

"And she was forever without musical entertainment?"

"No. She appealed."

"And what was the holding of *this* opinion, Mr. Marquart, in the Court of Appeals?"

"It reversed the lower court and ruled that the installment contracts *were* unconscionable."

Norris slammed both hands down on his podium, leaned forward, and stared into me: "*Whyyyyyy?*"

"The court looked at the terms of the contract and Ms. Williams's lack of sophistication and decided that the contract was simply not fair."

Norris tightened his grip on the podium and leaned farther forward. He squinted at me incredulously. From seat 125, I felt the moisture of his breath on my face.

"Not *fair*, Mr. Marquart? Not *fair*? Is it *fair* to refuse to hold people up to the terms of bargains of which they were well aware when they made them? Or, better yet, is it *fair* to deprive every honest, paying customer of Walker-Thomas of electrical appliances because the courts have unilaterally decided that installment lease contracts are not *fair*?"

"Maybe not. But if this resulted in no more installment contracts in the market, then that's because those types of contracts should not have existed in the first place!"

I gambled that that last question was more of a statement. He resumed his upright position and loosened his hold on the podium. For a moment, my ass cheeks loosened their grip on my boxers. Then, he turned to the side and shifted his focal point upward, out the window and into space. He put his left hand in his pocket and his right index finger on his chin. His expression shifted to one of thoughtful contemplation. Norris was about to get to the *what-do-you-think* line of questioning. Opinion territory was always the most treacherous ground to navigate in Socratic dialogue. It was where the theoretical became personal. I thought back to my earlier run-in with Mr. O'Toule and my attempt to pose as a highbrow. If it had to get personal, I was at least going to be myself.

"What do *you* think, Mr. Marquart, is the goal of the doctrine of unconscionability?"

"To rewrite contractual terms that a reasonable person would never agree to."

"Isn't that paternalistic? Does not the very *term* 'unsophisticated party' smack of elitism?"

"Of course it's paternalistic. The law shouldn't be in the business of correcting every single instance in which someone got duped, fair and square. But every now and then you have a situation where both people clearly know that one of them never would have accepted the deal had he known about such-and-such term. Then, a little paternalism isn't a bad thing. It's not a statement about the unsophisticated person's intelligence, just his position at the time of the deal. Anyone who's picked someone up at a bar after a few too many knows exactly what I'm talking about. 'Course, they don't get to undo the deal."

My weak, largely off-point line got a small spattering of laughs. Even Professor Norris seemed moderately pleased.

"Thank you, Mr. Marquart. You've certainly given us some valuable insight into the human elements of unconscionability and true *empathy* of the lives it affects. That's our goal here, people. To bring the law to life."

Professor Norris was scrolling down his chart looking for a new name, when I blurted:

"Thanks. I always did see myself in the position of the unsophisticated party."

Ooh, that didn't come out right, I remember thinking, as a murmur of chuckles emanated from its epicenter, Seat 135, Mr. O'Toule. I had not heard O'Toule's specific snicker, but it must have been the Brahmin equivalent of "no *shit.*" Sometimes, if you can smile naturally enough right away, you can be in on the joke. But that window passes quickly. I scanned the room with a confused look. My throat muscles flexed and my Adam's apple made the pronounced up-and-down motion of a hard swallow. They were subtle gestures, but their meaning was apparent—I was surprised to hear laughter, which made it obvious that I hadn't meant to make a joke. The murmur grew to the point of all-out laughter. The last time I felt like that was when I went to school with Winner's Choice shoes, the kind made of plastic meant to look like leather, with a swoop where there should have been a swoosh. My mom paid $8 for them at Bill's Dollar Store (Wal-Mart for the ultra-poor—the prices were higher, but you could walk there). The kids on the playground were relentless. But that was third grade. And they knew me.

The rest of class passed in a haze. I stumbled out of Austin Hall not feeling all bad about my experience. I knew my unconscionability law, even by Norris's standards. Still, I couldn't look back on the whole thing without a wince. Fortunately, Contracts was my last class that day. I headed back to my room to sit alone and run through it all about three hundred more times. Or maybe try to call Elise again. Then, on my way to Gropius:

"Hey, Marquart!"

I turned around and recognized the guy with the Texas A&M cap: Brian Green, a fellow Texan from my Introduction to Legal Studies section. He had been running after me.

"I gotta admit, Marquart, I for one could relate to what you were saying in there. I've been seeing myself in the position of the unsophisticated party quite a bit lately."

"Thanks. You might be the only one, though. Texas had its share of assholes, but at least they had the courtesy to talk behind your back. I never thought I'd say this, but I could go for a few more of the passive-aggressive type right about now."

"Sounds like you've been running with the wrong crowd. Wanna come grab a beer later? Bar Review's tonight."

I hadn't actually been running with any crowd, and I was preoccupied as hell about keeping up with my assignments. Brian was my first taste of the familiar in a long while, though.

"Sure, how much damage could one beer do? But I've got to hit the library first. I'm still trying to figure out what this Fraud Statute is all about."

"Perfect. I'll go with you. We can head to Bar Review from there."

After four productive hours in the library, Brian and I went to Bar Review. For law school graduates, Bar Review is the rite of passage that transforms them from law students into lawyers. It is review for the Bar Exam. But for Harvard One Ls, Bar Review is a survey of a different Cambridge pub held once a week. It is one of few organized social events for One Ls. That night, we were at Grendel's, one of the oldest and most trafficked bars in Harvard Square.

"Can you believe that?" Brian said as he brought back two Buds. "Four-fifty a bottle? That's three longnecks where I come from. Hey, there's Edgar from Intro to Legal Studies. And he's got a couple of hot friends with him. Let's go introduce ourselves."

"*They're* hot?"

"They are at Harvard. Have you taken a look at your Face Book lately? It's the Saturday Night Theory of Success. It explains why a disproportionate number of butt-ugly, socially inept people get into Ivy League schools. It all comes down to what everyone was doing on Saturday night in high school. When the cheerleaders and football players were out at various movies, parties, and backseats of Trans-Ams, these guys were reading Shakespeare, learning classical piano, and going to the opera with their parents. Now the cheerleaders and football players occupy various Wal-Marts and secretarial desks across our great country, and the butt-ugly people are making the real buck, working out, tanning, driving Porsches, buying new tits and teeth, and signing the cheerleaders' and football players' paychecks."

"That's cruel. Funny, but cruel."

"Maybe. But I wasn't in that great a shape myself for a time there. Scratch that, I was downright fat! And then I hit puberty. Since then, everything I've done has been about one thing: getting the hottest girl I could get. I was smart enough to know sports wasn't gonna be my in. So here I am, Harvard Fucking Law."

Brian's efforts had not gone unrewarded. In addition to his recent law school boon, he wasn't bad looking. Brian's fashion of choice was waist-up crazy. You know, the kind of guy who'd wear the nutty bowling shirt or hip Hawaiian print, or maybe the thrift store chic, vintage 1965 avocado-green button-up, but only with khakis or Levi's. If you shot him from the waist up, he'd fit right into a Butthole Surfers video. Below the belt, he looked like your dad. Waist-up crazy guys will take a small leap into the unusual, but they always have to anchor it with something safe, something Gap. They do pretty well in the clubs, but they are no match for the guy who rolls up in bright orange corduroys with paisley bell bottoms and a patchwork shirt. That's head-to-toe crazy. But Brian was just waist-up, like me.

On Brian's lead, we walked over to Edgar and his female friends.

"Hey, Edgar, right? We're in your section. I'm Brian Green, and this is Jaime Marquart."

Edgar smiled and shot a confirming nod at me. As I turned to introduce myself to his friends, one of them remembered where she'd seen me hours earlier:

"Oh yeah, the unsophisticated person."

They laughed, but unlike Mr. O'Toule's, their laughter was inclusive. Taking the invitation, I laughed along and took a strong pull of Bud. I was beginning to think this might not be so bad after all, when the other of Edgar's not-so-butt-ugly friends spoke up:

"Did you see Friday's Contracts assignment? It's got *ten* cases!"

"I know," said the other. "I spent three hours with *Black's Law Dictionary* sorting through all of the legalese, and I'm only through the first *two!*"

It was just Monday, and there were two more Contracts classes before Friday. Brian and I had just spent four hours in the library, and only managed to knock off the first half of Tuesday's assignment. Brian tried to save the conversation.

"Anything else besides law going on for you guys these days? Any good movies?"

"Who has time for anything else?" Edgar exclaimed.

"Yeah, Scott Turow never had time for a movie his first semester at Harvard," one of the others added.

"I think it was the whole first *year*," added Edgar. "It's a good thing *we've* got Bar Review."

My hopes for a law school respite were waning, but Brian had a more immediate escape in mind. At the first conversational out, we said our good-byes and moved on. The single bottle of beer I had allocated for myself was drained. I stepped up to the bar to get the next round while Brian scavenged for worthwhile conversation.

Next conversation: all guys, no better than the first. This time, at least, they weren't talking about a bunch of cases I hadn't read yet. Instead, Brian and I had stumbled upon a real-life nonalcoholic beer commercial. Edgar caught up with us, his friends having opted for their casebooks and class notes a little earlier than expected. The talk went something like this:

"Did you see the game last night? Man, that Shaq is huuuge! And Rodman's a madman on the boards."

"And everywhere else!"

Or:

"How about Gingrich and that Contract with America?"

"More like Contract *on* America."

And so on and so on, each punch line affirmed with an "Oh, yeah!" that would make the Koolaid man proud. Now, before you all crucify me,

I know we've all had those conversations. In fact, that brand of small talk usually *starts* any conversation. But the small talk tends to trail off in a few seconds, and the conversation moves to another level where something original or honest comes out. Not profound, mind you, just original *or* honest. These guys managed to talk for more than fifteen minutes without going beyond the first paragraph of any financial or sports article in *USA Today*. Worse, any kernel of honesty in anything they said was wrapped up in so much innuendo and bad pun that it was more unbearable than the rest of what they said. One of them, Wellington Ford, continued:

"You know, that Martha Miller is actually in pretty good shape for a law school professor. I bet she's a great *oral* advocate, too, *if you know what I mean.*"

Who wouldn't know what he meant? I expected a little more flavor out of so-called smart people. But it was all conversational tofu.

"No, what do you mean?" I asked, hoping to at least get this guy to say blow job.

"Oh, nothing. I'm just saying I'd be honored to proof *her* briefs."

Ah, briefs. The name for legal documents and also the name for underwear. Another clever one. I pressed further.

"Are you saying you want to go through Martha Miller's panties?" I asked.

"Yeah, tell us what you *really* think, Wellington," Edgar added gleefully, reminding us of his presence. He had not picked up on the satire.

"No, no! Of course not. I can't believe you just said that. That's over the top, man! Don't even go there!"

Don't go there? If you think you're tired of hearing that phrase on Ricki Lake, you can't imagine how bad it sounds coming from a third-generation Harvard guy named Wellington. At one point in Wellington's backpedaling, I caught a glimpse of Brian's expression, free and clear of any awareness of my watchful eye. It was the look of playful disbelief, about to become mockery. It was mine. A split second later, we met eyes and shared an unspoken dialogue, which I continued in spoken form:

"I don't know about all that, Wellington. But I for one would love to slip my cock in Martha Miller's mouth, *if you know what I mean.*"

Brian choked up beer convulsively and banged his chest to recover. Then we turned to leave. Edgar was bewildered by the comment. He wore the contemplative look of someone on the cusp of a great decision. He glanced at a slack-jawed Wellington, then back at Brian and me. He followed us. As Brian and I were walking away, Brian rested his hand on my shoulder, and he looked at me and smiled. For the first time at Harvard, I felt light.

Then, an earful of feminine screams came from deep within one of Grendel's dark corners, followed by an exodus of humanity. The crowds parted to reveal a man in his mid-twenties, wearing Mighty Mouse boxers, his pants around his ankles.

"Goddamn, here we go again," Brian sighed.

The quiet that descended immediately after the incident melted into an inquisitive chatter.

"Who's that? Does *he* go to Harvard?" a girlfriend asked.

"Not likely," the boyfriend sniffed.

"That's The Kankoos," Brian said.

"*Does* he go to Harvard?" the girlfriend asked Brian.

"I wouldn't exactly say he goes—"

"As predicted," the boyfriend quipped.

"But he *is* enrolled."

"Unbelievable," the boyfriend pleaded, dragging his girlfriend toward the door.

"Let's go see what the hell he's gotten himself into now," Brian said, motioning for Edgar and me to come along. "There's The Dynamo. He'll know what's up."

Jonathan Strong, aka The Dynamo, had the look of an old college linebacker four years after his playing days were over; more Ivy League than Florida State. His only passions were sex, food, and mind-altering substances of any kind, and he was perpetually loaded with all of them. The sum effect of these forces was a permanent, sedated grin. Yet despite The Dynamo's base outer layer, he held more beneath the surface. He also happened to be a Yale-educated English literature major who would switch without transition from the latest *Hustler* beaver-shot layout to a conversation about how he found *Hamlet* to be "busy, not one of Shakespeare's five best tragedies." He was walking casually away from the dark corner toward the bar, as though nothing unusual had happened, when Brian and I caught up to him.

"Hey Dynamo, what the hell happened over there?"

"What?" The Dynamo asked. If it's possible to slur the word *what*, I'm sure The Dynamo pulled it off. Brian elaborated:

"The screaming, the running away...? Was everybody that freaked out cuz The Kankoos pulled his pants down?"

"Nah, pants came off an hour ago. Kankoos just guzzled a pint of his own piss."

"Piss?" Edgar asked.

"His own. Took the whole thing down in one throw. No gagging either. Those were the rules."

"What the hell did he do that for?" I asked.

"The short answer is sixty bucks. If you want the long one, you're going to have to hang around for a while. Action, in pure form, is always simple. Motivation, though, is where the complex layers of character reside. The Kankoos is *not* a simple man. I'm Jonathan Strong. Friends call me Dynamo."

"How's it goin'?" I muttered, shaken by the fact that the same guy who struggled with a monosyllabic question seconds earlier had oozed a stanza of what sounded to me like poetry.

"What are you guys drinking? I'm buying."

The Dynamo's question temporarily resuscitated my conscience. In all the commotion, I had forgotten my amended two-beer rule. I had labored through Wellington's don't-go-there chatter with two more Buds, and I was now on number four. But even an anal-retentive, guilty Christian knows when there's no reason to look back. I dispensed with the scorecard.

"Two Buds."

"Make that three," Edgar said, reminding us of his presence a foot and a half behind us.

Brian and I headed over to the dark corner and I introduced myself to The Kankoos. Edgar trailed deliberately, maintaining his foot-and-a-half cushion.

"Hi, I'm Jaime Marquart."

"Hey. Kankoos."

The Kankoos. Despite his enigmatic qualities, he had the most inclusive personality I've ever encountered. The Kankoos was capable of extracting life from apparent lifelessness, yet always left everyone he came into contact with feeling like they had received more than they had given. They had. And yet, so had he. The Kankoos had a *life* wish, a gift for hope, a hunger so great it was at once a gift and a curse. There's a big difference between someone who rejects life and someone who has to live it so fully that nothing but 24/7 action will do; but self-destruction and lust for life start to look a lot alike sometimes. The Kankoos was socially aware, but ambivalent. He knew what actions were dictated by a social situation, but often did the opposite. He detested convention of any kind. He never used the truth to maim, but never reserved the truth to spare feelings. He never asked for more than he gave, and he didn't ask for much. With The Kankoos, everything was unconditional and never situational— sometimes for the better, sometimes for the worse. The Kankoos's fashion choice was irrelevant.

After a parched fifteen minutes, The Dynamo came back with our beers. I took a glance at my watch. *Damn!* Ten 'til eleven, and I still had about three more hours of Criminal Law and Civil Procedure reading to finish off the study session Brian and I had started in the library before Bar Review. The Kankoos caught my anxious glance and spoke a one-and-a-quarter-word sentence that everyone but me understood immediately:

"Mmmm . . . Foxwoods."

Everyone leapt into action. The Dynamo picked up his cell phone and began dialing 24-hour rental car outlets. Brian and The Kankoos headed out the door. Edgar moved with equal urgency in the other direction, back toward Wellington and crew. I ran after Brian and The Kankoos.

"Wait! What's Foxwoods?" I asked.

They laughed incredulously, as if I'd asked what Fenway Park was.

"A casino. Come on, gotta get to Christy's. Need road sodas."

"Road sodas are not sodas, *if you know what I mean*," Brian said.

There was never time for the question, "Are you in?" Never time to formulate an answer, to weigh the pros and cons. I was in.

Five minutes at Christy's quick stop, a twenty-minute cab ride, and twenty minutes at Alamo later, we were speeding down I-95, energized by a night that was going from mundane to memorable. An hour and forty minutes after that, we were rolling blearily through dense Connecticut wood, fending off yawns. The thought of my unfinished Contracts reading was just re-entering my consciousness when, around one last windy bend, it came into view: an immense, glowing castle blasting out of the darkness. Posture improved by 45 degrees, car speed increased by ten miles per hour, and energy returned to the level of a brisk morning walk.

This was Foxwoods. The largest casino in North America.

Inside I got $60 from an ATM. That was my entertainment budget for the week, but I was trying my best not to look like a neophyte. I had turned twenty-one a few months before leaving for law school, and this was my first time in a casino.

"Big spender?" The Kankoos asked, glancing at the three twenties I had just withdrawn for a three-dollar surcharge.

"Hey, that's still a lot of money where I come from."

"It's a decent amount of money anywhere. But we'll see if sixty bucks gets your rocks off after a few more trips."

A few more trips? The thought was both enticing and unnerving. I was still in the throes of the first one.

"I'm gonna take a look around for a while."

"Alright. I'll either be at one of those blackjack tables over there, the cash machine, or the pisser."

I had never considered what adrenaline smells like, but on that first visit to Foxwoods I was certain it was a cross between expensive cigar smoke and cheap perfume. The casino was teeming with hyperkinetic senior citizens and fleet-of-foot, obese middle-agers moving with urgency from machine to machine and table to table. Some of these same people wouldn't part with thirty-nine extra cents to supersize their Extra Value Meal on the way to Foxwoods. Now they all reflexively dumped several dollars a minute into machines that pinged and clanged with cascading coins. They diverted from their purpose only to yell at big-haired waitresses who zoomed by with "complimentary" drinks and wore fake squaw outfits, one part Pocahontas, one part Madonna. Lights flashed, sirens wailed, and hearts pounded in perfect harmony. I looked at my watch. It was 3:00 A.M., Monday night/Tuesday morning. Not much time. I changed my course and joined The Kankoos and crew in the blackjack pit.

By 4:00, I'd turned sixty dollars into two hundred. Choice, rules, and strategy offered the illusion of control. I felt more smart than lucky. As I was coloring up, The Dynamo commented:

"That was the worst thing that could have happened to you."

I was hooked from the get-go. Why? At the time, I didn't consider it much. I just loved the rush and liked winning a dollar a little more than I disliked losing one. It did occur to me that the money I was risking could have bought me a new winter coat or a new pair of shoes. But you never come home from the store with a sixty-dollar box of shoes, open it up, and find your shoes in there along with a hundred and forty dollars. If the chance of that actually happening is worth about two pennies to the dollar more to you than the chance of coming home with an empty shoebox, you're a gambler. It was worth it to me.

"Would somebody please stop that goddamned ringing?"

I slammed the alarm clock. It continued. I unplugged the alarm clock. It persisted. Somebody, Brian I think, finally realized it was the phone.

"Hello . . . What? . . . It is? One more hour . . ."

"Fuck that, one more day," muttered The Kankoos.

"One more hour will be great. Thanks."

What the ringing could not fully do, the odor did. I was now completely awake, still struggling to figure out where in hell I was. And what was that smell? And:

"What time is it?"

"One o'clock," said Brian. "That was the front desk. Just a courtesy call. One's usually the latest checkout time. But they'll give us as long as we need, thanks to The Kankoos's stellar play last night."

"Stellar play?" The Kankoos asked.

The Dynamo, who'd been calling dinosaurs in the bathroom, poked his head out and answered:

"The casino host deemed your play stellar last night. How do you think we ended up in this suite?"

"Comcheck?" asked a pensive Kankoos.

"Comcheck."

"Son of a cunt!"

Comcheck? The Kankoos patted his pockets. They crackled. Money? He reached into his right pocket and pulled out a receipt—$500 dollars, Citibank Visa.

"Pissing Jesus!"

He reached into his left pocket and produced another receipt. $700, MBNA Platinum.

"Oh, for shit's sake!"

One more reach into the left pocket yielded one more receipt. $1,000, MBNA Platinum again.

The Kankoos sat there for a few seconds, his head down and in the palms of his hands. Then, his head tilted upward and to one side and his brow lifted as a hopeful thought entered his head. He pulled out his wallet. Empty.

The Kankoos laughed.

I couldn't laugh. The last of my classes, Contracts, had just ended. Three lectures meant two hundred pages of reading and thirty pages of notes, gone forever. In my stomach, Maker's Mark, Cuervo, and chili-cheese dogs fought among themselves at the entry point of my intestines.

"What's wrong, Marquart? Hung over?" Brian asked.

"Something like that."

"So much for all that work in the library yesterday, huh?" Brian said.

"Yeah."

"We'll catch up. I'm heading straight for Langdell as soon as we get back."

"Brian, you're an idiot," The Kankoos replied, a strange claim for a guy who just discovered he'd blown $2,200. "How many times do I have to tell you, you're already ahead of the game."

Before responding to The Kankoos, Brian leaned toward me and explained:

"The Kankoos spent the first week of school copying old exams, which are all available in the library, and collecting old student outlines for all our classes. By the end of the week, he had put together a four-inch stack of papers that he claims contains everything he needs to pass our first-semester courses. After that, he swore off going to class."

Brian then turned to The Kankoos:

"Kankoos, *you* are the idiot. Your plan would be perfect, except for the fact that you've ignored about a hundred and five drawbacks. For one, your teachers are going to call on you. And then there's the matter of new material. What are you going to do when the professor throws in an issue decided by a new case? Or what about something someone brought up in class? And what about the fact that you're going to have to take the Bar when this is all over? Then, of course, there's the law job after that."

"Teachers have to contact you and ask you to show up before they fail you. New stuff and class discussions are in notes and new outlines, which I'll borrow or steal later. There's a two-month course after we graduate that teaches us everything we need to know for the Bar. I don't have to take a law job when this is over. But if I do, whether I'm any good at it won't have a damn thing to do with knowing the law. You might be right. I probably have overlooked some drawbacks. But so far no one's come up with any I haven't already thought of. And I can give you some damn solid drawbacks of *going* to class, too, not the least of which is going to class."

"Well, I choose the library. We'll see soon enough who's right."

"What about you, Marquart?" The Kankoos asked. "You look like ass."

"This was a bad idea."

"Hey, look on the bright side: you got a new hobby and made some new friends. Not bad for one night's work."

"Yeah, too bad law school isn't a popularity contest."

"No, it's not. It's a *perspective* contest, and you're all losing it. Let's get outta here. I gotta go sell some stuff."

The ride home from Foxwoods gave me a chance to assess my situation. I made over a hundred bucks at the tables, but would spend the rest of the week catching up in school. Around me in the car, everyone but The Dynamo (driving) was asleep.

"Dynamo. I hate to ask you this, but it's really important. I need to borrow your cell phone to make a long-distance call. I'll pay you back as soon as we get home."

"Whatever," he shrugged, tossing me the phone.

I dialed. She answered.

"Hóla?"

"Hóla, Elise?"

"Sí. Hi, Jaime! Is something wrong?"

"No, just wanted to see what was up. Did it sound like something was wrong?"

"Oh, no, it's just . . . I wasn't expecting your call for another couple of days."

"Well, I came into a little money so I thought I'd call."

"Oh, cool. But you actually *just* caught me on my way out the door. Can I call you back?"

"Oh. Where're you going?" I asked.

"Just out to grab a drink or two."

It was 8:00 P.M. in Bilbao.

"Great! Who are you going with?"

"Well, I told you about Tracy, right, the British exchange student?"

"Cool..."

"...and her friend Maria..."

"Great..."

"...oh, and Ariel."

"."

"Jaime? Are you still there?"

"I'm here."

"OK. Well, I gotta go, so I'll talk to you later. OK?"

"OK, bye."

As I hit the End button, The Kankoos, who was apparently awake the whole time, laughed conspicuously.

"What Kankoos?"

"Girlfriend?"

"Yeah."

"I figured," The Kankoos said.

"What's funny about that?"

"You wanted her to be miserable too."

I shrugged off the comment, but he was right. I needed her to feel miserable, just as badly as Tom O'Toule needed me to feel stupid.

"What kind of name is Ariel, anyway?" I asked.

"I think it's Middle Eastern," The Dynamo said.

"That's not what he means, Dynamo," The Kankoos laughed. "He wants to know if it's a dude or a chick."

"No. Just curious."

"OK, whatever. Well, if you *do* care, I think it's about fifty-fifty."

"No way," The Dynamo said. "It's a chick's name all the way. You know, The Little Mermaid."

"That's a cartoon, Dynamo," The Kankoos said.

"What, cartoons don't have real names?"

"All I'm saying is, I knew a couple guys named Ariel, too. It's fifty-fifty."

"It doesn't matter," I pleaded. "That's not why I asked."

But it was why I asked.

CHAPTER 8 | # PRICE OF ADMISSION

"I'm Lucy. Heard you used to be a bike messenger."

Those were Lucy Faar's first words to me. She knocked at my door one afternoon in September. She'd brought her bike.

"My ex just mailed it to me from New York. I have no idea how to put the thing together."

Nor did I. The disassembled bike was in a box. Tim Apparel emerged from his room, took in the scene, and headed out. I told Lucy I would get her bike rolling, but that I'd need a few days. She came into my room, dropped the bike box, and sat on my bed.

By the time of Lucy's visit, a pattern of bland contentment had taken shape. Wake up. Bike ride. Torts. Another ride. Dinner at Breakers, the eating club. Evening bong session. Splash of bourbon. Sleep and repeat. Sunday mornings I cooked breakfast at Breakers. Lucy amended the pattern without destroying it. My time with her felt clean and unspectacular—the simplicity I had sought in law school. Rather than pure solitude, though, I felt as if I had scored an unexpected bonus, a little human contact.

Most afternoons, after Lucy's last class and my last bike ride, she would set up in my room. Lucy always sprawled herself across the same spot on my floor, always borrowed the same blue pen. We talked and shared the bong, listening to our local radio DJ, Carson Daly. At night we listened to *LoveLine,* with Dr. Drew and Adam Corolla. Adam would say, "Drew, that's ricockulous," and Lucy would say, whenever blowing off most of my classes came up, "Byrnes, that's ricockulous." Lucy always headed home at night and, after a phone call to say she'd gotten there safely, we'd each sleep. The phone calls, I think, kept me from falling back into that edge-of-sleep longing for the past, Helen in particular. Had I been truly bare and alone I might have been grounded by the futile wish that I should have just stuck with Helen; thus no Weld and no law school. Instead, if you had asked me then, I would have lazily told you I was enjoying law school, when in fact it was only my time with Lucy, not really law school itself, that kept me from looking backward.

The Lucy Period was brief—a seven-week slice of law school's first semester. One afternoon, she hit a serious note for the first time. Before law school, the New York boyfriend had ditched her without warning:

"I had to beg Stanford to let me come. I'd already turned them down. But when I said I was bailing out on *Yale* they got cooperative."

It seemed as if everyone at Stanford had been dinged at Yale and had gotten in, but affirmatively chosen not to go, to Harvard. Lucy was the relatively rare person who had said no to Yale. She was at Stanford because she wanted to be, needed to be—in California, outside New York's emotional reach. She couldn't be bothered to hint at things you'd eventually discover or figure out.

"I got 176 on the LSAT," Lucy told me. "First time I ever missed points on a standardized test. How'd you do?"

I told her.

"Jesus. I'm nine smarter than you," she said.

Lucy was proof that the LSAT is a predictor of some useful real-life talents. There's a funky section on the LSAT known as "games." It's where people fuck up the LSAT. Meltdown is possible; missing whole chunks of six, eight, ten questions, not uncommon. Blowing the games section can be enough to get you the heave-ho at the most snooty law schools, even if you had kick-ass college grades.

The LSAT games section[3] isn't so uselessly abstract as it first appears. It gauges whether you function well amid a flurry of information and action, a circumstance Lucy sought out and prospered in. Sitting in my room she would steep tea, listen to Howard Stern, read from two (sometimes three) casebooks at once, get high, tell the story of her life before law school, speak dolefully about her ex-boyfriend, ecstatically about Mozart and The Clash, all simultaneously, and, exactly four minutes after she put the steeping cage into the simmering water, she'd remove it, then sip the perfectly produced tea as her mind stored a just-read case and directed its thoughts toward how that case might figure on the final exam, still months in the future.

Lucy's instinct was to expose rather than conceal. She told me:

"The break up freed me to act on desire."

"So you . . ."

". . . got a ton of action. None of that wait-'til-the-third-date bullshit. I stopped worrying about my 'number.' Turns out, though, it's other women who can be the worst sexual oppressors of all. They're the first to whisper 'slut.'"

"Resentment masquerading as rectitude."

"It's already happened here, after my little hookup with Bobby Boylan."

"Bobby?"

"That troll Becky Klamm found out and told Tabitha that *it makes Lucy look like a not very serious person . . .*"

"You and Bobby Boylan?"

"It makes Becky Klamm look like the twenty-five-year-old virgin she is. Yeah, Bobby Boylan. The guy with all the wine. First week of school. Before classes started. Forgettable, but not entirely unfun."

---

3. An LSAT "game" might go like this: Each jam package contains three different flavors. Apple jam is always packaged with blueberry jam; currant jam can be packaged with marmalade. If there is currant jam in a package, there must also be quince. Quince jam and marmalade can never be packaged directly next to each other. Which of the following is a possible jam package:

(A) Currant, Apple, Blueberry

(B) Currant, Quince, Blueberry

(C) Currant, Marmalade, Quince, Apple

(D) Marmalade, Currant, Quince, Currant

(E) Apple, Apple, Apple, Blueberry

(The answer is at www.brushwiththelaw.com.)

Lucy was a serious person. She always went to class, always read all her cases. Around a law school, though, Lucy was threatening. She mixed her seriousness with a vitality that exposed the anxious types—like her early antagonist Becky Klamm—as being self-consciously dull and overwrought. Lucy believed nothing so much as that she had found life's golden balance between work and play, reason and passion. She took to task extremists on either side of her. When Lucy chided me for not going to class, I explained, as Tim Apparel had to me, that outlines would suffice.

Tim Apparel and I had been on little more than hey-what's-up terms since our costly bike store trip and the dinner conversation where he had advised me against buying law books. I imagined Tim Apparel would play out as a male Niccola; that he would have thwarted the whole get-the-hell-out-of-Boston-and-go-clean thing. But after Lucy's first visit I had to call on him. It was Tim Apparel who would assemble Lucy's bike. Tim Apparel was always either locked in his room, riding his bike, or going on cryptic errands. He rarely turned up to eat at Breakers. In stray moments, I began to guess what the glass pipe and his distaste for pot, taken together, might mean. In one way, Lucy and Tim Apparel were alike. As he put Lucy's bike together, Tim Apparel smoked a cigarette, read a novel (Don DeLillo's *White Noise*), watched *Beavis and Butthead,* and traded options online. They were critically different, though. Lucy was safety, Tim Apparel risk. And I liked the idea of Lucy's friends—Bobby Boylan and Tabitha Mullen—becoming my own friends. They did, for a time. Bobby yelled to me one day after Torts, as I was heading back to Leland.

"Hey Byrnes, we're punting class. Come to The City."

We took Lucy's car to San Francisco. Halfway there, Tabitha asked:

"How the fuck did you go from being a bike messenger to a speech-writer?"

This had never come up with Lucy. So it would be a fresh story for everyone. I told them: about Helen, all about Helen, and how I answered that phone call at Helen's place. Then, the next part, which I'd never really told myself:

"That afternoon I went out to play hockey and the whole time three prophecies swirled in my mind: *I'll be the randy young aide to the governor who might be president . . . . The Boston Globe will do stories about me . . . . I'll get tons of action.*"

"All true?" Tabitha asked.

"Sort of. Everything came to pass in the specifics, but the specifics turned out to be trifles. Weld still *might* be president; he just never will. Davis Mund has a better shot. The *Globe* devoted all of a column inch to me the whole time. And I'd have traded the tons of action for an ounce of Helen."

"So she could be *here*," Bobby said. "Teaching at Stanford, right? If she got the job the professor was calling about?"

"Kind of spooky if you run into her," Tabitha said.

"I'm pretty sure that won't happen."

After the usual San Francisco parking search. . . *shit, a driveway . . . hydrant . . . too small . . . a spot!* We settled into a Noe Valley bar and another afternoon buzz, a privilege reserved for the idle rich, the terminally down-and-out, and law students. There was nowhere we absolutely had to be until early January—exams. In this regard, law school was less burdensome than college, with its periodic papers and midterms, and far less so than high school, full of daily quizzes and a truancy policy with teeth.

"No place to be—best place of all," Lucy said.

As the night crowd appeared, Lucy suggested heading over to Berkeley. We meandered on the way, stopping to look at the abandoned *Real World* house on Lombard, taking a detour across the Golden Gate, smoking a joint in the Marin hills, and then making our way back through San Francisco, across the Bay Bridge, into Oakland. Inside a windowless bar, we sat thigh-to-thigh: me and Lucy, Tabitha and Bobby. We then did a little drunk driving, parked, and set out on foot in Berkeley, with its street hawkers checking on us at least once per block . . . *bud? . . . tickets? . . . need anything? . . . rock? . . . all set? . . . change?*

Tickets? Natalie Merchant. Face value. Good seats. But not together. We went. Bobby and Tabitha sat together in the balcony, Lucy and I took the floor seats.

After the concert, we drove the long way home, via the Pacific Coast Highway, to Half Moon Bay. Lucy tossed blankets and pillows from her trunk, and we claimed our distant spots, sleeping in pairs on the beach.

In California, the sun doesn't rise over the ocean. The big hills that abut the Pacific kept the sun from waking us until ten in the morning. We gathered the bedding and headed back to school, for Torts at 11:15. We wound up a canyon road, reaching the top of the mountain ridge, above Silicon Valley, Stanford's red roofs a distant blot between the hills' base and the Bay. We traveled along the top of the ridge, Skyline Boulevard, then descended the other side and headed toward the Law School. I reaffirmed the goal of reaching Skyline—on a bike—something I took to have ultimate purpose, in the way I imagined others in law school aspired to *Law Review*, a swank clerkship, or a job that makes people say *wow!* I kept this to myself, tuning out the conversation in the car, so blithe and formless on the way to San Francisco, which, only now I recall, had turned to grades, law review, clerkships, and law firm jobs. We rolled up to the Law School five minutes before Torts was to begin.

In the Law School courtyard, a group from our Torts class sat wearing shorts, shaded by palm trees, with laptops and casebooks opened. As we approached them, I glanced down at Celia Shackles's casebook. She had underlined the day's assigned reading in four different ink colors, a sign of industriousness seconded by her evident lack of sleep.

"I hear you guys went up to The City yesterday," Celia said.

"I feel *so* guilty for missing Crim," Lucy said. "But it was such a beautiful day. We just drove up, had dinner, and headed right back. It was nice, though. Nice to get away, take a little break."

We all made our way to Torts. Professor Howard walked in and snapped her notes on the lectern:

"Last night you read about the doctrine that is known as assumption of the risk. Can anyone tell us how assumption of the risk might arise in tort law. Bobby Boylan?"

"Could I get back to you on that one?"

"Fair enough," Howard said. "We'll give you a few minutes to assemble your thoughts, Bobby."

"Actually, I was thinking more like tomorrow."

There was a slight murmur of chuckles, which might have settled into snickers had the prevailing mood turned against Bobby. It didn't. Professor Howard was convulsively amused. Following her lead, the class let out one of those communal laughter blasts that makes people in adjacent classrooms wonder what they're missing.

"OK, then. Does anyone—other than the indisposed Bobby—recall how Judge Cardozo described assumption of the risk in the *Murphy* case?"

A student attempted an answer that began with blustery confidence but trailed away in confusion. "Murphy concerned an amusement park ride, called...It was a ride at Coney Island that jostled people around, I know that... that was the whole point of the ride. The plaintiff was injured, broke his...sprained...and, and, anyway, sued, but the amusement park. They..."

The stumbling answer put me into a temporary dissonance. I recognized this person. But, then, he couldn't be who I thought he was.

"Burley, thank you. That's getting us there," Howard said.

Burley. A. Burley Mahnmeets. The always-closed door in Leland. The business card. Big pompous fuck. The shirtless photo on Tim Apparel's Web site. The Barrister. He must have been one of those geniuses whose ideas best found expression in the written rather than spoken word.

"Anyone else?" Howard asked, relieving The Barrister.

Celia Shackles's right hand floated into the air. With her left hand, she turned her casebook pages in smooth control; first multiple pages, then a single page forward, and then two pages back. Celia didn't look tired anymore. Her index finger came to rest on the passage Howard was looking for, and Celia knew it.

"Celia?"

"The ride was called the Flopper, which Judge Cardozo noted was itself 'warning to the timid.' There was no recovery for the plaintiff, Murphy, despite his broken kneecap. He assumed the risk because, quote, 'a fall was foreseen as one of the risks of the adventure. There would have been no point to the whole thing, no adventure about it, if the risk had not been there,'" Celia said. She added, "Judge Cardozo appears to be saying that assumption of the risk arises when the risk associated with an activity is merged with the very essence of that activity."

"Such as?" Howard asked.

Answers flowed:

"Rock climbing."

"Skydiving."

"Not doing your Torts reading." (Bobby again); Howard guffawed.

"Snowboarding."

"Rollerblading."

This was too inviting an opportunity not to inoculate myself against being called on when a real legal question was in play.

"Mountain biking," I said.

"Let's stop there for a moment," Howard said.

Shit.

"Suppose . . . " Howard said, looking at her seating chart, ". . . suppose, Robert, you've had a mountain biking accident. You incur enormous medical expenses. A broken leg. Serious internal injuries. You're unable to work. Lost wages—lots of lost wages given what they're paying you guys right out of law school these days. [Laughter] Are you out of luck simply because mountain biking is *dangerous?* What isn't? Life is dangerous. Does that mean we all just assume the risk? Should we scrap tort law altogether? Is assumption of the risk the exception that swallows the rule?"

"Compound question!" Bobby said.

The resulting laughter opened a space to come to my first and most enduring revelation about law school: there is no answer, only analysis between the extremes. So, a good starting point: *it depends.*

"It depends," I said, "how broadly you construe assumption of the risk. Obviously the 'life is dangerous' position hasn't been adopted or else we wouldn't be here."

"So what about your mountain biking example? Too dangerous an activity to sue for resulting injuries?"

"I'd say you assume the risk. Crashing's part of a good ride."

Torts ended. The night before was starting to manifest as full-bodied staleness. My instinct was to head back to Leland, take a nap, then go for a bike ride. I didn't. Instead, I went to the Coffee House with Bobby Boylan. Bobby pulled another bottle of wine from his "bag." We sat with four other first-year law students I had seen, noticed, but never before met. This was the same foursome Bobby had pointed out to me during our first after-Torts drinking spree. *Those four are up for adventure.* The conversation again turned to Bobby's law school vision: *take everything pass/fail, don't be like the uptight dorks at Harvard, suck the marrow out of life.* Then, Bobby got specific:

"Law school could be our last chance at sexual abandon. I don't have to tell Byrnesie here any of this."

It was Bobby's second allusion to knowing something about my past. The Four asked Bobby what he was talking about. He explained:

"A kinda-sorta college girlfriend—Niccola Renton. . . "

Niccola. Bobby had been one of the hundred or so guys she'd done at Yale—they'd run into each other in Boston at some point, and they had the so-what-have-you-been-up-to exchange. Niccola told him. Apparently I'd figured in several of her stories, stories Bobby told with amazing accuracy. Bobby related, for instance, how Niccola and I, along with several of our fleeting groupies, found ourselves on the roof of a Boston townhouse, coked up and looking to land softly on the comedown. With a big group, there are so many preferences to accommodate that Niccola diagrammed, on her Office of the Governor notepad, who would be where and doing what to whom, at least to start. By group sex standards, it was a successful venture. Like a good summer camp or cruise, there was an abundance of activities to satisfy diverse abilities and desires.

Bobby finished telling the story, my story. Then he got up to leave, to go to Criminal Law. Bobby was an odd person, pitching an orgy that he would not himself participate in. I remained with The Four. We exhaustively considered the costs and benefits of group sex, tallying more benefits than costs. Toward the end the conversation drew toward a consensus.

"A lot of straight guys worry that they'll have to suck cock."

"Price of admission?"

"At least no one goes puttering around wondering, how long should I wait to call the eight people I just boned?"

"There's no 'I don't do that on a first orgy' either."

"Still tough to get it started."

"Someone still has to be brave and say let's do this."

"A leader."

"And at that point you're pretty sure no one will dissent."

"Or you're ready to pass it off as a joke."

Then someone, not me, said: "So, it's decided then. Orgy on Halloween."

October rolled along. Most days, Lucy would come by my room and then phone before sleep. We made a few more San Francisco trips with Bobby and Tabitha. The Barrister's closed door continued to suggest scholarly dedication. Tim Apparel's door stayed closed, too. Subsequent talks with The Four refined our orgy plans, which might otherwise have faded away as a onetime conversational lark. In Torts, Professor Howard took up causation. To be liable for tort damages, in addition to being negligent, you also have to have caused the injury alleged. Causation, in torts, is limited

to immediate as opposed to attenuated, quirky, or faraway causes. Suppose
you call me on the phone and delay my departure just long enough that I
leave my house precisely as an anvil falls on my head. You have "caused"
my harm, in that I wouldn't have gotten plunked if you hadn't called. The
phone call is a "but-for" cause. It is not, however, a "proximate" cause.
(And, in any event, making a phone call isn't generally a negligent act.)
Whoever dropped the anvil, on the other hand, was likely negligent in
some way, had a running duty not to drop anvils on others, and is the proximate cause, the legal cause. In other words, all proximate causes are but-
for causes, but not all but-for causes are proximate causes. All events
have a potentially infinite but-for causal history. For instance, had I not
gone to graduate school I wouldn't have met Helen. No Helen, then no
phone call about the Weld speechwriter job. No Weld, then no Niccola.
No Niccola, then no group sex conversation with The Four, without
which I wouldn't have been in that pulsing bedroom as Stanford Law
School's Halloween party thumped beneath us.

The orgy had hit a lull. Handling the knob of a foreign cock for the
first time ever, I passed on the chance to give a blow job, fuck or be
fucked. A penis attached to someone else has a grotesque ominousness that
can drive a wedge between abstract desire—something you would do—and
actually doing. I needed a little time away from the orgy.

Out in the main party, an impromptu bongo line wound up the stairs.
Standing at the bottom, The Plumber was dressed as Jesus. He offered me
a Eucharistic wafer with an off-color blot at its center and the last inch of
his joint. Davis Mund stood in happy conversation with Jana Lee and
Becky Klamm. The Barrister was there, costumeless, in effect as himself. In
the living room a second- or third-year student wearing a Bill Clinton mask
sat watching a *Beavis and Butthead Moronathon*, getting baked, and making
video quips drawn on a subtler intelligence than even Beavis or Butthead.
His quite smashing girlfriend sat next to him. Bobby, accurately as it turned
out, referred to him as The Future Supreme Court Clerk. He was a stunningly funny person, as most truly brilliant people are. The Future Supreme
Court Clerk was no dork, though. Bobby hadn't gotten that one right.

I reached the door and spotted Lucy, Bobby, and Tabitha, outside, in
the distance. Nearer to me, alone, was Celia Shackles. She was inscrutably
done up, seemingly as Rococo Woman.

"Celia?"

"It is I. Simple skirt and sleeveless becomes you," Celia said. She angled her head high, with imperial pensiveness. "There is an undeniable fecundity to this night."

Celia was more right than she knew. I sensed vibe from her. Fresh from an orgy, though, you feel as if you're getting vibe from everyone. Then, someone else's words rumbled between us:

"Celia! You embrace the pagan ritual with all the aplomb I expected." It was The Barrister. They seemed a match. I was off.

"Gotta run, Celia; see you in Torts."

As I made my way outside, toward Bobby, Lucy, and Tabitha, I had no thoughts, only sensation, a tingly trance. I joined them as they were drinking beer, passing a bowl, and talking about why they had come to law school. Lucy asked me:

"So, Byrnes, why did you?"

Lucy's simple question undid my trance. Yet another basic matter that had never come up between us: *why law school?* There was the official reason, the second and successful application essay:

APPLICATION TO STANFORD LAW SCHOOL
ROBERT BYRNES

My boss turned to ask me the location of an obscure Boston street.

"You know that from your bike messenger days," he presumed, correctly. He added: "Probably the best job you'll ever have."

Bill Weld could never have been a bike messenger, living outside the expectations of his social class. For the first time he (public figure, prominent family) showed a streak of envy.

And he might have been right. Some jobs dominate your mind, others your body. Biking dominated my body, but my thoughts were always my own. A romantic image of life as a bike messenger survived my actually doing it.

Growing up, I also had a romantic image of politics. I remember watching Governor Dukakis speak on television, when I was in high school. Dukakis's words seemed to have been delivered from the heavens. I had no idea his speech had been written by an actual person, and that for Dukakis's successor, that actual person would be me.

The romance of politics also survives. In my work, I live beyond the expectations I had for myself, and my thoughts can live beyond me, as well.

In a bar, I once watched Governor Weld deliver a televised gay rights speech I had written. There were no cheers, but there were no derisive remarks—a small victory for tolerance. I told Weld his gay rights position would probably be his most significant contribution as Governor.

And while my mind can never be entirely free writing his speeches, it can travel paths I once thought off-limits to people like me.

Like most official documents, the essay lacked complete candor. And, anyway, it didn't say a thing about law school. Among friends, I told the truth:

"I needed to get away from Boston."

Lucy was costumed as "Justice," with what looked like drug scales in her left hand and eyeholes cut in the blindfold. She took a hit off the bowl and handed it to me. I got high instantly—happy high, not paranoid high. Grouped not far from us was the Public Interest Crowd. They always had the best weed and were fortunate, then, in having come to law school for strongly felt reasons; better off now, too, in that they tend to like their jobs more than those who work in law firms. Lucy's face went comically expectant. An animated thought bubble appeared over her head, reminding me that her question lingered: why *law school?* Bobby and Tabitha were both entering the early stages of an involuntary smile. I continued:

"I just..."

Bobby began to chuckle, for no outward reason. Then Lucy chuckled, then Tabitha. I laughed fully as I forced out the words:

"*The Paper Chase...*"

With that, the laughter virus claimed us all. We fell to the ground. Giggly pot: a marginal joke or no joke at all, even a single word, and you're clipped by knee-weakening hilarity. We tried to keep up the conversation.

"Do you love the law?"

"The life of the law is the law itself."

"Admission to Stanford Law School *is* very competitive."

"What was that thing?"

"Thing?"

"The admissions thing."

"The one about..."

"About how hard it is."

"What was it..."

"Rigorous?"

"No, I know... *competition is...*"

Then, at the same instant, we all tapped an identical memory source and used our last available speaking air to say the same word, in the most farcical voices we could manage:

"*Severe!!!!!!!!!!!!*"

"*Severe!!!!!!!!!!!!*"

"*Severe!!!!!!!!!!!!*"

"*Severe!!!!!!!!!!!!*"

An image lit up in my mind:

Admission to Stanford Law School is based primarily upon superior academic achievement and potential to contribute to the development and practice of the law. Competition is

severe:

the 180 members of the Class were selected from among 4,000 applicants, and most were drawn from the upper 5 percent of their undergraduate class and the upper 5 percent of the LSAT pool.[4]

And the satisfaction was this: Lucy, Bobby, and Tabitha were all seeing the same thing.

We stayed on the ground. The laughter would fade. Then someone would say *Severe!* and it would begin again. We would still ourselves, fighting the laughter waves into faint sputters. Finally, the word lost its comic force. Unprovoked, I started churning again, and Lucy put her hand on my forearm, as if to say: *stop . . . if you laugh we'll all laugh.* She was right. It was time to head back to the bedroom, back with The Four.

---

4. From the Stanford Law School Web site.

I peeled off the ground, away from Lucy, Tabitha, and Bobby; then past Celia, alone again. Celia Shackles had her problems, but she also had the rarest poise: standing comfortably alone among the usual social constellations. I walked by The Future Supreme Court Clerk, The Barrister, and The Plumber, back through the house, up the stairs, and into the bedroom.

The Four had arranged themselves in an oral sex Möbius strip. I slid out of my Ann Taylor skirt, unhooked a front-clasp bra, and made a gentle leap back onto the bed. Bodies reconfigured to accommodate me. And you know what? It's all that. Lives up to its mythology. This wank fantasy is indeed fantastic. I'd had other glossy images growing up. Politics for one. Don't laugh. When you're fifteen and you hear grown men talking in that full oratorical lather, it's natural to think they're onto something cosmic; that they're sincere. So they turned out to be a bunch of windbag flabasses (with juiced-up flakes writing their shit for them, at that). Scratch politics. You move on to the next and last unexplored myth. Law school looked to be looped into the Bigger Things. Check out *The Paper Chase*. Professor Kingsfield inspired more fear and awe than the Great and Powerful Oz. By contrast, I hadn't seen my own real-life Contracts professor since early September. Law school wasn't quite matching its movie mythology. But your basic three-on-two orgy is bigger, better, and more alive than in the catalogue picture. No letdown. Just like they say—it's lounging on a cocaine-sand beach, with rose-juice water, gourmet oxygen, palanquin transports, and a massaging, noncancerous sun. There are more reality-bound reasons to like an orgy, too. Having so quickly traversed sexual intimacy, here were four people to grab for lunch, phone on a whim, and chat with in the dead time before Torts. Solitude's a fine thing in theory. And I've always had a lusty admiration for people like Celia Shackles and Dawn, even The Barrister and Tim Apparel, in their own ways, who look to be most at peace when they're alone. I just prefer to have someone next to me.

Halloween night, 1995: sweet thoughts, summary sensations. Whatever the reason, there I was, in law school. I had found friends, a spicy sexual counterlife and, when it was all over, I'd have a swank credential that more or less guaranteed a job for life. On the edge of sleep, I thought, *My life has been populated for all of time and*... Then there was one last thought before drifting off. I resolved to stop going to all classes, even Torts. I would devote myself to biking, at least until the rainy season began; just biking, no law school at all for a couple of weeks. I envisioned finally hitting Skyline, which I knew would deliver sensory overload: the Pacific Ocean to one side, the Bay to the other, Silicon Valley below, that unmistakable nugget cluster at the tip of it all, San Francisco, the most enchantingly beautiful city I have ever seen, and... *and sleep.*

CHAPTER 9 | **DISSONANCE**

I didn't sleep the day after my first trip to Foxwoods. I got back to my room at three in the afternoon. By 3:30, I'd borrowed Edgar's notes from that day's lectures. From 3:30 until 6:00, I rewrote his notes into my notebook. Then I turned to the reading I hadn't finished in the library the day before. I was done by 8:00 P.M. I spent the next twelve hours finishing all of my assignments for the next day. Then, I ate my first meal in twenty hours—plain bagel with low-fat cream cheese and coffee (black)—and made it to class ten minutes early. Prepared. I was not called on.

The rest of September and first part of October were the same: study until midnight, wake up at six, study until class, go to class, do it again. I limited my contact with The Kankoos and crew to the dining hall, necessity errands, and the occasional movie. I quit gambling. Coasting on the fumes of guilt and fear, that regimen lasted three weeks.

At the beginning of October, I was snoozing from 6:00 to 8:45 every morning, waking up just in time to walk to class. By the time 11:00 P.M. rolled around, I told myself I would study better lying in my bed and reading. I would crash inside of five minutes. By mid-October, I had put together a reward system to keep myself alert and motivated. For reading a page, I claimed a chunk of chocolate. For twenty pages, a little Internet exploration. With a full day's assignment for one class came a television interlude. And all of my assignments for a day meant a couple hours in Harvard Square.

That incentive system lost its punch by Day Ten. Just in time, I discovered a new, unlikely source of motivation: sparse Internet bandwidth. In the fall of 1995, two factors defined Internet usage: (1) graphics were rapidly replacing text as primary Web content and (2) connection speeds were crawling along at 14400 bps. This implied two things: (1) high-quality porn was available with the click of the mouse, but (2) you needed the patience of a nun to enjoy it. Downloads could take up to fifteen minutes a picture. And if you made the mistake of falling for one of those phony free sites, you could end up in Pop-Up Window Hell. Three-hour-plus tugs-of-war were common back then. This must have been frustrating as hell for sneaky husbands and horny teenagers. But for me it meant at least four pages of case reading per download. And the best night's sleep short of prescription drugs. I'm convinced the phrase "sleep like a baby" lives on only because the phrase "sleep like a man who's just yanked off to Internet porn" is too cumbersome and less well-received as elevator chatter. As it turned out, alternating Jenna Jameson money shots with Oliver Wendell Holmes wasn't exactly the most efficient way to study. Still, morale was up and burnout down. And the New Incentive Regime was born. Read four pages, kick back to the Internet, read four pages. The reward-to-work ratio came in at around seven to one, and there was always the Protestant guilt to contest (which I had not gotten over), but at least there was work.

But burnout wasn't the only source of my dwindling work ethic. In my second month at Harvard, healthy skepticism was replacing fear. By late October, the Harvard myth was losing its shine. First, there was the woman in our Contracts class with the amazing capacity to generate organized, complete-sentence, hypersyllabic commentary on the fly every time she spoke. In the middle of one of her filibusters, I mentioned to Brian how impressive her command of the parol evidence rule was. He pointed to a set of three-by-fives beside her, one of which was wedged upright in the crease of the table that held student name placards in days past.

"Cue cards," Brian whispered.

But nothing had me calling bullshit more than my brief time in a study group. Study groups are made up of five to seven students who meet weekly to talk about sketchy points from past lectures and prepare for upcoming classes. The only tangible item of value that comes from a study group is an outline of all the lectures and case reading for each class. In theory, a study group is both efficient and therapeutic. It allows for division of labor and helps each student realize he's not alone with his anxieties. Scott Turow's study group was his academic lifeline in *One L*. And it might have been for other people in my class. Not me. Three sessions in a study group were all it took to confirm my suspicion about my classmates. As The Kankoos once put it:

"If these people ran into a talking dog on the street, instead of saying '*Holy Shit, that's a talking dog!*' they'd be more likely to correct the dog's grammar."

Like The Kankoos, I never planned on joining a study group. But when Edgar invited me to join his, I figured I'd give it a try. During our first session, Scott, a twenty-eight-year-old married guy from New Hampshire, reminisced about his college days—homecoming tailgates, naked Olympics, and quarter-beer nights. In the spirit of the moment, I offered up the story of my night gambling with The Kankoos. The group's reaction was unified. Their faces were simply blank, as if they hadn't heard or understood what I'd said. They apparently could not fathom that a *Harvard law* student would drink his own piss, or gamble away $2,200 in a sitting. I had the impression they doubted that anyone did these sorts of things. At the time it was happening, I didn't know what would possess someone to drink his own piss either. But it was at least worth a *Holy Shit* or two. Without a word spoken about my story, the group shifted the subject back to Contracts and never brought it up again.

But the indifferent reaction to my Foxwoods story wasn't the reason I ultimately bailed. Midway through our third session, I began to suspect that the primary agenda of each group member was to boost his own confidence by undermining everybody else's. The group dynamic went something like this: We'd start with a legal question in our casebook or one raised by the professor at the end of class. Someone, often Edgar, would mention the general rule applicable to the problem, usually from the leading case on the subject. Then the others would take turns undermining his comment by way of obscure references to optional reading that went against the general rule. Occasionally, someone would mention a case that was never even assigned, optionally or otherwise. The trick to winning this pissing contest was twofold. First, find a rule of law so obscure that no one else had heard of it. Then, act like it was the most obvious and important point to be made on the subject. The grand prize was a seed of doubt in everyone else's mind.

I swear you could see the transfer of energy from one person to another. Edgar, once enthusiastic and proud to have memorized and called up a relevant legal rule, now lost an inch or two in posture, his chin down 45 degrees from horizontal, lips curled inward and brow furrowed. The others, originally ravenous, now spoke with the perky falling-all-over-yourself tone of an ungracious winner, suppressing self-congratulatory laughter with every word they uttered, as if they were performing some lavish endzone dance in their heads.

The dominant study group behavior was an underevolved way to achieve personal happiness, always at another's expense. And we're all guilty of it at one point or another. But at Harvard Law School, people were *defined* by it. Most of them were just spooked themselves, and the only way they could cope with their own suspected ignorance was to look for someone who knew less than they did. They probably didn't even know the harm they were doing, and they were victims of the behavior as much as they were perpetrators. Others, like Mr. O'Toule, seemed to know exactly what they were doing all along. They were intentionally collecting status by depleting everyone around them, propelling their achievements on false confidence mined from others. Regardless of their motives, I had had enough of it. I left my third study group meeting in midsession and never went back.

As of the first of November, I had missed just three lectures: the classes I hadn't attended because of that first night at Bar Review and Foxwoods. I was entering my second week under the New Incentive Regime, the bandwidth was sparse as ever and my tolerance for late-night studying on the rise. I was reading everything assigned to me, except for the one hundred-page law journal articles that made their point in a summary paragraph on the first page. I was starting to feel on top of things again. My whole life, that kind of confidence has always meant one thing. Time to fuck off.

The slacking epicenter at Harvard Law School in 1995 was a Gropius room known as The Parlour, the counterlife headquarters of The Kankoos and his horde of gifted misfits. I had spent some time there during October, but only during the day, when the place was a shadow of its nocturnal self.

The odor of warm beer and cigar butts filled its cramped confines. Mellow tunes from Simon and Garfunkel or Pink Floyd soothed two or three weary revelers who slept off the night before. Black poster board covered the windows. Plastic wrap and duct tape sealed the smoke detector. Its walls were bare, except for a Scotch tape–bandaged topographical map of the Appalachian Trail.

The Parlour's only regulars at the time were The Kankoos, The Dynamo, and Brian Green. These three were The Parlour's lifeblood, but its continuity was maintained by its many visitors, people with one foot firmly planted in the mundane, still ruled by the fear of failure and age-old myths about Harvard's rigor. People like me.

At 8:00 P.M. on November 1, I phoned The Parlour. No one answered. Maybe the phone wasn't working. I walked downstairs. The Parlour's door was shut. And locked. I knocked. No one was there. I had walked by that place a few hundred times, and it was never empty. It was the Denny's of law school ditching. I took The Parlour's sudden inaccessibility as a sign and returned to my room. I thanked God for looking out for me, then asked him to forgive me for what I was about to do, if in fact that sort of thing was still wrong. I logged on at www.cumshot.com and opened my Contracts casebook.

Three hours later, I was on my third legal case of four and jenna-bj.jpg was millimetering its way down the screen. I heard a knock at the door. Instinctively, I jerked up, hit the Home key, and minimized Netscape. The thought of being watched, maybe even discovered, resuscitated feelings of guilt that secrecy and solitude had suppressed. I eased out of my chair without a creak, tiptoed to the door, and looked through the peephole. I saw The Kankoos. What kind of sign was *this*? Or was it a test? For a moment I thought I wouldn't answer. I looked through the peephole again. He hadn't left. I opened the door.

"What's up, Kankoos?"

"You whackin' off in there?"

"No," I said, in a tone far too agitated to pass for honesty.

"Whatever. I've been trying to call you for the last hour. Phone's been busy."

"That's weird. I just tried to get a hold of you for the first time in days and now you knock on my door for the first time ever. What made you come down here, tonight of all nights?"

"Caller ID. Wanna smoke some pot?"

"Sure," I said without pause. I had never smoked pot and figured I never would. In high school, many a party passed where some miserable guy bugged me to take a hit. I never did, mainly because of the implied statement I would have made—I'm doing it just because a guy with more first names than front teeth told me to. Now, with nothing more than an innocent question, asked without any knowledge of my views or experience, I said yes. That's usually the way walls fall, for me anyway.

When we got to The Parlour, I noticed The Kankoos was alone that night, which must have been the other reason he came by my room. He pulled a Skoal can filled with pot out from under his mattress, along with a contraption devised from an old Dr Pepper bottle, the clear plastic shaft of a Bic ballpoint, and duct tape.

"This is The Monsignor. You do the honors."

"Nah, you go ahead."

If my casual response in any way disguised my inexperience, I quickly removed any possibility that I had the slightest idea what I was doing. Of course, I coughed too much, didn't inhale, messed up the hit. But that wasn't what blew my cover. I called it "marijuana."

"Mara-what?" The Kankoos laughed. "Figures. Let me help you out there, Cheech. You're melting the Monsignor..."

Three hits each later, we were both making a shitload of sense.

The Kankoos swung his right leg all the way over his left until his knees were touching, an almost feminine pose. His left hand laid upon his right knee and his right elbow rested upon that. He massaged the stubble on his chin with his right index finger and stared out the window, which was now open. His expression was less the contemplative look of a Rodin than the perplexed look of a final contestant in a national spelling bee. Then his expression brightened, as if he'd just remembered how to spell *psittacine*. He spoke:

"You still think it's wrong."

"It?"

My posture was now defensive. He could have been talking about any number of things: pot smoking, gambling, excessive drinking, excessive drinking and driving, missing class.

"Masturbation," he said in a sarcastically formal tone, a playful tribute to my earlier "marijuana."

That one had not crossed my mind, but I instantly knew what he was getting at.

"I don't have any idea what you're getting at."

"Don't misunderstand me. I know you've had your moments of enlightenment. First, there was the question of why dancing and drinking were wrong when they did it in the Bible. Then, what happens to people who lived their whole life and never heard of Jesus? Or what about all the other religions of the world? Do those people go to Hell? You answered them all by converting yourself into some stripe of modern believer—probably nondenominational Christian, maybe even a spiritual agnostic. Now, you can have your sex out of marriage and drink your beer without the obligatory sting. But you can't ask the ultimate question—the preliminary question—the only one that matters. Something lingers. You feel it from time to time. In fact, you feel it most when you stroke it. Especially right after your man-chowder gets uncorked. It's like the hand of God has come down upon you, leaving you as spent as ashamed, wondering why you ever bothered. Swearing you'll never do it again. But, of course, you will."

Uncannily, The Kankoos had described every single emotion I'd felt when I beat off, emotions I had ignored for the last five years. I could only sit there in silence, transparent. There could be no pretending I didn't know what he was talking about. He knew it. But how? Before I could ask, he too became transparent:

"Last night I prayed for the last time. I told God I just didn't believe anymore. That's the first honest prayer I've had in years. Now, there's nothing more to say."

"Then what the hell have I been feeling?" I asked.

"Here's how it works, Marquart. You take a little bit of history, some artifacts from the real world, mix in some questionable logic, and you've got religious doctrine. But doctrine only gets you partway there. You need *faith*. And faith requires more than logic. It needs emotion, *feeling*. It's only when extreme human emotion meets and confirms that shaky logic that you get faith. The mind says: *What are the chances I could feel so low, so spent, right after doing what the Bible said was wrong? I didn't just memorize that for Sunday School. I felt it. I experienced it. I always feel like crap right after I grease the gibbon.* The mind rarely considers the fact that all of that shaky logic and history—the doctrine—came from those experiences to begin with. It was no coincidence. The whole religion thing started with a noble effort to explain those intense human experiences. But when things go in reverse—when logic and history come *before* intense emotion—everything feels *confirmed*. You are born again. Foucault was all over that shit. And Skinner showed how your dick will get hard when it rains if you whack off in the shower enough times. You know, conditioning. But Nietzsche summed it up. All the time-honored things you think have inherent meaning are really nothing more than bad habits. I just dropped one of mine."

I'm not sure if it was The Kankoos's musings or my fourth bong hit, but I was sent back to that earlier Contracts lecture. Duress. Unconscionability. Especially duress: more responsible for the proliferation of Western religion than love and inspiration. Just about every reason I'd ever heard for someone deciding to become religious involved a crisis of some sort. I thought about all the testimonials I'd heard in my evangelical days. Starkly absent from the list was the one that went like this: *One day, I found myself with a brainy piece of ass for a wife, a high-paying, high-powered job, a cut midriff, and a resting pulse of 48 . . . so I decided to give my life to God!* Instead, some crisis or another—best friend's fatal car accident, addiction to painkillers, ball cancer, you name it—was always the catalyst for enlightenment. When I questioned my faith, my mother would always tell me, "Just you wait 'til you're feeling down and out, when things aren't going your way, then you'll come back to God."

Who wouldn't? The law was skeptical about the terms of any contract struck under those circumstances. In Norris's words: *A contract formed under duress is voidable by the party under duress.* Yet neither cancer, death, nor substance abuse preceded my faith. What were my reasons? The Kankoos must have been wondering the same thing:

"Ever watch a squirrel gathering and eating nuts in Harvard Yard? Sometimes I'll watch one for hours. What do you suppose he's thinking? He sure as hell isn't thinking, *I'm alive and soon I'll be dead.*"

I understood. The human condition was the source of my duress. Mortality is shared throughout the animal kingdom, but awareness of one's mortality is a sick joke reserved especially for humanity. Still, that's no reason to go making shit up.

That night, I declared my contract void. Then there was nothing more to say.

The Kankoos was the youngest child in a born-again Christian family. Like me, he was raised to fear things he couldn't see and obey voices he couldn't hear. Like me, he believed. But in his teen years, he grew curious. Curiosity bred experimentation, and that led to mischief. Normal stuff: stealing street signs, breaking into abandoned buildings, skateboarding where it wasn't allowed. Typical for seventeen. But The Kankoos got a little more than the typical amount of punishment, and his parents experienced a little more than the typical share of disappointment. Finally, one night when the police called to tell Mrs. Kankoos her son had been arrested, she came upon the answer she had prayed for: The Bay River Institution for Tough Love. The institution's literature promised revival and rebirth. It must have gone something like this:

> No child is a lost cause. All children at BRITL are God's children, though most have special needs. Through hard work, firm rules, and discipline, BRITL graduates emerge . . .

The details of The Kankoos's time at BRITL are sketchy. Some of it he honestly can't remember, and the rest of it he was never quick to share. But it's safe to say that BRITL promised to be some sort of Christian boot camp for wayward teens—one part tough, two parts love—and that it over- and underpromised. And it's safe to say that kids were taken to the woods and beaten by other kids; that The Kankoos was leagues smarter than all of the kids and the counselors at BRITL; that this made life there harder, not easier; that his days were filled with informal rap sessions with the Future Felons of America and his nights were filled with the whimper of children calling for their mothers and the stench of fresh urine; that he cried every time he phoned his parents and begged to come home. It's also safe to say his cries were hard for his folks to hear. Is everything better now? It's not safe to say. All we know is that he eventually got out of BRITL, finished his final year of high school, got straight A's in college, and somehow found his way to Harvard Law School when most of BRITL's alumni were destined for machine shops and prisons. That, and he was the best friend I ever had.

"By the way, I was surprised to see you alone tonight, Kankoos," I said.

"Oh, that's right," he exclaimed, looking at his watch. "They should be back with the rental by now. Let's go."

He didn't have to say where. On the way out the door, he put his hand on my back and held it for a second longer than usual.

"I was wondering when you'd call."

My second trip to Foxwoods brought about a handful of firsts. I was introduced to "chasing," and I made the first of what would be many Com-checks. Chasing, or chasing losses, happens when a gambler's losses get to the point where he is so distraught (and/or indifferent to further losses) that he cashes in for more and tries to erase his earlier losses. He's lost so much already that he feels like he has nothing to lose. Chasing losses is the second leading sign of problem gambling. (The leading sign, and the converse of chasing, is not quitting when you're ahead. They're basically the same thing, but there's something worse about a guy who can't be happy with what he's got, compared to a guy who feels like he's got nothing to lose.) Chasing isn't bad in and of itself. The odds of winning or losing a particular bet are the same whether you're chasing or not. But chasing increases the overall volume of a gambler's betting beyond budgeted levels and tends to exaggerate losses. I also learned about exaggerating losses that night. I started out at the tables with $200, lost it in minutes, cash advanced $100 more to chase my losses, then borrowed another $100 from The Kankoos and blew that too. Then I borrowed more, chased more, lost more. I blew a grand that night.

If winning made me feel more smart than lucky, losing made me feel all the more stupid than unlucky. Gambling is ultimately a losing proposition, after all.

It was 7:00 A.M. when we rolled back to Harvard. My first class of the day, Contracts, began in two hours. I had written off classes when I left for Foxwoods. But now, the possibility of attending all of my classes left me with a resolve to cut my losses.

"Kankoos, you mind dropping me off before you return the car?"

"Why are you in such a hurry to get back?"

"Contracts."

I braced for the backlash. It didn't come.

"OK, but stop by The Parlour before you go. There's something I've got to give you."

Back in The Parlour, The Kankoos reached into his three-ring binder and pulled out an eighty-page outline from Professor Norris's 1994 Contracts class.

"Take this with you. It's too long to be of any use to me. But it's perfect for your purpose. It's got everything you need."

I shoved the outline into my book bag and headed to Contracts. As I settled into my classroom seat, I remembered that I had a one-out-of-ten chance of being called on. I had not done any of the reading. So I packed up pen, notebook, and casebook and was halfway out of my chair when Norris entered the room. Then I reconsidered. I had a 10 percent chance of being called on if I stayed, but a 99 percent chance of Norris screwing with me if I tried to leave now. I'd seen it happen. I got back in my seat. I left my casebook in my bag and pulled out The Kankoos's outline instead. I turned to the part of the outline that began with our assignment for the day, as Professor Norris called out the first name on his list. It was not mine.

The entire discussion—the facts of the case, its holding, how its reasoning might be reconciled with an earlier case that reached a different conclusion, even Norris's impossible-to-anticipate what-do-you-think questions—were transcribed almost word for word in the outline. It had to be a coincidence, I thought. Yet Norris called on his next student, then another and another, all with the same result. In a matter of minutes, Norris's Socratic dialogue was reduced to a three-page, unfunny sitcom sketch.

Two minutes before class was over, Norris tossed out an economics question that was answered in the middle of one of those one hundred-page law journal articles I'd stopped reading a month before. I scrolled down the outline. The answer he was looking for was there. In note form, of course, but it was there:

> *Posner Article* (1996): Coase Theorem (people always bargain to share mutual advantage) fails most often b/c of status quo bias, an irrational fear of change.

Norris scanned the room for volunteers. There was less than a minute left in class. I would not have to speak today. Unless I volunteered. Norris began to call out:

"Mizz . . ."

I swallowed hard and raised my hand.

"... ter O'Toule."

O'Toule steadied himself and read from the page in front of him:

"The Coase Theorem fails most often because of status quo bias, an irrational fear of change."

PART 5 | **NOVEMBER AND DECEMBER**

| **CLAMPDOWN**

"Surprise!"

Middle of November, an unexpected Boston face at my door: Niccola. Weld was making plans to run for the Senate, against incumbent John Kerry. Niccola had come with Weld on a Silicon Valley fundraising trip.

"Only have a few minutes. I'm meeting Big Red in Sunnyvale. Just wanted to see how you're coping with solitude. Got enough bikes?"

I told Niccola everything, about Tim Apparel and the bikes, about Lucy, and about how Bobby Boylan had laid the groundwork for Halloween.

"Mmmm...Bobby Boylan. I sort of remember that one. They still haven't filled the speechwriting job. Any interest in bailing on this law school thing?"

Had it been two months earlier, I might have. Even then, I would have been too lazy to pack up and pull all the administrative levers at Stanford and in Boston. Back in September, before classes had begun, staying in law school was easier than quitting law school. Since then, things had improved.

"Friends for life. Orgies. No homework. All good reasons to stay," Niccola said. "The lovely Helen isn't here by chance, is she?"

"Looks as if she stayed in New Haven."

I raised my shades and saw that all-day clouds had established themselves with a permanence the gone-before-noon clouds never did in September. It would be the day I resumed going to Torts. In the two weeks since Halloween, I hadn't gone to any classes. I still hadn't hit Skyline on a bike, either.

Niccola asked if I had any suggestions for a new speechwriter: "What about that edgy intern in the biker jacket? The one you thought looked like Chrissie Hynde. She interviewed last time."

"Dawn. She's gone. To graduate school, last I knew."

"You were quite smitten by her, no?"

A few months before I left for law school, there had been an opening for the second speechwriting job. Looking through the résumé stacks, I found Dawn's. I called and told her I could arrange an interview, but not the job, which was Weld's call. Dawn passed by my office on the way to her interview with the same sparkle I remembered, but she left looking defeated. Between my call and the interview, a Mario Cuomo speechwriter had established herself as the immovable front-runner. I called Dawn again and, my heart thumping like it was eighth grade, asked what she was doing that night. She told me: something with the boyfriend, whose existence I had all along suspected. I feigned enough composure to learn Dawn was planning a move to New York, the Columbia writing program, so she hadn't staked too much on the speechwriting job. Because I would be heading off to law school around the same time, I believed I hadn't staked too much either.

"Gotta go," Niccola said, never one not to act instantly on her whim.

Niccola walked with me toward the Law School. Outside Leland, there was commotion. An undergraduate had committed an act of performance art—a psychedelic painting covering the Leland basketball court and backboard. The artist sat on the pavement, absorbing his completed work. Two campus cops stood above him. Davis Mund and The Barrister stood with the cops. Niccola and I stopped to watch things unfold.

"One of you the one who called 911?" an officer asked.

The Barrister answered: "I did, sir. I do not want to be forced to put up with this eyesore every day."

"You see him do this?"

The Barrister answered again: "I did not actually observe the vandalism being committed. However, he did indicate to me that he had produced this quote-unquote art."

"That so?" the cop asked the artist.

More than anything, the artist looked perplexed. The law students who reported him were only a few years his senior. Yet they appeared to be in full dress rehearsal for the role of suburban property owner, aesthetics enforcement division.

"I'm talking to you. *That* so?" the cop asked the artist again.

"Fuck yeah."

Davis Mund and The Barrister expressed variations on the same theme: solemn head shaking as their minds silently hummed an ode to schadenfreude.

"*What* did you say to me?" the cop asked the artist.

"I confessed, sir."

The promising row ended there. The artist was arrested.

"What petty little cunts you go to school with," Niccola said. "I do like the sound of that Tim Apparel chap, though. I'll visit again. Call."

"Mail me my stuff. I'm here to stay."

I headed to Torts. Not having been for two weeks, I reacclimated myself. Davis Mund had taken my seat, next to Bobby Boylan, so I found a new seat in the last row. There were other changes. Bobby was now wearing high-fashion eyeglasses instead of his contacts. The Plumber had cut the shoulder-length hair that allowed him so convincingly to be Jesus on Halloween. And in the time before Professor Howard arrived, the section conversed as a noisy, familiar whole rather than in the discrete units that characterized the earlier days. There was some common topic that I could discern no more specifically than *it*. *It* was hard, impossible, frustrating at times, most agreed, but *it* was fairly straightforward toward the end of *it*, Becky Klamm said, and most agreed, seemingly relieved that *it* had recently ended. *It* appeared to be unrelated to Torts.

When Professor Howard started speaking, I listened to her orienting remarks with extra care, tuning out the *it* conversation, to discover exactly where we were in the course. Negligent Infliction of Emotional Distress, I heard Howard say. I flipped my outline to that section. Howard snapped her notes:

"OK, let's get going. Robert, perhaps you could start us off. Just a brief sketch of the facts in the *Gammon v. Osteopathic Hospital of Maine* case . . ."

It was a light punishment for my two-week absence—just a brief sketch. That's what outlines are: brief sketches, notes. I found the case name in Tim Apparel's outline.

"The plaintiff's father died in defendant's hospital," I said. "The hospital sent plaintiff a bag that plaintiff believed contained his father's personal effects. In fact, the bag contained a severed leg."

"'A bloodied leg, severed below the knee, and bluish in color,'" Howard said, reading from the casebook.

"Right," I said. "After he received the leg, plaintiff began having nightmares and his relationship with his wife deteriorated. He sued the hospital for negligent infliction of emotional distress."

Others picked up the case from there. The class moved with astonishing fidelity to the outline, which even noted Howard's giving emphasis to the rotted body part. When Bobby Boylan spoke, though, he ventured into territory that appeared nowhere in Tim Apparel's outline. Bobby was as thorough as when he blathered about California wine. But his classroom bearing had become more George F. Will than the jester of classes past. Having done my bit, I left class sometime after the midpoint, to go to the campus bike shop, across from the Law School.

The bike shop was jammed with people wearing Stanford Cycling Team windbreakers, so I wandered—first to Leland for a bong hit, then to Breakers to post my Sunday breakfast menu, then to the Stanford Bookstore for coffee, and finally back to the Law School. As I reached to open the classroom door, words came from behind me:

"Looked as if you were riding full-time these days. What are you doing over here?"

It was Tim Apparel.

"Torts. What are you doing here?"

"Meetings. Bike team. *Law Review.* We should ride or head up to The City sometime."

"Yeah, sometime."

I stepped back into the classroom. Torts was winding down, with Howard praising everyone for a "robust" discussion. Bobby had the last word, a point so complex and subtle that I could never replicate it. Class ended. I left the classroom again, still feeling an octave off the world around me. I had been displaced from my seat. I was clueless about the conversation before Torts began (*it*). Bobby had gone serious. And what was the story with Tim Apparel—*Law Review?*

I chose to put it all out of my mind with a bike ride, a quick failure of a ride that ended with a blown tube, closer to the Law School than Leland. So I went to my Civil Procedure class, already in progress, and gleaned that the professor had just announced a potentially disastrous policy: closed-book final exam. The Barrister was leading a rearguard action against the rules being changed midgame, however. The Professor relented. She would allow a single page of notes to be brought into the exam. The Barrister asked for clarification: could the notes be in microscopic print? on both sides of the page? produced by someone other than the student using the notes? The professor set about to define what a "reasonable" page of notes might look like. The Barrister responded, "There is nothing intrinsically unreasonable about, say, a seven-point font." This left the professor in a bit of a rethink. After a long, agitated pause she said:

"Alright. Never mind. Bring whatever the hell you want to the exam."

Civil Procedure ended on that acrimonious but slacker-friendly note, and I never dropped in again. Heading back to Leland, and still feeling off balance, the familiar revisited me. Lucy. We'd spoken on the phone but hadn't seen each other since Halloween. She asked:

"The City?"

We retrieved Lucy's car and headed back to the Law School. As we approached, I saw that there were two additions to the group that had gone to San Francisco the prior times: Celia Shackles and Becky Klamm.

"Shit. Why is Becky Klamm coming?" I asked.

"She's a really amazing person," Lucy said. "We've been hanging out a lot the past few weeks."

Bobby and Tabitha sat in the front passenger seat. I sat in the back, between Celia and Becky Klamm, my feet on the transmission bulge.

"I really need to get away from here," Becky Klamm said. "I was so stressed out I almost didn't finish it. Question three was so . . . "

"Impossible," Tabitha said.

It again. "What was so impossible?" I asked. Becky Klamm started an answer:

"Have you been on Neptune for the past . . . "

Celia intervened:

"The Contracts Problem Set." Celia rejoined the main conversation: "It was rather taxing. My first of what I suspect will be countless law school all-nighters."

In addition to being The Contracts Problem Set, *it* was also the reason for this trip to San Francisco, a celebration to mark the end of a travail.

"What if someone just didn't do it, the problem set?" I asked.

Becky Klamm had all the information: "The only component to your grade for the course is the final exam, which is graded blindly. Law school policy. The Problem Set is more of a reputation maker. I bet Davis Mund is on cloud nine today."

"Davis Mund?"

"Because the model answers the professor handed out—I heard they were *all* Davis Mund's. I also heard he did nothing else for a week."

"*I* did nothing else for a week," Celia said. "Virtue must be its own reward, I suppose. But I do fear law school is becoming an all-consuming, sexless phantom. God, I need a drink. I have an appetite for the *unvirtu-ous* right now."

"This *is* law school," Lucy said, unhelpfully.

I saw an opening to be helpful, seizing on one word in Celia's lament. And so I told them all about Halloween, about the orgy.

I would have been better off producing a bloodied leg, severed below the knee, and bluish in color. There were polite, confirmatory words— *really? . . . huh . . . is that right . . . no kidding*—as if I had said my college major was in some offbeat discipline. There was no invitation for me to elaborate, and the conversation reverted to The Contracts Problem Set. I looked to Bobby, but saw no trace of his earlier orgy boosterism. Nothing. I still existed in their eyes, but only insofar as I consumed space.

We arrived in San Francisco, a Noe Valley bar. Bobby said he wouldn't be drinking, mainly to Lucy; she handed him her car keys. Celia ordered expensive Scotch. Tabitha drank tea. The conversation took up whether Davis Mund, The Contracts Problem Set *primus inter pares*, had set himself up as an early front-runner for excellent grades, better career prospects . . . buildings bearing his name, beatification, titanium arteries. I sat, unable to contribute. When you're a part of things, you feel weightless, nimble, dancingly engaged. In my unwanted silence I felt bulbous; my skin sizzled with self-awareness, the bad kind. After finishing an Amstel Light, Becky Klamm proclaimed a moratorium on further conversation about The Contracts Problem Set, adding:

"And I think my decision on which class to take 3K[5] has been made: Contracts."

My mouth moved to say *me too* but my voice was insufficiently revved for actual words to issue. The conversation took another mysterious turn.

"I don't know," Lucy said. "I've heard professors who are just starting out tend to be clumpers. You could be safe for a grade in Contracts if he turns out to be a clumper."

"I totally agree. If you're only taking one 3K it should be Torts. Howard is a notorious spreader," Bobby said. "You could really get hosed on the low end in Torts."

"Actually," Becky Klamm said, "I've heard Howard has become more of a clumper over the years."

"Even a clumper will do *some* spreading," Lucy said.

Then Tabitha said: "That obnoxious English guy..."

"The Barrister?" Lucy clarified.

"Him. He actually went up to Howard after Torts and asked her, 'are you a clumper or a spreader?'"

"That is *so* inappropriate," Becky Klamm said.

"I can't believe he did that," Lucy said. "Did she answer him?"

"She said she's a spreader," Tabitha replied.

"That really surprises me," Becky Klamm said.

Clumper? Spreader? I didn't ask. I just listened and figured it out. A professor who's a "clumper" clumps grades tightly around the mandatory 3.2, B+, mean. A "spreader" spreads the grades out, giving more high grades, but also more low grades.

At nine o'clock, Becky Klamm signaled the next move:

"I think I'm becoming slightly inebriated. Maybe we should think about getting back."

Bobby drove back to Palo Alto, the cruise control pinned at fifty-five. They dropped me off at Leland.

Shortly thereafter, Lucy commenced never to call again.

---

5. 3K—Stanford's pass-fail option, which isn't strictly pass-fail, but rather pass (K = Credit), fail (NK = No Credit), or barely pass (RK = Restricted Credit).

CHAPTER 11 | **ZERO SUMMERS**

In November, Harvard Law School became a picture of opposites. Pot and cigar smoke wafted a beckoning odor out The Parlour's little window on any Tuesday night. Drunken cackles and playful yelps resonated throughout the lonely, utilitarian Gropius courtyard, as head-hanging silhouettes of students practicing their roles in the Socratic dialogues that greeted them every morning passed obliviously by.

I was unequivocally in between. I began to spend more time in The Parlour than I spent studying, less due to Harvard's lost luster than my confessional with The Kankoos about my religious faith. The Kankoos was right: law school was a perspective contest. And nothing gives perspective like having your expected life span go from infinite to negligible in your first pot-smoking session. Deferred pleasure is bound to lose some ground to instant gratification. Still, I continued to keep up my class attendance and skim most of what they gave me. One day in mid-November, as I was rolling into The Parlour from my Criminal Law class, The Kankoos took issue with my hesitance:

"You do realize that well over 99 percent of all students who make it to exams pass?"

"Yeah, but that makes it all the worse to fail. Failing sucks bad enough when there's company. But when you're the only one . . . that's bullet-in-your-head depression."

"All our lives we've been hearing stories about how hard it was going to be to get to the next level. It's always been a load of crap. I have an honest memory of getting all check-plusses in Writing, second grade, and Ms. Tugbotham telling me it would not be that easy when cursive came around in third grade. But it was that easy. There's no reason to think this is any different."

"Maybe. But every other asshole here has done the same and more. At more big-name schools than we came from, Kankoos. And if you judged any of us in here by our study habits or knowledge of the law, everyone in The Parlour has to be in the bottom 1 percent. One percent of our class means five people. Where are those five going to come from, if not here?"

That comment reduced the rest of The Parlour to silence. The Kankoos reached under his bed and pulled out his three-ring binder, ripped out one of the past year's exams—Contracts, I think—tossed it to me, and said:

"Look at that exam. There's your bottom line. Two questions, each a page long, each as broad as a Russian housewife's shoulders. One of 'em only asks your opinion for fuck's sake! Even Joe Shit the Ragman has an opinion. You've got three hours to answer both questions. Those answers are all your professor's ever gonna see from you, and he doesn't know you from O'Toule when he's grading it. Now, when you're in that exam room sweating your ball hairs off, do you think it's more important to know that there are only three types of damages in contract law or to be able to state the facts of *Felcher v. Felcher?* Is it more important to know what Duncan Kennedy said about the Statute of Frauds in footnote 21 of his 1972 article in the *Harvard Law Review* or to have spent half an hour arguing over brews about why we don't punish people who breach contracts? I'm not saying all the future Supreme Court clerks out there aren't better off cuz they know 'em both, but that's the *other* 1 percent. The top 1 percent. I'll tell you what happens to the *bottom* 1 percent: they flip the fuck out. Maybe they actually go catatonic, I don't know. But they probably just lose sight of the big picture. They read too far between the lines and convince themselves that an optional case from the District Court of Wyoming is right on point. But I ask you, what are the chances that the professor picked this year, for the first time out of his twenty-some-odd years, to make trick questions out of the only two graded questions he's ever going to ask you? I'll take my chances this ain't the year. Now, shut your hole and get me the Face Book. I gotta make some new friends. On second thought, make it the Yellow Pages. I'm not taking any chances."

Despite The Kankoos's superb and heartfelt performance, that conversation—which must have taken place twenty times from late November until grades came out—always ended in a standstill. None of us really knew who that 1 percent were. I, along with the rest of my class, suspected I was part of the bottom 1 percent.

Part of that fear was rational. Everyone at Harvard was summa cum something. My grandfather once said, if you're in a room full of people for more than fifteen minutes and you can't pick out the dumbass, you're it. But if you apply that reasoning in a Harvard Law School classroom, you'll always end up feeling like the dumbass. That explains why everyone was so goddamned elated when someone messed up in class. They just found the dumbass, and it wasn't them.

Despite the rational reasons to be afraid, the largest balance of the fear was not rational at all. It was habitual. Deconstructing religion is a rational exercise. But guilt and anxiety are reflexes. Logic can correct a misconception, but only time can cure a compulsion. Time was in short supply.

For most One Ls, the last half of November was one of the darkest times of the year. Classes ended in about a month. After that came a three-and-a-half-week break, then a nine-day study period, and then exams. Just as everyone was starting to get the hang of Socratic classroom dialogue, they were taking stock of the prior months and realizing that they didn't have any idea how they were doing. In college, everyone would have had their midterm grades in hand by then, a decent chunk of their academic fate decided. But here, regardless of whether you'd read every single thing they told you to, volunteered in class, or smoked pot all night and never saw the light of day, you were in the same position as the next guy—nowhere. That alone was enough to drive any anal-retentive career student mad. As Thanksgiving rolled around, it was safe to say we were—I was—losing it.

Thanksgiving: four days off, distraction, good food, home. For the first time in months, Texas occurred to me. I cringed.

"Then don't go home!" The Kankoos said, weary of my deliberating. "When's the last time you've seen that girl of yours anyway?"

"Elise?"

"Yeah, Elise. The Girlfriend. Where the hell is she?"

"She's in *Spain.*"

"So go to Spain."

"I don't have enough money."

The Kankoos substituted action for a verbal response. He fired up his laptop and started typing. A few seconds later, he looked up from his screen victoriously.

"Here it is. Five hundred dollar student fare to Bilbao. That's a couple blackjack hands to a high roller like you."

"What about the seven-day advance?"

"No seven-day advance required on international student tickets. Got a passport?"

"Of course," I said, omitting that I'd never used it. "But what about the money when I get there? It's got to be a fortune to spend five days wandering all over Spain."

"I saw you Comcheck your Gold Card for seven hundred bucks the other day, and I know there's more where that came from. Don't worry about those escalating balances. It's all about *available credit*. You're gonna pull down twenty grand as a summer associate. Before you know it, money won't be your problem. Time will be the scarce commodity. Get it now, while it's cheap. You're in an enviable situation. It actually *makes sense* to leverage your future. Just get on the plane and let fate take care of the rest. This ain't Eagle Lake, Texas, Bubba. People here cart off to Europe on a moment's notice all the time."

It wasn't until after I'd bought the nonrefundable ticket, and as The Kankoos was dropping me at the airport, that I confessed:

"I'm really a little nervous. I've never done this. I only have this passport because I was starting to feel stupid without one. Is there anything I need to know?"

"Fuck if I know," The Kankoos said. "I've never been out of the country. Have a nice trip!"

Four hours into my flight, equidistant from Harvard and Elise, dissonance grabbed hold of me. I could not reconcile *Jaime the One L, Friend of*

Kankoos with *Jaime the Boyfriend of Elise*. Like anyone, I spent most of my life in a handful of worlds. But I was always me, the same in each of them. And Elise was always there in each, if only on the other end of the phone line. But there was nothing law school about Elise, and nothing Elise about law school. I shrugged off any premature conclusions and saw that for the good thing it was. It was easy enough to stick to basics. I had four days to get in three months' worth of sex and affirmation.

Thankfully, there was nothing law school about Spain either. Everyone in the small villages scattered throughout the Basque Country was engaged in a strangely healthy social contract. It was as if they all recognized that if they just relaxed, no one would get behind. Of course, even these societies do not exist in a vacuum, and maybe the rest of the world is "getting ahead." But try explaining comparative advantage and fluid global economies to a *carneceria* proprietor in the little village of Derio. There, everyone's lives were blessed with time and reflection. They were alive. I'm sure I won't get a thank-you from the Spanish government for this one, but Spain to me represented the slacker's ideal—relaxed, beautiful, and indifferent to prestige or upward mobility.

Spain had isolated all the qualities I'd most admired in Elise, edited out a few inconsistencies, and amplified the result. Her hair, once long and flowing, a tribute to her parents' debutante virtues, was now short and light, calling attention to her other features—an attention they'd always deserved. We each bore the effects of an abrupt leap into a foreign world; but where my points of change were scattered, hers formed a straight line pointing to the heavens. Someplace else, I might have ignored, scoffed at, or worked to squash those things going on inside Elise. But then, thankfully, I couldn't help but follow. The unchangeable prevailed—we were young and in love in Spain.

I returned from Spain with two weeks of classes left until the end of the semester. Having drastically underestimated the time it took to get through customs, I got to class—a Criminal Law lecture about deterrence—a few minutes late. Professor Quivers's Criminal Law class was the best to arrive to late; he rarely used the Socratic method and relied on volunteers as much as possible. As I found my seat, Professor Quivers was introducing the class to law and economics:

"The school of law and economics is one of the most influential in legal scholarship today. Economics is the study of the distribution of scarce resources. With only so much to go around, economics asks who's going to get what and how we are going to determine the allocation. Law and economics questions the role of legal institutions in maximizing the distribution of resources. It also studies the effect of incentives on human behavior. That's where deterrence comes in. The debate over the efficacy of deterrence in criminal law concerns the core microeconomic premise that individuals are rational maximizers of their own utility—in other words, that people calculate whether an action will make them better or worse off, and that they make the calculation before they act. Would anyone care to disagree with that premise?"

Edgar raised his hand. "I believe it depends on the crime you're trying to deter. If you're talking about parking tickets, I think people act in a way that minimizes their costs. But with violent behavior and other emotional crimes, I don't think a person considers the costs prior to committing such an act. They just do it."

Vicky Sentence, a card-carrying member of Mr. O'Toule's gang, took issue with Edgar's comment:

"People are always acting to maximize their own utility. It is true that they make errors in calculations from time to time, and their ability to estimate the benefits and costs of a particular course of action falters in the heat of the moment; but they are always calculating. In all things."

Professor Quivers's curiosity was piqued:

"Does that mean you utilize a calculus to determine whom you love, or estimate the future cash flow from every ounce of affection you shed upon others?"

Vicky had never impressed me as an affection-giving type. She began her response by clarifying her earlier statement:

"Not necessarily future *cash flow*, but yes, future utility. Love and hate are not immune from the laws of economics. The decision to marry at a particular moment in time, for instance. That choice is a binary one: to marry now or to wait. Whether you marry or wait is a calculus determined by the likelihood of meeting a romantic partner in the future who supplies you with utility equal to or greater than the current prospective spouse. There are other variables as well—time, risk preferences, and so forth. But yes, love, hate, passion, you name it. Emotional life is not above utility analysis."

"I see. But economics concerns the distribution of finite, *limited* resources. Would you be willing to say there's a definite, limited amount of love and affection to go around? That the quest for love itself is a zero-sum game?"

"*Life* itself is a zero-sum game," Vicky said.

Life a zero-sum game? As Vicky spoke those words, I raced over the past three months—Mr. O'Toule's intimidation tactics, the goofing on people who stumble in class, the hidden cue cards, my study group partners' frenzied attempts to undermine each other's confidence, and my own hope for Elise's misery when I was insecure. With one comment, it all made sense. I had uncovered the name for, and the source of, Mr. O'Toule and his ilk: Zero Summers.

In a zero-sum game, the total number of points to be scored is fixed from the beginning and never changes. So the total number of gains and losses always adds up to the sum of zero. As a Zero Summer sees the world, every time I get credit for an accomplishment or win someone's affection, that is less credit or affection left for the Zero Summer. And it goes one step deeper: my success is directly linked to and inversely correlated with his self-worth. A Zero Summer would prefer 90 percent of a ten-dollar pie rather than 40 percent of a million-dollar pie, though he'd be the first to tell you that the hypothetical is ridiculous, because the size of the pie is fixed and is never affected by the actions of those scratching and clawing for its ever-diminishing morsels. A Zero Summer's universe is always in balance. For each person's happy moment, someone else must experience tragedy or loss. And so all Zero Summers have a personal stake in each other's unhappiness. Zero Summers thrive at Harvard Law School.

Two weeks later, classes ended. As I stepped on the plane to make my first trip home to Texas since arriving at Harvard, that sick, sinking feeling returned to my stomach. It wasn't like me to miss home (I left when I was sixteen), but it wasn't like me to *dread* going home. The source of my malaise was no mystery. As Scott Turow pointed out in *One L*, the first year of law school is all the more trying because it is "a time when law students typically feel a stunning array of changes taking place within themselves." But Turow was a married Amherst College graduate who had lectured at Stanford for three years before going to Harvard. He had lived off-campus, in a nearby suburb, Arlington, as a One L. I was a single, twenty-one-year-old, state school graduate from Eagle Lake, Texas, reared in single-parent poverty. Naturally, I was due for more than the usual "stunning array" of changes, and that made going home all the more difficult. And lonely. The transition from one social sphere to another is bumpiest in the time *after* you've grown beyond the old circle but well *before* you've grown into the new one. I was there.

On the surface, the scene at home was as usual—a dozen screaming little children running around, idiotic bigotry that made me treasure my education, and dirty old uncles telling old dirty jokes. Uncle Enis launched into one of his favorite pastimes, berating me for my social tolerance:

"You know there ain't nuttin' natural 'bout two men gettin' it on—I never seen two boy monkeys doin' it on the Discovery Channel..."

Of course, I never saw two boy monkeys discussing Nietzsche on the Discovery Channel, either, but by the age of thirteen I had learned it was easier to just keep quiet and let Uncle Enis go.

Amid all of the chaos, my grandfather held court from his vintage 1975, burnt-orange, velvet recliner, taking time out only to yell at my grandmother about their dog, Roosevelt, who was always trying to get at the people food.

"So, Boy, d'ya hear ol'... Honey! Control that damn dog of yours; he's gonna burn himself surer'n shit!... D'ya hear your cousin Pootie shot himself in the foot at work again the other day?"

"No, I didn't hear that. What, d'he get drunk and give Mr. Paulson some lip again?"

"No, dammit, he shot himself in the foot! Nail gun, right through the pinky toe. Damm thing bled for two days. I tell ya, that boy could throw a football through a tractor tire forty yards away and rollin' downhill, but he couldn't pour piss outta boot if the directions were written on the heel.... Honey! If you don't get that damn dog outta here, I'm gonna put a foot so far up his ass..."

"A foot in his ass? You tryin' to encourage him?" Uncle Enis chimed in.

"That damm Roosevelt humps every dog on the block, boy or girl."

This time, I couldn't resist:

"I thought homoeroticism didn't exist in the animal kingdom, Uncle Enis?"

"Homer-who? You know, I think you're turnin' into a gay yourself. Hey, y'all remember the time we got halfway to Houston before Jaime realized he left the rodeo tickets on the counter? Got damn, that boy'd forget his own head if it wern't attached."

A sharp canine yelp interrupted Uncle Enis's active-aggressive resuscitation of my horribly outdated self-image. Roosevelt, dissatisfied with the yield from his begging, had hopped up on two legs to take a peek at what was on the stove. As Papaw predicted, he burned the living piss out of himself and ran under the Christmas tree to cool down. As the laughter was subsiding, Papaw turned to me and said:

"See that, Boy. That dog ain't never gonna touch a hot stove again. But he ain't never gonna touch a cold one, neither."

My grandfather didn't know his Pavlov from his Pennzoil, and I'm sure he never read Twain, who was the first to write that saying down. But I think many of my classmates would kill for such simple wisdom.

Roosevelt's antics spared me from any further sparring sessions with Uncle Enis, but he couldn't save me from the five-cousin inquisition that greeted me as we sat down to eat. It was as if I'd just returned from lunar orbit.

"Is it true everybody walks around in fancy suits and talks like that rich guy on *Gilligan's Island?*"

"No, but a couple of them do."

"What's class like?"

"The classroom is in a castle of a building that's older than Texas. The teachers pull people's names out of hats and grill them for as much as half an hour with a lot of hard questions in front of a hundred other people. It's nerve-racking as hell. It drove us all crazy for the first couple months."

"No way! Wait a minute, what happens to you if you mess up?"

"Actually, nothing. They go on to the next person."

"If somebody pays fifteen bucks for a BB gun, but it turns out it was stolen—uh, hypothetically speakin', a' course—do they have to give it back when the real owner comes for it, even if they say they didn't know it was stolen and there ain't no witnesses to prove any otherwise?"

"I have no fucking idea, Pootie."

"Do you like it there?"

That one gave me pause. There were any number of ways to read that question. I chose the broad reading, Parlour included.

"Yeah."

"Are you doin' good?"

I was surprised it took them as long as it did to get to the bottom line, but the question shook me just the same. For the first time, I could feel the distance I'd traveled from that first stroll through Harvard Yard to the revelations of the previous month. I couldn't help but smile.

"Yes, I'm doing just fine. It was foreign as hell at first, but now it's just like riding a bike."

This exchange caught my grandfather's attention. He had only one question for me:

"What are your grades, Boy?"

"We don't have any grades yet, Papaw. We take our tests after Christmas and then the grades come out in..."

"Then how the hell do you know how you're doin'?"

CHAPTER 12 | **ROAD TO NOWHERE**

After Halloween, things changed.

It turned out that Bobby Boylan didn't take all—or any—of his classes pass-fail, though he did become the most ubiquitous One L running for student government. His platform had one signature policy: mandatory pass-fail in all first-year classes. Bobby limited his former gregariousness to weekends. For a few consecutive Saturdays in November, the same message was on my answering machine:

BEEEP: *Byrnesie!!! Play eighteen tomorrow? It's a fucking awesome course! We go out the same time the Stanford team does! We see Tiger Woods!!! Every day!*

I detested golf and sucked at golf, and either sucked because I detested it or the other way around. Soon, Bobby stopped asking. After Thanksgiving, I ran into Bobby in the library, where he had encamped to begin studying for finals. There were only two more weeks of classes, then two weeks off over Christmas, then finals at the beginning of January. As we met eyes, Bobby said:

"One down, three to go."

He'd just finished his Contracts outline. This was where outlines came from; people make them. Bobby's was a real outline, too, something more than the "just notes" sort Tim Apparel favored. In Bobby's ninety-page Contracts outline, points were distilled and synthesized. Cases from November illuminated classes from September. Someday Bobby's outline would become another student's voucher for ditching class, getting drunk on a weeknight, or just slouching in front of the television. Before they are uploaded, downloaded, filched, and exchanged, though, outlines were created by someone's actual industry. Part naiveté, part arrogance, I'd assumed outlines to be as free and abundant as air.

Bobby and I chatted. It would have been awkward to bring up the early days; the forgotten, implied plans made around afternoon, after-Torts beer and wine; the Natalie Merchant concert and sleeping on the beach; the pot-induced laughter jag on Halloween. Bobby was looking severe.

"I'm basically in study mode for the next month," he said.

Then, the grip of restraint loosened, and Bobby glimmered as he had when he leaned over to speak to me that first day in Torts. From behind me, Tabitha had arrived. She and Bobby had recently become a regular handholding couple.

"Great news," Tabitha said. "I've got a decent flow chart for deciding whether the UCC applies. Hey Byrnes, what's up."

Contracts talk—the UCC, Uniform Commercial Code. The old currency just wasn't being honored any longer. If I'd told Tabitha I was having pangs for Helen, and that I was thinking of contacting Helen, writing her an e-mail, attempting a long-shot reconciliation, quitting law school if need be, Tabitha would have known what I was talking about. She just wouldn't have been interested. Contracts talk, then:

"Contracts still staying on the *Emmanuel's* script?" I asked.

"Word for word," Tabitha said.

"Professor still blows?"

"That's kind of harsh," Bobby said.

Throughout November I would wake at 4:00 A.M., thinking or hoping I'd heard the phone ring and looking for a message that was never there. Lucy did call occasionally, in the afternoon, but with ventures as unappealing as golf. Once, missing her, I took what was offered. I went to a Spike Lee movie—*Clockers*, about crack dealers—with her and Becky Klamm. I would have been better off, freer anyway, playing golf with Bobby Boylan. When we got into the theater, Becky Klamm insisted that we sit dead center, although the place was jammed. She required that Lucy and I stand in the back of the theater while she scouted for seats. I had the impression that sitting in my own separate seat would have established me as more of a deviant in Becky Klamm's mind than my being a group sex practitioner. So I sat, miserably, in the putative best seats, the ones Becky Klamm chose. On the drive back to Stanford, Becky Klamm repeated her only reaction to the movie, three times: "That was *so* depressing."

After that night, Lucy never called again, nor did I call her. And what of The Four from the orgy? Based on what I heard, they were irate—that I told Celia, Lucy, Bobby, Tabitha, and Becky Klamm, who had evidently told others. Exponential gossip quickly reaches a class of 180 people, a law school of 500. By Thanksgiving, it had become common lore. "Group Sex in Leland" resonated throughout the law school. Only the Leland part wasn't true. Or, if it were true, it was an orgy I hadn't been at.

At the beginning of December, therefore, I was alone in my room, down to a pinch of pot, and with an unwavering zero on the answering machine. Niccola had finally mailed my CDs and Pavoni espresso maker from Boston, along with boxes of once-valued possessions that were now starkly useless—notes and doodles from Weld staff meetings, framed diplomas from college and graduate school. The ground was slicked by increasingly frequent rain, so biking became more infrequent. Niccola called with news of her latest conquests. For my part, the conversation turned to a harangue against all my former law school friends who had gone from libertine to Puritan in the time since Niccola's surprise visit. She listened, but didn't speak. Niccola never traced emotional damage back to a point of original fault. *Assumption of the risk*. I told Niccola I'd call her when I had new adventures rather than backward-looking gripes to talk about. I hung up and went for a bike ride.

I headed south on El Camino, helmetless, on the road bike, away from Stanford and San Francisco, parallel to the Santa Cruz Mountains and Skyline, toward nothing. With a tailwind, I was holding at thirty-seven miles per hour. Night rides have a soothing, clandestine feel—a little too clandestine.

A mile from campus, a minivan was making a turn. The minivan driver didn't see me and we would crash in less than a second. There was a frozen fearlessness—no time for meaningful choice—the outcome was fixed, death among the possibilities. I'd been there before, bike messenger days. Those times, though, it was at half the speed, half the impact, and on a chunkier mountain bike. I gave the brakes my hardest pull. Then I let go with my left hand and fisted a passage for myself, smashing the minivan's side window. My front tire hit steel, snapping the bike's fork. I went airborne, to where I didn't know. Yet there was no wailing, writhing, or regret. No fear. Not me, anyway.

"Oh my goodness! *I am so sorry!* It was my fault," the minivan driver said. "Can you *walk?* ... can you even *move?* ... *I am so sorry, it was my fault.* ... Just tell me what I can do. Anything. I'll take you to a hospital."

I shook myself back into awareness. Sprinkled with glass confetti, I'd been projected through the side window and *into* the minivan. From the rear seat I looked to the driver and said:

"If you could just take me to Stanford ..."

Back at Leland, I took pictures into a mirror while the blood was fresh. And there it was—game, set, and match in tort law.

MEMORANDUM

TO: Gene Blue, The Blue Insurance Group
FROM: Robert Byrnes
RE: Claim Code #Y3lT7AH-8H-I

I have enclosed photos of me and my bike following the accident, as well as receipts for the bike (destroyed), bike shorts (torn, bloodied), halogen front headlight (smashed), and eyeglasses (crushed).

My first legal memo was a winner. I was fully compensated—"made whole" in tort argot. All new bike stuff, plus another five hundred dollars for "pain and suffering." When she asked why I was all cut up, I told Professor Howard about my real-life tort. Her face couldn't resist transmitting what she thought of my story: *dumbass.*

"Hmmm ... five hundred dollars? Hit by a car on a bicycle is usually worth ten or twenty grand."

Even so, it was five hundred bucks from nowhere, money to compensate me for a supposed loss, even though I would have paid at least that
much—not to be hit by a car, but to have *been* hit, because it gave me a
strain of peaceful resignation I'd never known before. Death still looked
awful. But dying, if it's fast, might be kind of mellow. I'd scored that valuable assurance. And some spare cash. Had the driver not offered up her
negligence so willingly, though, there might have been a tort suit that took
up whether there was "contributory negligence" on my part, which could
have eroded or even negated the driver's admitted negligence, leaving me
with nothing. *Was Mr. Byrnes's headlight wattage such that would be utilized
by a reasonable person? Did Mr. Byrnes assume the risk of an inherently dangerous activity? Was Mr. Byrnes himself prima facie negligent by traveling in
excess of the posted automobile speed limit? Was Mr. Byrnes under the influence
of a controlled substance? Was the minivan driver even negligent in not seeing
a bicycle that she simply did not see?* There was no trial, no "litigation," no
inquisition into fault that would have produced an answer—*whose fault?*—
but not necessarily the right one, if there even is a right one, or only one.

A rainy, solitary time filled mid-December. The crash wounds remained.
Scabby abrasions textured my ass and forehead. One incisor's tip had
been chipped off and is now just another El Camino street pebble. My
tongue passed a lot of time sliding along a new, rougher, tooth-feel. The
bike's front chain ring had triple-punctured my shin's soft side, leaving an
irritated Orion's belt. I sat alone in my room listening to Frank Black and
P. J. Harvey and began reading through outlines. Exams started in two
weeks. Then one afternoon—*snap, snap, snap.* At my door: Davis Mund.
He said:

"Heard you had an accident, old sport."

I pulled him an espresso, which, along with the story of my brush with
mortality, seemed to make him chatty. He said, "One of the perils of
being ambitious is a tendency never to look up. You're always concentrating, eyes to the pavement. I have a little ritual where every time I leave
the dorm I gaze up at the hills."

I loaded that last pinch of weed, took a hit, covered the bong's mouth,
and, by a gesture, offered the whirling smoke to Davis Mund.

"Don't want to destroy my political viability," he said with a wink. He actually winked, and I found it charming, not ridiculous or contrived. Davis Mund unlocked the quick grin—*you thought I didn't know the fucking score*—the one that good politicians beam sparingly to their intimates.

As I exhaled, Davis reached into his satchel and flipped a floppy disk my way. "My outline. Contracts. So far. He covers a lot of stuff in class that isn't in *Emmanuel's*. Could get someone who doesn't attend class into a panic on the exam." Davis stood up and moved toward the door. He asked, "You going to Bar Review?"

"Not tonight."

From my window I saw Davis leave Leland, and he did pause to look at the hills, the sky; to absorb nature in a way that was both theatrical and real. The ocean had sent its moisture up, a marshmallow puff blanket holding an edge at Skyline. Immobile and content, I started reading Davis Mund's Contracts outline.

I strayed from the outline to confront myself. Before the crash, I could have just ridden to Skyline any time I pleased; it wasn't Everest. I hadn't because, on a ride like that, you return feeling as if your body and spirit have been reconstituted into what you want to believe is a finished state; a complete, stronger self. But that new self gets annihilated and reordered on the next ride and the next. Maybe you accept this cycle of remaking and destruction, content to be strong today, stronger tomorrow, even though it's strength and motion that send you deeper into solitude and separation. After even a small ride, I don't have anything to say to someone who's overheating because she's stumped by a bombastically cryptic professor who's written a casebook I don't own. Skyline, all the more, would have the effect of separating me from others, something I didn't need to any greater degree that December.

Then, I fell asleep.

The next morning there was a confident knock at the door. Not Davis Mund—it was Tim Apparel.

"Heard you wrecked your bike," he said.

I showed him the disfigured bike and its identical replacement.

"Nice crash. Can I have this one?" he asked.

"No use to me."

"Come check this out," Tim Apparel said.

He led me to the Leland bathroom, where a note had been taped on the mirror:

Gents:
While it is all well and good as a sanitary measure to insulate one's bottom from unwanted contact with the porcelain arse crescent, I make only the modest request that you

FLUSH THE TOILET PAPER DOWN AND DON'T LEAVE IT DANGLING THERE AFTER YOU TAKE A SHIT.

And another thing: STOP LEAVING THOSE PUBIC CURLICUES ON THE BOWL RIM!

anon

We headed back into my room, leaving the note posted, where it remained until Tim Apparel whisked it down the next semester.

"Any idea who wrote it?" he asked.

"Maybe Davis Mund."

"My money's on The Barrister," Tim Apparel said.

Tim Apparel walked to my door carrying the twisted road bike. He gestured toward the stacked boxes Niccola had mailed me and said:

"Ahhhh, you want to go up to The City tonight? I've got a storage space. You could put all this crap there. And as long as we're up there . . . "

"A little clean living?"

"I'm out of that phase."

"Me too."

We went to San Francisco. Tim Apparel drove.

Clogged in San Francisco's outer-rim traffic, Tim Apparel and I stayed motionless next to a gold-brown 1973 Beetle, FOR SALE, $2000, OBO. Two grand. Same as my Perkins Loan, "for the neediest students."

"You could use a car," Tim Apparel said.

"I could use a driver's license."

"California driving test's the hardest exam you'll see all year," Tim Apparel said. "I tubed it three times. Now go claim the pride of ownership."

I got out. Traffic started to move. Tim Apparel craned from his car and said:

"I'll be at PoMo. Lower Haight. Bathroom."

After a dash to the bank, I bought the Beetle and drove it to meet Tim Apparel at PoMo. I parked and a woman walked up to the Beetle.

"You Burns?" she asked, and I nodded. "I'm Clara. Come park up by your friend's car so I can watch 'em both."

Technically a bar, PoMo felt like walking into a Kandinsky. I couldn't find Tim Apparel. Then I remembered. *Bathroom*. I knocked on the door farthest from PoMo's core. There he was, on the floor, breaking small, pearlescent rocks into smaller pebbles. Tim Apparel's thumb, callused from holding a lighter under the glass pipe, dabbed one of the pebbles and held it over the pipe until it lost adhesion with his thumb and fell into the pipe. He sparked the lighter and spoke in a staccato I'd never before heard from him:

"Clara find you? She watches cars. Does general lookout for a few more bucks. Just quit rock. Got a mind for business. She'll give head for a cheeseburger. Kind of a shaky part of town. Hit the lock. Have a seat. Do you know that according to Zeno's Paradox you can divide something in half forever? Even a little bitty thing."

Tim Apparel dropped another pebble into the pipe and held the flame to the pipe's bottom. There was a sizzle, then state-change; elegant, orderly, melting, becoming liquid, clear and hot, but not turbid; then hotter, never boiling, then::::::smoke...so much smoke Tim Apparel couldn't take it all in. He spoke, retaining the smoke:

"Here."

I inhaled the surplus. When we exhaled, an involuntary memory struck: the first day I met Tim Apparel, at his door. It was, after all, a good smell.

"At least now you've got a secret worth keeping," Tim Apparel said. "The Barrister claims you were a part of that Group Sex in Leland thing. True?"

"Basically. What's with that picture of The Barrister on your Web site?"

"I torment him. The Barrister also claims all your classmates talk shit about you."

"I don't even know the fucking Barrister. What's everyone got against orgies?"

"They're Dullards." Tim Apparel's eyes widened. He nodded vigorously as he absorbed another hit. "All law students are Dullards. It goes like this. Begin at the beginning. You're five years old. You're smart. You've been safe at home and your parents praise you for being sharper than dumb adults eight times your age. The affirmation feels good. Then you start school, kindergarten, elementary school, and it's easy. All your papers come back from the teacher with '100%' written on them. It feels good—just like home. Affirmation. Then one day, you're at school. Someone writes a swear word on the blackboard. No one knows who did it. There's wide suspicion, but no finger points at you. You're an established rule follower. You're left alone. The kid who did the bad thing gets caught and, not coincidentally, he's a dreadful student. He's crossed the line, like he always does. Now he feels the pain of punishment. It's a spectacle; all eyes look down on him. You never want to be where he is; never want to cross the line—and be observed, suspected, disfavored, punished."

"Or you could have written the dirty word and gotten away with it."

"Or done something truly clever and disruptive," Tim Apparel said. "Anyway: a young Dullard takes things in the other direction. If rule following keeps you beyond suspicion, why not go far beyond the general rules and make your own? Show the world you love its rules. And you want more. The basic rules are: come to school, get B's, and stay out of trouble.

You go light-years beyond. Perfect attendance. Perfect grades. Little touches like handing in papers a day early."

"Mainline 'extra-credit'..."

"Regular people need to be watched. Radar guns. Sign in, sign out. Punch the clock. Jail and God are there for the ones who need full-time supervision. A Dullard doesn't need supervision. Ever. Dullards live to be praised. Check+, A+. Valedictorian. Phi Beta Kappa. English Award. Order of the Queef. *Law Review*. *On behalf of the admissions committee I am delighted to lick your balls*. Each achievement is a sword that slices the way to the next achievement."

"And a shield against punishment," I said.

"As a Dullard you supervise yourself—to be sure you don't violate any of your rules, which are far more onerous than anything the world requires of you. It's Foucault's Panopticon, with credit to Bentham. Topic of my college thesis. Which would have been a lot more lucid if I'd had the advantage of some rock cocaine."

"Speaking of which, Zeno, apparently you can't break something in half forever."

"Time to find Paris," Tim Apparel said.

Paris? Tim Apparel folded three twenty-dollar bills into one-inch squares and put them in different pockets, arguably an *actus reas* sufficient to sustain a criminal charge for attempted possession of a Schedule One drug. We moved out of the bathroom and into PoMo's main room. Tim Apparel continued:

"So, your record is clean and sparkling. And in case you haven't guessed already, orgies aren't part of the mix. Then you go to law school to do what... *why do you go to law school?*" He answered his own question: "You go to law school because rules are your friend. In law school, you learn what the rules are. And because you've done so well making your own rules, you learn how to make rules for everyone else.... I'll be right back."

Tim Apparel left, then promptly returned. He had come up short of money, but had proposed a barter deal with Paris, the dealer: "something of value" in exchange for a palmful of rock, five peanut-sized nuggets, going price one hundred dollars.

"What do we have that's valuable?"

"Your car," I said. "My Beetle."

"Too much. Anything cool come with the Beetle?"

"Bike rack."

"We'll need that. Anything in my car, in your boxes?"

"Just stuff I haven't unpacked ... books, a juicing machine, my diplomas."

"From?"

"Brown, Harvard ... "

"A Harvard diploma?"

"Grad school."

"Good enough. Why the hell *did* you come to law school, anyway? Seems like you had a good life before this."

Tim Apparel headed back to the street with my Harvard diploma.

You could say that a short Dullard sprint when I was seventeen ultimately landed me in law school. By the end of high school's All Important Junior Year, I was an accomplished truant and ranked dead last in Oyster River High School's 155-member class. My juvenile arrest record was gaining some heft (drinking, shoplifting), and school authorities seemed inclined to invoke the technical device that none of my absences over three years was properly excused (self-forged notes, amorphous "appointments"), which would have put me, at best, in the impossible position of recommencing high school as a freshman. There was also the matter of my doctoring the Latin teacher's grade book, to no good effect. I'd taken (and failed) Latin after getting the bum advice from a particularly obtuse social studies teacher that it would serve me well in law school, where class is conducted mostly in Latin, the teacher claimed. Even the baseball coach seemed in on it, suggesting that a flaccid junior season had put my place on the team in doubt. Leaving no failure unaddressed, I blew the SAT, getting an out-of-the-game 1100. The test was given at the burnout high school the next town over, so I arrived early, made some contacts, scored a nickel bag, and shared a rack of Genesee Cream Ale during breaks.

My friend Chris Dingmanio, by contrast, was the whole package: good athlete, great student, even better person, and he never broke a single rule. That I was good at some things (magic, biking, darts) didn't add up to the portfolio that would have me joining Chris at Harvard. More than getting into every college in the world, Chris's dogged Dullardness found favor elsewhere. Chris and I both fell for beautiful and brainy Aimee. My only advantage was that I had a driver's license and gave Aimee afterschool rides home. Aimee opted instead for walks home and make-out sessions with Chris, the valedictorian.

It was time for me to become a valedictorian. My father made good money selling Chevys, and he sent me to one of those steak-head private schools, Berkshire School, that had no interest in my plans for academic renaissance. It was a sports school, skiing and baseball, my sports. Although I sputtered in athletic mediocrity, I did graduate first in my class from Berkshire, which did me the considerable favor of factoring only the grades I got there into its class rank calculations. I fixed the SAT problem, too, scoring well enough to land a Princeton Review job (the hardest job application ritual I've ever seen), during the Boston bike messenger days.

So when the time came for college, I went Ivy League—not real Ivy, just Dartmouth. Dartmouth was the stupidest place I've ever been. More than a few times I saw students go arm-in-arm, swaying to and singing the school song . . . *Men of Dartmouth . . . with the granite of New Hampshire in their muscles and their brains.* Dartmouth was big on "tradition." Tradition: rules masquerading as revelry. Dartmouth wasn't my place, though I did settle in happily with the campus communist crowd. What I didn't know was that right there, in my class, was Helen Lynn Rogers. Helen. We never met at Dartmouth; destiny deferred. A note from the dean of students regarding an incident (CIA recruiter, exercise of my First Amendment rights) had me looking to pursue my education elsewhere. My romantic sights were already elsewhere, anyway. Aimee and Chris ended, and within hours there Aimee and I were, marveling at how I'd gotten my shit together. Aimee was at Brown.

I transferred to Brown. Brown University: a happy and virtually rule-less place. Except for an eccentric C in Existentialism, I finished up at Brown with A's in every class I took for a grade. With Aimee, there were idyllic moments, but like a lot of college romances we had turbulent times. In our breakup conversation, Aimee was declaring her grievances. I flipped the discussion, telling Aimee of my own dark vision: that as good as I was at doing college, I knew I'd be an incompetent at anything thereafter. Wearing a suit, getting up early—it was a future too brutal to contemplate. Turning from aggrieved to helpful, Aimee told me:

"You could get into any law school. Just do that, and you'll at least buy yourself an extra three years before the misery sets in."

With all the stops along the way—running for office, graduate school, Helen, bike messenger, Weld—I ended up buying myself ten years. Finally I went to law school and now, there I was, thirty-some miles north of Stanford, in San Francisco, at PoMo, taking a little downtime from the first-year law school grind.

Tim Apparel returned to PoMo, my Harvard diploma in hand. For Paris, apparently, the diploma held no value.

"Here, I've come into some money," I said, handing over the five hundred dollar pain-and-suffering windfall.

Tim Apparel set aside the diploma and headed back to the street. I waited for him in the bathroom. He returned with a handful of rock and a stack of outlines he'd grabbed from his car. We bolted the door shut. First-semester final exams were in two weeks. We never saw the diploma again.

PART 6 | FIRST-SEMESTER EXAMS

CHAPTER 13 | **TESTING**

I got back to Harvard a week before the designated nine-day studying period began. Everyone else was already there. A lot of them had never left. Zero Summers were everywhere, scaring up conversations with unsuspecting One Ls. The Zero Summers' currency was no longer obscure case reading. They now spoke of hard-to-spot legal issues in past years' exams. By my third day back, these conversations were avoided by everyone in their right mind—all ten of them. I was among the ten.

Then it happened, the first year's most unsettling moment. I was walking by The Parlour the day before our first exam. It was quiet. It reeked of aerosol roses. It was empty, save for The Kankoos, who was hunched over a standard-issue dorm desk. That desk was the centerpiece of every One L's life, but I'd never seen one in The Parlour. I had always figured The Kankoos threw his out to make room for the bar. But there it was, and there he was, dissecting an old Civil Procedure exam. Granted, he was using *Gilbert's* and an outline he ripped off from Tom O'Toule earlier that day. But I still can't think about it without grinding enamel off my incisors.

On Monday, January 8, 1996, I turned twenty-two. It snowed twenty inches. Public schools were closed. I took my first exam at Harvard Law School. It was a "take-home" exam in Civil Procedure. First-year exams came in two forms—in-class and take-home. Take-home exams lasted all day. One Ls picked them up between 8:30 and 9:30 A.M. and returned them between 3:30 and 4:30 P.M. I showed up at 8:15 to get my exam, and the line was already two hundred deep. One Ls had lined up outside the rooms where the tests were distributed at seven that morning to save themselves as much as a half hour of waiting in line. For the first time, I was glad I lived in Gropius, just a five-minute stroll in a heated tunnel away from where I would turn in my exam.

The exam was typical for Harvard Law School, or any law school for that matter.[6] It had two questions, each with a 1,500-word limit. Both questions were "issue-spotters." An issue-spotter is a one- or two-page narrative in which a number of legal problems, or issues, arise. On the surface, the task is simple: spot each issue, isolate the facts that matter, and apply the law in your outline to those facts. The professor makes the questions hard the same way a mystery writer makes you surprised that the real killer was the P.I.'s best buddy. First, she throws in a bunch of useless facts that have no significance to the outcome but might lead you down a wrong path. Then, she creates a number of different characters, each of which might have harmed the others. Finally, she makes it so that a number of different legal rules might apply. Every now and then, these legal rules conflict with one another. If she's done her job, it will take you an hour or more of diagramming to figure out that the killer was Miss Scarlet with the pipe in the study.

I'm no expert on answering issue-spotters, but I know a thing or two about fucking them up. The best way to do that is to jump on the first issue and start writing for a page or two before considering the thing as a whole. That's like trying to look at a Seurat with a magnifying glass—all dots and no pretty ladies with parasols. In the end, it's all about the big picture. The game is to spot, briefly discuss, and move through all of the legal issues instead of exhaustively answering one or two of them.

---

6. The actual exam I took is at www.law.harvard.edu/Administrative_Services/Registrar/exams
_95-96/exams/civpro3.html.

I picked up my Civil Procedure exam at 8:58 A.M. For seven hours and thirty minutes, I did not eat, drink, or piss. I read, circled, underlined, and typed. And saved my work compulsively. In all, it was not a bad experience. I was prepared. I had reread every major assignment the week prior to the exam and made my own outline. I rarely looked at my outline. I turned my test in at 4:28. At 4:30, I stopped by Harkness Commons to get a bite to eat. By 5:00, I was back to rereading my Contracts assignments and finishing up my outline. Contracts was on Wednesday.

The Contracts exam was in-class.[7] It was more the frenetic speed drill than my first test. It started at 1:30 and ended at 4:30 and had three questions instead of two. My Contracts exam was a lesson in perspective; or, more specifically, how to lose it. The first issue I spotted on the first question was one Norris had spent two lectures on. I blew my load on that first issue and started writing before I'd read the entire question carefully. By the time I realized I'd gotten a couple of the parties mixed up and missed a critical issue, the first fifty minutes of my three hours had passed. I still had two more questions to answer, and my first answer was going to need a lot of crossing out and rewriting. It was no coincidence that Contracts was the only class in which I had briefed many of my cases. Briefing is a notetaking process that results in a one-page summary for each case assigned. Unless you want to be the next Professor Norris, briefing is a colossal waste of time. One sentence per case, instead of one page, is a better treatment. But by the time I figured that out, I knew way too many specifics about way too many issues. When one of them came up, like that first issue in the Contracts exam, I was beside myself. I had to empty my mind of all its brilliant thoughts before I lost them. I didn't lose them. I just lost everything else that mattered for the next fifty minutes. I finished rewriting my answer to the first question at 3:30. There was only one hour left for the second and third questions. I spent forty minutes on the second issue-spotter and twenty minutes on the tell-me-what-you-think question. My answers to those questions were not thoughtful.

When the exam ended, I violated another personal rule of test-taking—no postmortems. For Zero Summers, postmortems were an opportunity to undermine everyone else's confidence. For the rest of us, they were a

---

7. www.law.harvard.edu/Administrative_Services/Registrar/exams_95-96/exams/contr3.html

masochistic exercise in reinforcing fears. As I descended the stairs that led from Austin Hall into the tunnel that would take me back to Gropius, I stopped and joined an after-exam conversation that went as it always does. Inevitably, I had spotted and addressed the majority of issues everyone brought up. Inevitably, I brought up one or two issues that some people had not spotted. Inevitably, someone brought up one or two issues I had not spotted. And inevitably, each of us ignored all the issues we spotted and obsessed over the few we missed.

I finished my postmortem and headed to The Parlour, where The Kankoos and The Dynamo were already lighting up bowl and bong. My plan was to have a beer in The Parlour, go back to my room for a nap, and wake up at midnight to study. Instead, I had eight beers in The Parlour, traded the nap for a road trip, and substituted *mens rea* for a couple hundred blackjack hands. I woke up on Thursday afternoon in a motel room somewhere in Connecticut, just down the road from Foxwoods, with 33 hundred-dollar bills wadded up in my pocket.

It had been a good night at the tables. My best ever, in fact.

I couldn't enjoy it. It was 2:00 P.M. on Thursday. I was closer to Foxwoods than law school; one hundred miles and less than twenty-four hours away from my Criminal Law exam. Ten minutes later, The Kankoos, The Dynamo, and I were speeding back to Cambridge. I tried to put it all into perspective. I had been gone for only a day. And I had made it to almost all of my Criminal Law lectures. I had even read most of the assignments. Still, I couldn't catch up on the hundreds of pages I had planned to read the day before. I sank down in my seat and began to not move.

It was 4:00 P.M. when we got back to The Parlour. The Kankoos gave me a good swift kick in the ass:

"Relax, Marquart, you're starting to make *me* worry. You don't need to know a thousand pages of text; you just need to know one three-hour exam."

He reached underneath a pile of empty Keystone Lights and grabbed two of his outlines, which were now condensed to twenty pages each. Twenty pages: everything I needed to know, or so said The Kankoos. Then, he gave me three old exams, along with a couple "model" student answers, and laid out my schedule:

"You got a whole night until the test. That's more time than I spent studying for the other two. Read these outlines three times each. Then read and answer the questions on these three tests. Write your answers out. Bring what you write to the exam. If you feel compelled to read anything, read the mini-outline in the front of *Gilbert's*. Go to sleep by 3:00 A.M. and don't wake up until noon. And sleep on this: dumb people do go to Harvard Law School, and you're not one of them. Meet me at The Parlour after the test to celebrate our victory."

"Victory? Are you referring to the $3,000 I just took from Foxwoods or the $20,000 I wasted on tuition?"

"Neither. You won three grand last night? I gotta talk to you later. But right now, just do what I say. We'll talk at 5:00. Oh, and one more thing—"

"Yeah?"

"At least we'll finally see who was right."

I do my share of needless worrying before any big event, but I've never been one to wilt in the throes of it. I did almost as The Kankoos told me to. I got to bed at 5:00 A.M. and woke up at 11:00. I took nothing to the exam but the two little outlines and my answers to the old tests, where I had scribbled some abstract musings. The musings were my own contribution. Every issue-spotter is also a broad philosophical question on some level. A few minutes discarding the *how* and writing about the *why* would make me sound like I spent a lot more time thinking about the law than I did.

The Criminal Law test was in-class. I had three hours to answer two issue-spotters. By the time the test started, survival instincts kicked in, and I was calm. I spent the first thirty minutes reading the first question carefully, underlining and numbering each issue. I then went down one of my outlines, writing the number of each issue next to each section of the outline that applied. I wrote about a paragraph for each issue. The first sentence of each paragraph stated the issue. The next two or three sentences paraphrased the parts of the outline I had marked off. The two or three after that applied the rules in the outline to the facts in the question.

Once I had written a paragraph for each issue, I added one more paragraph, copying word for word some of the philosophical bullshit I had scribbled into my practice exam answers. I finished by filling in the five or six lines I had intentionally left blank in the beginning of my answer with a summary paragraph, in the hope that this would create the impression that I knew what I was doing all along. I was done early.

I walked out of the test alternating between opposing thoughts. I was scared as hell that I'd be found out. But I couldn't tell the difference between my exam answer and the sample answers The Kankoos had given me. I even felt like I had a decent understanding of criminal law. I wasn't going to be bailing my cousin Pootie out of his jams anytime soon, but I could probably tell him what law he'd broken and what his rights were. As I entered the tunnel, I came upon another group of students rehashing the exam. I walked by. I got to The Parlour at 4:30, ahead of The Kankoos. He showed up five minutes later, claiming victory.

I hesitated. We would have to wait two more months to find out if The Kankoos was right. Grades wouldn't come out until the end of February. Never one to worry over things that can't be changed, though, I grabbed a Keystone and let it all fade into numbness. No postmortems.

CHAPTER 14 | **SHOWING UP**

At the beginning of January, Stanford's final exams come in rapid fire. Contracts, day off, Civil Procedure, day off, Criminal Law, day off, Torts, month off. I wasn't nearly so far gone as to pull the easiest and most obvious fuck-up: don't show up, fail out.

During the pre-exam "reading period," Tim Apparel and I settled into the PoMo bathroom and rented rooms at the Red Victorian, a bohemian bed-and-breakfast in the Upper Haight. Contrary to what you might think if you watch Stone Phillips or read *Newsweek*, crack doesn't instantly hook you and leave you dead or dying. It's cocaine, of the amphetamine family, which in the legitimate and lawful world can have functional properties. Gets people going, keeps them focused. Plenty of coke-heads hold down jobs, even become president. In addition to giving propulsion, uppers edit out life's major stagnancies: sleeping and eating. There are the obvious risks when you go about it along your own terms. Without the benefit of medical supervision, you need to be adept at making your own rules, setting your own limits. A little Dullard blood is sometimes all that separates productive druggies and profitable gamblers from flat-out addicts.

Final exams are the time to flick on those Dullard turbines. I did. Tim Apparel and I rolled back from San Francisco the Friday night before finals began. Fresh and alert for the first exam on Saturday morning, Contracts, I'd committed Davis Mund's brilliantly compact outline to memory during six hours of unprecedented concentration at PoMo.

During the Contracts exam, I felt loose, not least because I was taking the class pass-fail. Add to that the fact that the exam was fabulously easy. It never broached the more difficult grit of contracts: sales contracts requiring application of the Uniform Commercial Code, which I had believed was a theory, merely an academic proposal, until I inferred from the conversations around me, as the Contracts exam was being handed out, that the UCC is live law, enacted in some form in all fifty states and applicable to the sale of "goods." Long and widely established as it is, the UCC is full of plainly stated rules that lend themselves to exam questions with only one right answer.

By contrast, this exam's questions were more on the "cutting edge" of contract law. *Is a surrogate mother's contract to turn her baby over to a married couple, for a fee, an enforceable contract? Is it an unconscionable contract?* Cutting edge is code for: knowledge of the law unnecessary. Why? Because law at the cutting edge is inchoate, uncertain. Before growing up and hardening into an axiomatic rule, an infant proposition of law is just another debatable issue. Anyone who's endured a little *Nightline* knows the pros and cons of surrogate mothering. On a law school exam you state a fact slanted one way (*the surrogate mother was vulnerable, unsophisticated*), then find the legal support in Davis Mund's outline (*courts will decline to enforce contracts where one party, in making the contract, has exploited its disproportionate bargaining power to the detriment of the other party*). Finally, to show you've read your casebook, note the leading case (*Williams v. Walker-Thomas Furniture*). Next, *on the other hand*, you consider the converse proposition—*as repugnant as the commodification of human life is, it is long settled that courts will not second-guess an arm's-length bargain between two competent and informed parties.* Finally, connect the specific to the general: *the surrogate mother made a difficult, controversial choice, but it was an informed choice, a fair bargain for consideration and thus a valid, enforceable contract, her vulnerability notwithstanding.*

Then do the same on the Civil Procedure exam and, after a self-congratulatory trip to PoMo, the Criminal Law exam.

It would be dishonest if I were to give the impression that I alone was calm in the face of law school's famously hard first round of exams. Around Leland at least, there was a lot of pool playing, television watching, and Scotch nightcapping. There was also the occasional exam quandary— *what's the difference between voluntary and involuntary manslaughter?* Or the stray musing—*is attempted manslaughter theoretically possible?*—that confirmed the person posing it already knew enough to do just fine. The sole break from exam week tranquility came early one morning. Bobby Boylan had locked himself out of his room and faced going to the Torts exam without an outline. I woke up to find several students offering vain help lifted from movies and detective books. Davis Mund fumbled with a credit card in the lock slot. The Plumber caught no give when he tried a hip-to-the-door breakdown. Watching in the distance was The Barrister. He stepped nearer, then back. The Barrister got a slight running start, only a matter of steps in the slim Leland hallway, and, amplifying The Plumber's limp lunge, put his ass and shoulder into the door. The thick, hard wood snapped, loudly and respectfully. It was the greatest triumph I ever saw The Barrister achieve.

For me, the ruckus was a fortuitous wake-up call. I also had Torts, my last first-semester exam, in twenty minutes. I would try to do well on the Torts exam. Not that I hadn't tried on the three prior exams. But during Contracts, Civil Procedure, and Criminal Law, I made time for a relaxing stroll at the mid-points and set the personal objective of being first to finish and leave. I had done this just for sport, a remnant of having written so many speeches under manufactured duress. With Torts, I wouldn't fuck around, partly as an experiment, to see if taking things seriously affected outcomes.

Although I had attended Torts regularly, I saw no point in transcribing my own notes. Tim Apparel's outline from the previous year was for the same course and same professor. His outline would be my shepherd, and a good one, until I reached three questions near the end of Professor Howard's exam:

There is a robbery at a fast-food Restaurant. The Restaurant has no security guard, so the armed Robber easily occupies the seating area. There is a thick, bulletproof, Plexiglas divider between the seating area and the employee/kitchen area (where the cash is). A plainly displayed sign reads: Not Responsible for Property Loss or Personal Injury on Premises. The Robber takes Customer #1 hostage and demands that the cashier give him the money from the register or he will kill Customer #1. The cashier ducks out of sight. The robbery has failed. But the Robber makes good on his promise. He kills Customer #1. On his way out, the Robber gives emphasis to his frustration and kills Customer #2. Customer #1's family sues by a survivor action on the theory that the Restaurant had a duty to Customer #1 to comply with the Robber's demands; that it breached that duty; and that it was therefore negligent. Customer #2's family also sues on the ground that the Restaurant had a duty to employ a visible security guard and thereby prevent robberies, a general duty to all customers including Customer #2, and was therefore negligent in not having employed a security guard.

Questions
What, if any, is the liability on the part of the Restaurant to Customer #1? Customer #2? What defenses on the part of the Restaurant?

The topic had come up in class. I'd been there. But I didn't remember which way the law went. It would have been convenient to just write *no liability* because of the sign. But you can't opt out of the law by announcing it doesn't apply to you. Tim Apparel's outline did have the heading "Robbery Cases." Apparently, though, Tim Apparel had not attended first-year classes as compulsively as he claimed. Beneath the heading, the outline was blank. With few exceptions, law school exams are "open book," and *book* is broadly construed to include casebooks, student-made outlines, and, in some instances, store-bought outlines. There was no time crunch, so I could avail myself of the open book option by finding the robbery cases in the Torts casebook. I could have, had I owned a Torts casebook. I left the exam room to go to the bathroom, where I thought about what to do. First I had a bad idea: torch the glass pipe. Then a good idea. If you don't own a book and need it right away, there are two options: bookstore and library. The Stanford Bookstore and the Stanford Law School Library were equidistant from where I was standing. Casebooks can cost three or four twenty-dollar bills each. Reasserting the cause of frugality, I went to the library.

"I need a casebook," I said to the librarian.

"You're either very late or very early," the librarian said.

I checked out *Cases and Materials on Tort Law and Alternatives*, Franklin and Rabin, Fifth Edition. At pages 186 and 187 I found my answers. Did the restaurant have a duty to employ a security guard? *It depends*. In one case, a judge reasoned that requiring a security guard would require businesses to provide a safer environment than exists in the world at large, an unfair burden to impose. A different judge, however, in a different state, under different facts, reasoned that if the history of the surrounding neighborhood indicates robberies are likely, then not having a visible security guard could constitute negligence. Customer #2 might have a case against the restaurant for not employing a security guard, then again he might not. Customer #1's legal position was more straightforward. There was only one case that considered whether there is a duty to accede to a robber's demands if he has threatened to kill a customer. That case clearly stated there is no duty. I finished the exam by quoting from the case—"*We cannot afford to extend to the criminal another weapon in his arsenal*"—and then pompously noting, in my own words, that *even where legal lines are sensibly drawn, they cannot function as an impervious barricade against all tragic consequences*.

End of first semester.

And there I was. In law school. With my friend Tim Apparel. California. Where mountain biking was invented. I had plenty of walking-around money, yet didn't have or need a job. I was feeling good.

PART 7 | **SECOND SEMESTER**

CHAPTER 15 | LIMBO

The day after exams ended, I woke up on a strange floor with a blunt pain in my back and a sharp one in my head. I reached up to massage my temples. As digits met cranium, I realized I was trembling. I looked down. I was naked, except for boxers. I sucked in a wet breath of stale Cuban Cohiba marinated in Pete's Wicked and realized I was in The Parlour. It was saturated with darkness. Had I lost time? I remembered that the windowpanes were cardboarded to keep out light. I felt my way to the nearest window and jerked it open, drinking in the cool night air. Night?

It's easier than you think to sleep through a January day in Cambridge. Still, the night takes on disorienting qualities when you've slept through the day before. With the aid of a diffused security light in the courtyard, I found my clothes and got dressed. I turned on a lamp. I took a quick survey of the room. The Kankoos was asleep in his bed. The Dynamo and his girl were on the floor, frozen in their entanglement like Pompeian lovers. A few others were slumped over against the wall. All were asleep, except Brian. Brian sat upright in a corner, his arms folded across his knees, his chin resting upon them. He was alert, but silent. I imagined he must have been watching me for some time, though he did not acknowledge my presence. Had the room been better lit, I would have seen his face. Had I seen his face, I would have kept silent. Instead, I whispered:

"What are you going to do, Brian?" I asked.

"Maybe get an M.B.A.," he said. "Nah, I've had enough of tests for a while. I'll probably go work at my dad's bank."

"What are you talking about? I was asking what you were doing for break."

There was a four-day break between exams and the second semester.

"Oh. I'm supposed to fly back to Dallas for a couple more interviews."

"Pretty messed up, huh? We already have three job offers apiece and you're talking about what you're gonna do if you fail."

One Ls had been sending out letters for summer jobs since December. Most of us got summer law firm jobs during the break before exams, two months before our first grades came out. Brian and I were both set to be summer associates in Dallas.

"Not *if* I fail, Marquart. *When* I fail. I'm out. I blew it."

"Everyone says that, Brian. I'm sure you did fine. We all did fine."

"You don't get it. I'm not that type, with all the false modesty and shit. I'm serious. I completely ran out of time on Contracts. I only got down about a page on the second question. I missed half of the issue-spotter in Civil Procedure. I was talking to Vicky Sentence, and she came up with an assload of issues I didn't find in Crim Law . . ."

There's nothing you can do to cheer someone up when they're hell-bent on being upset, especially if they're smart. With my cousin Pootie, at least I had a chance of saying something that he hadn't already thought of. But there was nothing I could say that Brian wouldn't have already anticipated and refuted. Still, I offered my best:

"I think you're overreacting, Brian. But I wouldn't believe that if I were feeling like you do. Why the hell were you talking to Vicky Sentence and those guys anyway? We're all going to be fine."

"You really suck at this, Marquart," The Kankoos interjected. The Kankoos was completely awake now. My eyes had adjusted to the sparse lighting enough to see that The Kankoos's comment got a half-smile out of Brian.

"You see, Marquart, when a guy's being irrational like Brian here, you don't try to change his concept of the world. It can't be done; he's too smart."

Brian smiled.

"You gotta accept his notion of reality and work with that. Now, Brian, let's say you're right. Let's say you really screwed the pooch. You know you at least passed Crim Law, right? Even in your whacked-out world, Quivers's never failed anyone and you're not going to be the first. So let's say you failed the other two. Not a problem! All you need is the Big Lie—one so cataclysmic and personal they'll never call your bluff. Like your girlfriend died in a kiln explosion a couple days before exams. Then you throw yourself on the mercy of Harvard and ask for another chance. Look at it from their perspective. They get ranked based upon their graduation rate. It does them no good to say they shouldn't have admitted you. Plus, you're a good guy with a decent excuse who wants to try again."

"What if they *do* check out my story?"

"We'll hop on Lexis and dig up a full story ahead of time. We'll find you a Fawn Lebowitz."

"You really think they'll give me another chance?"

"Why the fuck not? Who has any stake in your failing out, besides those people you talked to after the exam? Speaking of which, watch who you tell how you did. No matter how much you think they're trying to help, the possibility of your failure makes some people around here feel better. Marquart's got a whole theory on that one. He bored the hell out of me with it the whole way to Foxwoods the other night. He's right, though. I mean it, no rehashing with anyone that isn't us."

Brian left with a smile. He would spend the next few weeks breaking his promise not to rehash. After he was gone, I asked The Kankoos,

"Is that true about the second chance?"

"It *probably* is. We'll see in two months."

Two months. By that time, we would be halfway through the second semester. I was no longer willing to entertain ridiculous thoughts like Brian's, but I was not completely above the craziness around me. Only one solution came to mind, more evasion than solution. Spain, perspective, Elise.

Halfway across the Atlantic again, I felt a weightlessness I had felt only once before—October 19, 1991. That was the day I asked a pretty little brown-haired girl in a dark plaid skirt and white stockings to be my girlfriend. She said she'd think about it. The next day, she said yes. After that day, the sinking feeling was gone. Four years later, on a plane over the

Atlantic, it was back. I could have been refreshed. We had gotten way too used to each other, no doubt, and I could have welcomed a little newness. In a different light, I might have. Just not then. Not there. I checked the pocket in the back of the seat in front of me to make sure the little bag was there. I exhaled. My instinct to return to the familiar in times of worry had always served me well. But what of the familiar remained? I closed my eyes.

Two more months.

CHAPTER 16 | **THE SINGING OF SIX ON THREE**

On a January afternoon, the first year's second semester started with a new round of loans paying the tuition bill and bolstering the Wells Fargo card (balance: $6,789.25). The minivan crash wounds were healed and I had exactly one friend, Tim Apparel. The first thing I did after clearing the tuition violated that initial friendship pact between me and Tim Apparel. I bought law books.

I was at the Stanford Bookstore without purpose, meandering. Then, a nostalgia flash coupled with impulse buying, I laid out more than a hundred bucks for two casebooks. Outside, it was a gray and serious New Englandish day, which I think sent my mind back to *Paper Chase* images, in particular the one where Hart surrounds himself with law books and settles in for a library weekend. The image packed an attractive peacefulness: having a definite task, emerging from it fatigued yet enlarged. The books themselves were also elegantly enticing. The Property book was the ornate Little, Brown sort—red, black, and gold on the spine, like you see on the shelves in TV law shows. The Constitutional Law book was the thickest in the bookstore, with a no-bullshit blue cover and spare gold lettering.

Back in my room, I began reading the Constitutional Law book, with feet propped in the way of my hometown friends' parents, all professors, all

of whom had been candidly dubious of adolescent me, son of a car salesman. As I read the recent abortion cases (where Scalia pretends that
what he really deplores is judicial overreaching, not recreational sex),
there was a knock at my door. Tim Apparel. He saw the law books,
digested his disappointment, and spoke:

"Check this out."

He handed me the note about people not flushing their ass-protecting
toilet paper that had been posted in the Leland bathroom.

"So."

"Turn it over," he said. On the other side, a letter, on *Stanford Law
Review* letterhead:

Dear Mr. Mahnmeets:

I am in receipt of your appeal regarding the Editorial Board's vote
to decline publication of your article entitled "Civil(?) Procedure:
A Modest Proposal Toward Civility in Litigation." While I concur
with the assessment presented in your appeal letter (dated 15
November 1995) that the piece is both provocative and original,
I am loath, except in extraordinary instances, to "second-guess" the
judgments of my junior editors. Regrettably, therefore, the *Stanford
Law Review* remains unable to publish your article as submitted.

Sincerely,

Francine Lewis

Senior Editor
Stanford Law Review

"Stupid blunderfuck Barrister writes his anonymous note on the back
of a rejection letter." Having claimed battle victory in his strange jihad
against The Barrister, Tim Apparel then asked, "Bike ride? Then Bar
Review?"

After a mountain bike ride where Skyline stayed distant as ever, Tim
Apparel and I arrived at the Tool Shed, a crowded after-work Silicon Valley bar hangout where all manner of khaki pant and pastel shirt confirmed
membership in The Not-So-Great Generation. We crossed into the Tool
Shed, each of us still with a film of bikey grit, and our arrival was noted by

a demisemiquaver pause, or so it seemed. As much as I felt first-year law student eyes radiating scorn toward me, I sensed that Tim Apparel's second-year classmates thought him an even greater pariah. With me, the source of animus was attached to a widely known event. Tim Apparel was more the deviant without portfolio.

We dangled alone and ungreeted, something we didn't need to travel to the Tool Shed to experience. The Tool Shed did have two things our dorm rooms did not, though: steeply priced liquor and a dartboard. Tim Apparel headed for the bar. I went toward the dartboard.

As I attached my flights and sharpened the dart tips, a hand gripped my shoulder. Sloppy drunk words were directed at me:

"So, Byrnes, think you can just blow off the hardest first-year class."

It was The Barrister. He spoke again:

"OK, don't talk to me Mister Big-Shit. By the way, what was it? Seven people? Nine? That's really packing a Leland room, innit?"

I took that as a self-evident (though inexact) reference to the Halloween orgy. The Barrister's first comment apparently concerned my having gone to Contracts only once. That the two might have been connected didn't occur to me then. I now see how my approach to law school could have, to The Barrister's eyes, diminished his own efforts, both to get good grades and to shake his conspicuous sexlessness.

"I'm sure I'll get a perfectly shitty grade in Contracts, Barrister."

"Ah, dude, I don't go by that name."

I was coming to see Tim Apparel's dig with The Barrister. Behind all the English loftiness, The Barrister was an American frat boy, and apparently not half the scholar he imagined. I tried to stay amiable:

"Game of 501?"

"Hundred bucks?" he proposed.

"Bring it on."

The Barrister rumbled away to get a set of bar darts. His huge shoulder clipped Tim Apparel, who was approaching with a drink that, by size, could have been taken for a Coke if it weren't, by hue, plainly bourbon. I told Tim Apparel of the joust with The Barrister, and we made a rough plan to tell the entire Law School about the backside of The Barrister's bathroom note. The Barrister returned with darts and Tim Apparel left.

Taking a dart game off a Brit has special satisfaction. You start assuming defeat. And truth be told, The Barrister looked to be a better, more consistent player than I over the long haul. I was in a groove, though, pounding the treble twenties, then finding my out on a double sixteen, first throw. Game over. The Barrister handed me a hundred dollars, then I left. I stayed throwing. Then:

"So, you're Robert Byrnes."

Someone had been watching me all along. Thousands of internally satisfying darts matches had finally received external validation—from a woman I had never met, and yet she knew my name. How? Only one way I supposed, fresh from The Barrister's anti-orgy diatribe. But then again there are plenty of ways to know who someone is without having met. I knew, for instance, that she was Francine Lewis, a second-year law student. I knew this from her Face Book photo, radiant and no doubt much jacked-off to. I made my final throws toward the bull's-eye, a less rich target than the treble twenty, but more familiar to outsiders, like Francine Lewis. Only one hit bull, but the three darts were impressively grouped. I gathered the darts with a single grab and said:

"And you are?"

"This place is so white. I've got some killer weed at my place."

When we got to her rented house in the hills below Skyline, Francine Lewis began complaining with what seemed like rehearsed polish about her leading anxieties—bad ankles, unloving father, law school grades, disingenuous friends, clerkship and job after law school—each presented in order of its appearance in her life. Helen had had her own similar list, which she had grindingly worked her way through every night in New Haven when she arrived home from her job, which she hated. Francine Lewis, after outlining the grim prospect of whiffing on a Supreme Court clerkship, and thus having no choice but to work at a law firm, retrieved the most absurdly large bong I've ever known a woman to own. The pot clouded out her anxious ramblings, but it wasn't until the sex between us got fully rolling that I saw her face take on a peacefulness that suggested she couldn't access any of what had rankled her minutes before, even if she tried. Helen had transformed, within sex, exactly the same way. And in exactly the same way, after sex, they both would rediscover corporeal consciousness, wrap themselves in a sheet, and resume with the same complaint lists they had recited earlier. I saw for a moment that it was hard to argue with Niccola's often repeated question, really a statement: *do you think you maybe remember only the good things about Helen.*

As Francine Lewis continued to shroud herself, I took a bong hit and forgot most of that first night with her until I made a trip back to New Haven much later in law school.

I woke the next morning in a delightful confusion: wondering where I was. I had by then grown enough accustomed to my Leland dorm bed that I noticed the absence of its textures and bumps. This was a big, girlish bed with expensive sheets and a superabundance of pillows. I reached full consciousness on reading a note from Francine Lewis: she was gone, to an early class, then to a "fucking *Law Review* meeting." She also wrote that "(we should get together again sometime)" and that I was "not at all like what" she expected, a statement so indefinite it could mean a great deal or nothing at all. Rather than speculating into a paranoia spiral, I turned to the practical. It was the second semester's first day of classes and I headed straight to the Law School.

My first class that second semester was Constitutional Law. Stanford offered what must have been the most accomplished Constitutional Law professor lineup in the history of American law schools. There was John Hart Ely, whose book *Democracy and Distrust* seemed so famous and canonical when I was in college that I assumed he had to be dead. Still fully alive, even on the young side, Ely taught another course called Underwater Treasures, which Tim Apparel was taking this same semester. (Although Underwater Treasures was notoriously impractical, a few years later Tim Apparel called and told me he had just taken the California Bar Exam, which included an underwater treasures essay question.) Kathleen Sullivan also taught Constitutional Law. She had attended Harvard Law School, been a protégée of Laurence Tribe, and become a professor at Harvard. Sullivan then left Harvard for Stanford, a fact Stanford copiously advertises to prospective students. She would become Stanford's dean in 1999.

Although Sullivan was my professor for a third-year class on the First Amendment that I never attended, she was not my first-year Constitutional Law professor. Mine was Gerald Gunther. He was why I always went. Gunther was indeterminately "old"—older than sixty, younger than eighty. He had clerked for Learned Hand, and then for Earl Warren around the time of *Brown v. Board of Education*. The casebook we used was the most assigned, to all law students at all law schools: *Constitutional Law*, Gunther, Twelfth Edition. In the 1960s, Gunther had been hired away from Columbia Law School, an event that marked a shift in the elite law schools' sticky hierarchy. More than any single professor, he lifted Stanford's reputation from mediocre to elite.

There was also something adorable about Gerald Gunther, a playfulness that in no way diminished the impression that we were learning constitutional law from its greatest living authority. Gunther was as generous a professor as I have ever encountered, and he offered his kind-spirited genius to us. Not everyone shared this view, though. Bobby Boylan, Davis Mund, and The Barrister all came to the first few Constitutional Law classes and never returned, having failed to receive the charm in Gunther's anecdote-sprinkled presentation, which was more likely to give the dish on a Supreme Court justice than recite black-letter law.

"This geezer's boring the piss out of me," The Barrister mumbled to himself, on the last day I saw him in Gunther's class.

For my part, Gunther also represented the happier side of getting old. One of my earliest childhood thoughts was that there are two kinds of old men: the pathetically alone and those who, though they are near the end, radiate satisfaction in having lived a life of creativity and action. Gunther was this latter type, and he seemed to have entered life's last but most satisfying phase. He had nothing left to *do* but to give.

Attending Gunther's class was like watching a movie more for the star's energy than the underlying drama. Much of Constitutional Law concerned distinctions I couldn't have given a crap about. One example: whether the *federal government* can create Gun- or Drug-Free Zones around schools. It's uncontroversial that state and local governments can do this sort of thing—pass laws and post signs that say you're really, really fucked if you pack or do a deal in a defined zone around a school. But whether the federal government can do the same depends on a formalistic inquiry: *does it affect interstate commerce?*

The role of the constitutional lawyer, therefore, is not about stating the pedestrian position—drugs and guns are bad or good, abortion is necessary—but pretending to care about an abstraction. And it is an abstraction in the worst sense. It is meaningless. Everyone has opinions. To play lawyer, though, you have to dress common opinions in legal finery. If you hate guns and like federal gun laws, you gather up the reasons why guns around schools affect interstate commerce (e.g., fewer dead kids means more live interstate travelers). The Supreme Court might say the federal government can't make Gun-Free School Zones. In fact the Supreme Court did just that. Big deal.

The states and cities can enact identical laws, and they have, so the real-life consequence is the same. You tend to move your action elsewhere, somewhere outside the zone.

Even Gunther couldn't inspire me to care much about federalism. Embedded in nearly every Constitutional Law case, however, was some connection to real life. As Gunther finished the abortion cases with *Casey*, which more or less preserved *Roe v. Wade*, Lucy spoke:

"Though I do support a woman's right to choose, I am troubled that the Court has cast abortion as a constitutionally protected right."

This was Lucy Faar speaking, my good friend from first semester, with whom I had spent a night on the beach at Half Moon Bay, the same Lucy who had told me of her sexual awakening and succession of quick flings after the breakup with her boyfriend. I was feeling nipped at by a frigid Puritanism, an antisexual drift presented as if the Law commanded it. It appeared that law school had brought Lucy to a point of revelation and decision. Either she could derive her view on abortion entirely from her own internal instinct. Or that view could be qualified from a more exclusive and elite place: the Law. Everyone has instinct. Only the legally educated know the law. By putting her instinctive and educated selves in conflict, Lucy had done nothing so much as fashion a more "complex" self.

Class time was running short, and this would be the last of the abortion cases. For me, the moment was all about Lucy and, more generally, the gnaw of no longer knowing someone I once knew and believed I always would. I raised my hand. Gunther called on me. My point was short and unoriginal:

"The *Casey* majority couldn't save *Roe* with the Constitution. They had to get real and come right out and say we've all come to the point of relying 'on the availability of abortion in the event that contraception should fail.'" Then I said something like this, mostly to myself, because I get nervous and out of breath speaking in front of large groups: *Lucy says fall on the sword at the Supreme Court, then fight it out separately in all the state legislatures. Not me. I've always admired the Supreme Court's fuck-and-run. The state legislatures can't make abortion illegal. End of discussion. All the constitutional mumbling just forces abortion supporters to traffic in pious code. They prattle on about "privacy" and how they aren't "pro-abortion," just "pro-choice." Go to the source, though, and abortion is about sex. With all the recreational, nonprocreative sex going on, it would have been asinine to let state legislatures say a broken rubber means you're having a kid. Overruling* Roe *would have outlawed sex as we know it.*

Gunther nodded and gestured in a way that said that although he didn't share my analysis, and I hadn't been particularly trenchant, I had nonetheless fallen within a line of legitimate and recognized legal thought—so-called legal realism. It was probably the last time an older person I respected appeared to have thought well of me. And that was all I needed—a sense of belonging and affiliation; confirmation that the Puritans and Dullards hadn't extinguished all opposition. It's a fine line between healthy separateness and lunatic loneliness, and I can get edgy about being sure I'm still on the sane side of things.

Class ended and I made a common error among those experiencing paranoia waves. I got high. It was sweet Marin County weed. A Three L, who lived in San Francisco and was technically a Four L, dropped down to Palo Alto occasionally to attend a seminar and replenish the Law School's pot supply. Tim Apparel and I went in jointly on a four-finger bag. I got high in preparation for Property Law, because it had become my ritual.

Property law is the most basic and necessary of all law in a private property system. Nothing is more essential than knowing who owns what. If you don't, there's chaos from the outset, thus no chance to make contracts, no incentive to build and sell dangerous products, and no such thing as stealing. From that prosaic necessity, though, property law enters a psychedelic realm. At least it did for me. I attribute this partly to my professor, who laid out all the legal mechanisms for keeping track of property ownership and transfer, the deed recording systems, and rules governing future real property interests. None of it interested me, nor did I care about the seemingly thousands of alternate systems by which we could equally well manage private property. What did interest me was my professor's mad-genius ability to construct and deconstruct these alternate realities, each of which I absorbed and then forgot as soon as he moved on to the next, each successive reality seemingly bulletproof and grounded in something eternal and immutable, yet loaded with hidden contradiction and incoherence that only he could penetrate. Property seemed like the right sort of event to get high for. So I did, every class.

There was one property doctrine that I did remember. It was adverse possession. Adverse possession appeals to the baked mind because it involves getting something for nothing and doing next to nothing to get it. Say I own a plot of land, in the ordinary sense of having bought it and being free to sell it. I don't live on the land, though. You do—openly, continuously, and for a long time. You occasionally kick others off the land. By adverse possession you can come to own the land; sell it, build on it, whatever. I'm shit out of luck. Adverse possession seemed magical, medieval, self-executing—the way I imagined all law to be, as a child. Adverse possession also gave me an opening to be legally useful. I phoned my father and told him that he risked losing the triangle of land he had allowed our neighbor to park a Winnebago on. Then, after hanging up, I shot into the realization that I was completely wrong. It's called *adverse possession*—possession that is adverse, or hostile, to the original owner. It doesn't get any more *un*hostile than giving permission, as my father had, and acting consistent with that permission, as our neighbor had. I called my father back, and could only imagine a career in the law, if I were to have one, as being a series of similar blunders and retractions.

My other classes did little to allay a suspicion that the lawyer's temperament might not be mine. Yet I went, accruing a better-than-average attendance record, not that there is any actual "record," just my own recollection of having gone to class nearly all the time that second semester. Going to class ran no interference with biking. Tim Apparel and I managed a ride on the road bikes in the morning, the mountain bikes at night. After riding, we headed for dinner at Breakers. On Sundays, I cooked at Breakers, from which I always emerged feeling competent and functional. Laying out a gigantic meal gave the same rush and sense of simple achievement as making an under-the-wire bike delivery had. Physical, not intellectual, work seemed to be my calling.

Tim Apparel appeared during one of my Breakers cooking shifts to tell me that we had been summoned to the dean of students.

"Check your mailbox. I'm sure you got one, too. The Dean doesn't say why, but I assume we're being hauled in for exposing The Barrister on the *Law Review* thing."

I unlocked the Breakers supply room and handed Tim Apparel a case of Ramen noodles.

"Peace offering for The Barrister," I said.

"Probably best to lay off the e-mails now," Tim Apparel said, and I agreed.

The need to make peace arose because Tim Apparel and I had sent out a sequence of e-mails from an anonymous remailer address, all signed somewhat less anonymously, "The Barrister." To keep the e-mails from being traced to us, Tim Apparel and I would each engage our dorm room phone lines on long-distance calls. Then we'd find an on-campus computer we could use without identifying ourselves. From there, we sent out the Barrister e-mails to the entire law school. The Barrister's e-mail voice found an over-the-top haughtiness that mixed with a lingering bitterness toward the *Stanford Law Review*'s failure of insight in refusing to publish his civil procedure tome. On the Law School's e-mail exchange, The Barrister's solecism-spotted postings gained an angry following, particularly among One Ls, to which we posted a response:

```
TO: law-classifieds@lists.Stanford.edu
FROM: Bovine Remailer


Dear Classmates,

I do, as has been exhaustively noted, have an unfor-
tunate tendency to commit grammatical and spelling
errors—an affliction I share with Scott Fitzgerald,
President Kennedy, Robespierre, and Issac Newton.
Nonetheless, I press onward with mature revisions
to "Civil(?) Procedure: A Modess Proposal Toward
Civility in Litigation," confident that the occa-
sional vowel surplusage is of no moment in light of
the article's overarching substance. Seeing the
forest through the trees: therein lies the essence
of important scholarship and, indeed, success in
law school. Producing a great quantity of pointed,
well-organized observations also happens to be the
telltale skill common to those examinations judged
```

to be superior. As I poach on conversations between
classes, I note that the majority of you have drastically miscomprehended some of the central first-
year concepts (most notably in Propety and Civil
Procedure). Such is not my own fate. I have produced
treatise-quality, outlines which I will without
hesitation provide to subsequent classes because it
cannot possibly disadvantage me.

Cheers,
The Barrister

Eventually, The Barrister—the real one—sent this e-mail to us:

TO: rcbyrnes@leland.stanford.edu,
    tapparel@leland.stanford.edu
FROM: abmahnmeets@leland.stanford.edu
SUBJECT: Imitation

Gents:

Sincerest form of flattery, don't you think? Just
keep in mind that I know where you live, and as
regards the future you might take certain steps to
avoid a situation wherein this information must,
alas, be made accessible to third parties.

Cheers,
A.B.M., most assuredly not d/b/a "The Barrister"

We ignored the warning and kept sending the e-mails. Apparently
The Barrister executed his threat, bringing me and Tim Apparel to a
"third party's" attention. I had in fact been sent the same vague letter from
the dean as Tim Apparel had received: "Please arrange a meeting at your
earliest convenience." Tim Apparel and I decided to put a stall on meeting with the dean—one of us would always claim to be inundated with
schoolwork—until the meeting was unavoidable, sometime much later,
quite possibly never. In the meantime we'd cool the tension with Ramen

noodles from the Breakers supply room. We sent out a farewell Barrister e-mail, where he claimed to have quit the law in frustration at its small-mindedness.

From Breakers, Tim Apparel and I would head into the night. Our drug and entertainment rotation was a sensible one. A typical week: liquor and Valium on Sunday night for solid sleep; ecstasy and nitrous for a Monday rave; pot and hash on Tuesday for *Beavis and Butthead*; rock on sleepless Wednesday; then just plain beer at Thursday's Bar Review; another rave on Friday; leaving Saturday clean, maybe just an inch of Jim Beam to lubricate attendance at whatever movie or dinner Francine Lewis had arranged. (At some point she had asked, "does this mean I'm your girl-friend?" and I'd said "sure.") Up in The City, Tim Apparel and I devel-oped a certain familiarity and expertise. We'd spend a hundred bucks with Paris, enough for a month we figured, do a little test in the PoMo bathroom, wind up burning the whole thing, and then head back to Paris for another hundred, and another. Before long, it was as if Paris sensed the instant we emerged from PoMo, needy, on the way to the ATM. By the slightest nod his way, we confirmed our order. Paris would disappear to wherever the stash spot was. We'd restock our cash, sit at the Haight and Fillmore bus stop, drop the money on the ground, and Paris would pick it up with his toes and let the rock fall from his fingers, to the side-walk. After a casual linger at the bus stop, we'd head back into PoMo.

Fitting classes in busied things. But class functioned as a safe zone. It's one thing to wake up in the stairwell of a public housing crack factory, out of money, nowhere to go; quite another thing to speed straight back to Stanford and cleanse yourself with intellectual gymnastics in Property class. Property and Constitutional Law (like Torts, Contracts, Criminal Law, and Civil Procedure during the first semester) were required courses. The second semester also offered the chance to pick two of your own classes. I chose Modern American Legal Thought, and Law and Social Science, neither for entirely honorable reasons.

Modern American Legal Thought was about the law's attempt to define itself. Like a person, American law had an infancy, periods of self-doubt, tics of pomposity, waves of contradiction, and internal conflict. The course was a survey of these developmental phases and the schools of thought that characterized them. I knew the professor, Jo Howard, from my Torts class. Modern American Legal Thought also came with Tim Apparel's recommendation:

"Final exam's a two-*week* take-home. Kind of a fun class anyway. All about how law is bullshit. Legal realism they call it."

To a legal realist, whether abortion is constitutionally protected is all about whether the judges making the decision prefer that abortion be available. That's all. Judges have the same gut feelings as Joe Shit the Ragman does. The legal realist would say that while a judge looking to overturn *Roe v. Wade* might frame his opposition as a dispassionate legal finding, that view will tend to line up predictably with the standard "conservative" orientation millions of regular people share on other issues. Scalia, for instance, is against abortion and hate-crimes legislation; for the death penalty, antigay voter initiatives, all-male military academies, saying prayers at public school graduations, and, more recently, against Florida recounts. Ruth Bader Ginsburg comes out the other way on all those issues. Sometimes she wins, other times he wins. You can make the Constitution support either side on any well-traveled issue. They are "hard cases"—issues that connect with strong feelings and have developed coherent, conflicting legal arguments. The Supreme Court takes only hard cases. In contrast to Lucy's view, the realists say that judges consult their own intuitions first, and then send their clerks to go looking for the law that supports their intuitions. Lucy headed straight for the law. Still, Lucy did have a point. The dissent in the *Casey* abortion decision might win a few more debating points than the majority opinion. But the majority opinion got more votes—five to four—than Scalia's dissent. It's all about having the votes, not finding the law. There's law on either side of any hard case, and you don't have to be a Supreme Court clerk to find it.

The rebuttal to the realists came from the Legal Process School. Professor Howard read, with an unadmiring inflection, from Herbert Weschler's strangely famous *Harvard Law Review* article, "Toward Neutral Principles of Constitutional Law":

Lastly I come to the school decision, which for one of my persuasion stirs the deepest conflict.... Yet I would surely be engaged in playing Hamlet without Hamlet if I did not try to state the problems that appear to be involved.... The problem inheres strictly in the reasoning of the opinion.

Professor Howard explained: "In simpler language Weschler is saying that people of his *'persuasion'* of course deplore segregated schools. But because the 'school decision,' *Brown v. Board of Education*, lacks constitutional foundation, it is the wrong way to end segregation. Anyone have a thought or opinion on Weschler?"

The Barrister spoke up: "The realists were frustrated adolescents. They found that the world is not burgeoning with Kantian absolutes. So they rejected all generalizations about human nature, all first principles. Weschler saved us from the realists' childish nihilism. He brought principle back into our law. Quite eloquently, at that."

Professor Howard did make a last stab at ridiculing Weschler: "Is this idolatry of the trivial? Is what gets an A+ on a law school exam more important than ending segregation?"

The class stayed silent. There was an almost erotic allure to Weschler's formalism. Sitting in front of me, Lucy took notes and nodded. I still knew her well enough to know that her eyes said: *right all along*. Weschler's approach had been Lucy's when she spoke in Constitutional Law about the abortion cases. She and The Barrister were thinking alike.

I also took Law and Social Science second semester, but not because I had a special interest in the various clinical bases for the insanity defense or how jury size affects verdicts. I took Law and Social Science because you had a choice regarding its lone requirement (final exam or paper). I chose paper, a paper I allocated no more than a morning to writing, on the day it would be due, sometime at the semester's end. It would of course be a horrendous paper, so I took the course pass-fail. In that paper-writing morning, I could focus sufficiently to avoid either outright failure or the cusp of failure. I had written serviceable political speeches in far less time. I did, nonetheless, attend Law and Social Science, which is to say I showed up, invariably made a bathroom trip within the first eight minutes then, within the next five minutes, made another bathroom trip, which wasn't a bathroom trip at all. I'd wander back to Leland, grab my mountain bike, and head for the hills with Tim Apparel. The better part of the time Law and Social Science met, therefore, I was catching air on single tracks and stopping for hour-long staredowns with deer and coyotes. Outdoors and on a bike, that's what I'm good at, a revelation that was not without its troubling side. That I was basically enjoying "law school" was the problem. It put in higher relief the other side of law school: life in a law firm, which I took to mean wearing a suit and working on weekends, in an office. So as Tim Apparel and I rolled back toward Stanford from one of those rides, I made a decision. I would work as a bike messenger the coming summer, in San Francisco, the hilliest and fastest city of all, with the toughest riders, on stripped-down, one-brake speed machines. *Best job you'll ever have.* At the end of the summer, maybe I would return to law school, maybe I wouldn't. My summer plans were set. Dismounting our bikes outside Leland, Tim Apparel and I were next to a gathering of One Ls playing volleyball. I saw Davis Mund.

"Hey Davis."

Thirty first-year law students, Davis Mund included, stared blankly and silently at us.

"You see what I mean. I'm not imagining it," I said to Tim Apparel.

"Your orgy's old news, chief. Those guys are thinking about getting laid themselves, and about their GPAs and whether they'll land an offer from Cravath or Meeger Talley. You're far more forgotten than despised. Could be that's what's got you paranoid. Paranoia and vanity aren't so different. If you want a real worry, think about The Barrister."

The Barrister seemed almost touched when we gave him the case of Ramen noodles. At the same time he appeared unsettled that we had cottoned onto his base and unwavering eating habits. Tim Apparel tried to make a joke of it all, showing The Barrister the underside of the bathroom note that started the conflict and inspired our e-mails, the rejection letter from the *Stanford Law Review*. The Barrister was unamused. Reminded that he had written his snarky note on the back of an unflattering letter only forced him to revisit his own failure and stupidity. The Barrister puffed himself out, reasserting the physical power that had allowed him to smash Bobby Boylan's dorm room door during exams. Tim Apparel handed over the letter.

By March, we still hadn't found a mutually convenient date to meet with the dean of students. Nor had The Barrister ever conceded that he'd turned us in for writing the e-mails. That said, it was only our guess that we were being summoned to the dean at The Barrister's bidding. There were other possibilities. We came to prefer that it be about The Barrister, though, because the tensions between him and us seemed in decline a few weeks after Tim Apparel surrendered the letter. We'd stopped sending the e-mails, and The Barrister fell into a generally happier way when Jana Lee, a One L who lived in Leland, took an odd interest in his ideas about reforming the American civil litigation system. Jana Lee had also recently exited from a brief romance with Davis Mund. She visited The Barrister most afternoons.

One day when she knocked but found The Barrister not in, Jana Lee drifted by Tim Apparel's room and said she liked the sound of the obscure Elvis Costello he was playing. Listening to the complete works of Elvis Costello took the three of us deep into the night. Jana Lee was also plainly impressed by Tim Apparel's rogue-hacker persona. He owned up to masterminding the technical aspects around The Barrister e-mails, which by this point had been a cover-story topic of the Law School's newspaper, and I jumped on to claim some of the e-mail writing credit. This was unnecessary, in that the newspaper had already outed me. To Tim Apparel's dismay, I had sent out one of the Barrister e-mails from my own computer. It was easily traced. That only deepened the silence directed toward me by all my former friends from the first semester.

Jana Lee, though, wanted to hear more about orgies and e-mail shenanigans. So Tim Apparel laid out his plan to launch a Web site, after law school, using the code name "nowhitenoise." He told us, "I'll call it Greedy Associates. Salary and gossip exchange. It'll drive starting law firm pay up over a hundred fifty grand," he predicted, and I forgot about it, until a few years later, when Greedy Associates appeared on Yahoo! and did just what Tim Apparel said it would.

Toward sunrise, the Jana Lee conversation made a shift toward sex talk. Jana Lee told us she had heard the anti-orgy emanations around the Law School. "I was more intrigued than appalled," she said. At some point we became intertwined on Tim Apparel's bed, and at some later point Jana Lee began directing the action. Tim Apparel was assigned her upper half. My territory, she instructed, would be her legs, only her legs, and for the limited purpose of using one or both of them to beat off against, at the culmination of which, she further instructed, I was to make the deposit "right here," she said, pointing to her lips. A rule-bound three-way, it lost what little energy it had when Jana Lee asked flatly, "Which one of you is fingering me?"

Tim Apparel and I are quite certain The Barrister never found out we'd interfered with his romantic quest. By April, he had softened to the point of standing with us in the Leland hallway for a conversation about being a summer associate and whether we thought Jana Lee was an "attractive bird." We said yes. As to whether he might "get a little slap and tickle sometime before exams," we couldn't really say. The Barrister also told us that he'd gotten a "generous" number of summer associate offers and that he'd be working the first half of the summer at a Boston firm and the next half at the London office of a New York firm. He suggested a social outing:

"Law School Musical's tonight. You gents care to join me? Little rapprochement, eh?"

———————————

The Barrister, Tim Apparel, and I went to the Law School Musical, a pageant of in-jokes, mainly about lovingly lampooned professors. One skit, sung to the tune of George Michael's "I Want Your Sex," was about law students, particular law students. A lost friend from the first semester, someone I had known quite well, sang:

"Stanford Law Sex"

There's things you try to hide
And things the whole school knows
There's Two Ls you trust
and One Ls you don't

There's things you'd expect
And things you'd never guess
No one expected good sex in law school
But baby we did it and it was the best

Sex is natural—
Sex is good
Not many Two Ls do it
But many of them should

Sex is natural—
Sex is fun
Sex is best when it's . . . five on four
Six on three

"Six on three?" Tim Apparel asked.

CHAPTER 17 | **FEEDBACK**

The date grades will be released for Harvard One Ls is announced a few days in advance, to allow for buildup. When the day arrives, students scurry to assigned rooms and funnel into lines organized by last name to receive the envelope that contains their report card.

There are a few dominant grade-getting styles. Some students rip the grades open immediately, effusing their honest reaction, oblivious to any onlookers. Zero Summers calmly open their grades for all eyes to see, nod confidently as if they just got the excellent grades they expected, and then walk back along the line of waiting students with a satisfied grin on their faces, ever careful not to show their actual grades. But most One Ls retreat to a private place to get the news.

My plan was to take my envelope and walk as casually as possible back to my dorm room. Edgar and I agreed to open our grades together, over Scotch. I did not involve The Kankoos in all of this, for a couple of reasons. For one, I didn't want to be anywhere near him if he was wrong about ditching classes. But mostly, I knew he would think my ritual was immensely stupid, as it was. The Kankoos's approach was to get the envelope, rip it open right there, sort of shrug his shoulders as if to say *Yeah, whatever,* then crumple up the paper and toss it in the trash. Those who rummaged in the trashcan would have been at once astonished and disappointed by what they saw.

Unlike The Kankoos, Edgar suited my purposes. Edgar was a little more worried about grades than me. His nerves would calm mine.

Edgar hadn't missed a day of class and produced some of the most thorough outlines I'd ever seen—a hundred fifty pages per class. "*Too* thorough," The Kankoos often remarked. But Edgar was always the first to offer me his class notes the day after a binge in The Parlour or at Fox-woods. Even when the anxiety and pressure of exams put him at the edge of tears, Edgar stopped by The Parlour to explain an unclear point in one of his own outlines he'd given The Kankoos. And The Kankoos never gave Edgar any grief about his habits like he gave Brian and me. "Edgar's gotta do what Edgar's gotta do" was the only explanation The Kankoos ever gave for his disparate treatment of Edgar and us.

Come to find out, Edgar also had damned good taste in Scotch. Macallan, 18 Year. After a couple of drinks, we sliced open our envelopes. I reverted further into childishness. I covered up my grades with another piece of paper and uncovered each grade one by one. The first grade was Civil Procedure, the take-home exam, and my first-ever law school exam: B+.

My heart skipped as I edged the paper down farther. The next class on the list was Contracts, the test I knew I had blown. As I expected, it was worse. *Not* as expected: B.

The only class left was Criminal Law. I thought back to the two days before my Criminal Law exam—how I spent the first of them on a late-night Foxwoods run with The Kankoos and used his sketchy notion of cramming. I swallowed hard and uncovered my grade: B+.

Edgar seemed less pleased, perhaps disappointed. Before I could ask how he'd done, there was a knock at the door. It was The Kankoos.

"Hey, Marquart. How'd you do?"

"Fine. All B's of some kind."

"I'll spare you the I-told-you-sos. What about you, Edgar?"

"Not bad. Two B+'s. But a B in Crim Law. I worked my ass off in that class, too. What about you, Kankoos?"

"B+, B+, B."

Edgar's mood changed from displeasure to agitation and masochistic curiosity.

"What did you get in Crim Law?" he asked.

"B+."

"You're kidding me," he whispered, uncharacteristically deflated. "I never miss a class, make my own outline, and I get a B. You take a road trip to Foxwoods instead of studying and get a B+."

Edgar apparently expected to do better than The Kankoos and me by default. Still, I saw his disappointment for what it was. He didn't wish ill upon us. But our success represented a disconnect in the effort-reward paradigm that held his reality together. He had worked harder than us, knew more than us, and still got the same grades. He couldn't let it go. His disappointment shifted to denial.

"You couldn't have blown off Crim like you said."

"I wasn't lying to you," The Kankoos said.

"Well, maybe you got lucky. No, that's not fair. I'm sorry, Kankoos. I'm happy for you. And Marquart. I just can't believe you got away with it."

"I hear ya, Edgar," I said. "You deserved better grades than me. I never would have believed it could be that easy either, if I hadn't been forced to cram for Crim Law. But hey, look on the bright side. At least you don't have to work so hard anymore."

"Yeah, right. You're probably just a natural, Marquart."

"Don't get me wrong, Edgar, I'm glad to have someone I trust going to class and taking notes. But don't you think it's a little crazy to crown me kid genius? My LSAT score is two points below yours."

"I don't know, Marquart. All I've learned today is, if I keep making the same effort, reading what's assigned and taking good notes, I'll be fine. This is no time to start slacking. I've been burned before."

Burned before? Edgar's words touched off a recollection of Papaw's dog Roosevelt, at Christmas, and Papaw's prophetic words: *He ain't never gonna touch a hot stove again, but he ain't never gonna touch a cold one neither.* Edgar had been burned and he was not going to chance it again. I wondered what might have burned Edgar, but I stopped short of asking. It didn't matter. Everyone gets burned sooner or later—airs an unpopular view and gets ostracized, asks a girl to the prom and gets shot down. Most people come out of it only slightly scarred. But for some people, the wound is so deep, or their risk aversion so strong, they never touch that stove again. Often, a fear of particular stoves can become an aversion to them all. When that aversion rises to the level of a personality trait, a Cold Stover is born.

Though the stove at Harvard is room temperature at best, books, movies, and stories from just about every Harvard graduate confirm that the place is an inferno. For Papaw's dog, touching another stove after his sizzling encounter, even a cold one, was a leap of faith he wasn't willing to take. Same with Edgar and all Cold Stovers. To some degree, everyone at Harvard was either a Zero Summer or a Cold Stover. I was no exception. Only I had been forced to touch the stove. That gambling binge just before my Criminal Law exam gave me no choice but to test Harvard's rigor. The result: a tepid B+.

Edgar, as do all Cold Stovers, suffered losses of which he was generally unaware. Not your typical loss, the kind that comes from making a bad choice. Edgar was fully aware of that type of loss. He never made any unconventional choices. Everything he wore came from a department store, all his savings were in T-bills, and he never gave an opinion that hadn't been affirmed in the Sunday *Times*. But there is also the loss you suffer from not making a decision that would have offered greater rewards had you chosen it. Economists call this type of loss "opportunity cost." It is the cost of what might have been—of *not* being a fashion trend-setter, of *not* earning 30 percent a year in the technology sector, of *not* being lauded for your original opinions. It is just as real as the first type of loss. And just as damaging. It manifests itself in bitter marriages and midlife crises. I had a mental image of Edgar at forty-five—a law firm partner, a husband and a father, clumsily and pathetically living out his lost past with a paralegal while his kids waited for him after soccer practice. But Edgar was twenty-five and single now. It wasn't too late for Edgar.

The faint sound of my phone ringing down the hall saved us from prolonged awkwardness. I ran to my room. Brian was calling. He was right. He had screwed up, at least on Civil Procedure. He got a B–. B– is a bad grade, usually meaning you missed a handful of issues or wrote several things that were flat-out wrong. The rest of his grades were like everyone else's, B or B+. In fact, just about everyone got B's or B+'s. The Parlour's GPA mirrored that of the rest of the class, somewhere between a B and a B+. I heard rumors of people getting C's—i.e., your exam really, really sucked—but I never confirmed them. As for that supposed 1 percent, I didn't hear of anyone failing.

The night grades came out, Harvard became a world of boundless possibility. For one night, at least, damn-near honest, forthright conversations were the norm. Damn-near. There were faces in The Parlour I had never seen. We were opposing soldiers sharing cigarettes on the armistice; the coyote and the sheepdog punching out at the end of the day. All was good and light. Until, that is: Mike, a waist-up crazy Zero Summer/Cold Stover and occasional visitor to The Parlour, took up the mantle of rounding up entertainment. When two five-foot-eight, hundred-and-twenty-pound natural beauties with creamy skin and God-given C-cups arrived with a six-foot-four bodyguard in tow, The Kankoos instantly sensed that something had gone awry.

"Excuse me ladies, sir. I've got to talk to my friends here for a minute."

The Kankoos set the three visitors up with a beer in The Parlour and called a huddle in the hallway.

"What the hell is this, Mike?"

"That's the 'scorts. Pretty nice, huh?"

"OK, something's very wrong here."

"What do you mean? I can't believe you of all people are giving me shit about this. These girls are beautiful!"

"That's the fucking problem! There is no way these girls are 'scorts. They're way too pretty."

"What about porn stars? *They're* hot."

"There are no porn stars in Boston. It's too cold."

"That's preposterous," Mike said sniffishly.

"Preposterous, huh? Then who's the goombah? Have you ever seen a chaperone in The Parlour?"

"He must be the pimp."

"Just get me the ad, Mike."

Mike opened up the Yellow Pages to the ad. The Kankoos and The Dynamo inspected it nervously.

"Cock tease," The Dynamo sighed.

The Kankoos laughed. None of us knew what the hell had just gone on.

"Come here, Mike. Notice anything funny about this ad?"

We were all hovering over the ad, but no one noticed anything peculiar about it. The Kankoos gave another hint:

"What section are we in right now?"

"Engraving Equipment and Supplies?"

"Little lower, Mike."

Finally, it made sense to us. Apparently as he was paging through the E's in the Yellow Pages, Mike stopped at the first set of naked women he saw—Entertainers-Adult. Had he paged forward thirty more pages, he would have found the Escort ads. Other than the placement, there is essentially no way to distinguish the Entertainer ads from the Escort ads. Each ad promises the same thing, but one of them falls a little shy of its promise and the other over-delivers, in all of its ugly splendor. They even cost roughly the same, though entertainers were generally a shade more expensive. It sounds counterintuitive, but it actually makes sense if you think about it. It's a hell of a lot easier to give someone a five-minute, no-bones-about-it blow job than to dance around naked for half an hour trying to act like you're into it. Entertainers were never prostitutes. Escorts were never anything but.

The Kankoos turned to the situation at hand.

"OK, these ladies aren't leaving here happy without several hundred dollars of our money, and I'm not peeling off that kind of green for a pair of Southie prom queens and a turkey baster light show."

"Bachelor party," injected The Dynamo.

"Bachelor party it is!" The Kankoos said, reassembling the huddle. "Here's the plan. The Dynamo's our bachelor. Marquart, you and everyone but Mike fill the room. Mike's on procurement probation. I'll distract the prom queens and Big Daddy Kane over there."

The Kankoos went back into The Parlour and explained to our guests that they had shown up early for our bachelor party. He appeased them with well-chosen tunes (Boston, Kansas, and Aerosmith), booze, and the promise of good money. That gave the rest of us half an hour to round up wallets. My first move as Director of People Procurement was to excise Edgar from his expensive booze and Internet porn. Then, we called all the regular Parlour visitors. That netted us three extra bodies. We filled The Parlour's remaining square footage with rush candidates for Lambda Lambda Lambda in *Revenge of the Nerds*. The little room was hemorrhaging squinty-eyed, discombobulated freaks who might never have seen the inside of a strip club had someone not brought the strip club to them. When it was over, everybody was happy. The freaks got the story of their lives and the entertainers got their money. Even Edgar seemed to forget all his worries after a couple of lap dances. This was The Kankoos at his best.

It wasn't exactly Jesus feeding the multitude, but he had made a little bit go the longest way without anyone feeling unsatisfied.

The next morning, about six of the bodies we had packed into The Parlour were still there. The Parlour's mood was a hangover in many dimensions. Apart from the typical guilt and embarrassment that usually accompanies the morning after, our visitors were engaging in a massive denial and reconstruction of events. It began with establishing a consensus culprit.

"Who was it that called those girls anyway?" one of them asked, ostensibly joking.

"It think it was Mike's idea," one of them quickly offered.

Mike was not in the room.

"Oh yeah, *Mike*," another seconded. "I tell you, that Mike is *over the top*, man," he added in a tone of surface admiration (subtext: contempt and blame).

They all nodded and laughed in tacit agreement. Their laughs were actually a sigh. Their story was now straight. They had explained away aberrant behavior not befitting a Harvard Law student. This was the first stage of erasing the whole night from their minds. If anyone asked, Mike was the one. It was Mike's fault. With that out of the way, each of them did his best to relegate his own role to that of disapproving bystander.

The Kankoos was the hardest hit by the sudden change in *ch'i*. As usual, he didn't mope.

"Alright, anybody who's not going to Atlantic City with me in twenty minutes better get the fuck outta my room now."

The Kankoos's tone was half-joking, but the bad vibes cleared out in seconds just the same. The population in The Parlour was reduced to four: me, The Kankoos, The Dynamo, and Edgar.

"You in, Edgar?" The Kankoos asked.

"I'm in."

"You got credit?"

"Yeah."

"*Available* credit?"

"What do you mean?"

"Great, you can take care of me. Dynamo, call Brian. Edgar, you can reserve the rental."

All of this was happening a little faster than Edgar expected, but he had had enough of his hornbooks and highlighters. Brian was in, too. Twenty minutes after The Kankoos said the words, we were on the road.

Nothing brings people together like five hours of anticipation in a crowded sedan. And road sodas. And music—good, obscure, dorm room classics like The Replacements, Phish, The Jayhawks, and a little-known but soon to climb the charts Canadian band, Barenaked Ladies. Edgar played a necessary role, the guy hearing these songs for the first time, impressed by our broad taste and amazed that these songs weren't "on the radio." The most heavily rotated CD was Barenaked Ladies' *Gordon*. Track No. 7, "Good Boy," ushered us into Atlantic City... *We've got these chains hanging around our necks, people want to strangle us with them before we take our first breath*.... *Afraid of change, afraid of staying the same, when temptation calls, we just look away... This name is the hair shirt I wear.* After three consecutive silent listenings, Edgar interrupted the moment:

"So what is this song about anyway?"

"You, Edgar," The Kankoos said.

"Well I don't get it. 'This name is the *hair shirt* I wear?' What the hell is a hair shirt?"

"It's a coarse haircloth garment worn next to the skin by religious ascetics as penance," The Dynamo said. "The name can be anything time-honored to which you are connected. For someone born into a prestigious family, the name may be his surname. For Nietzsche, it is any time-honored institution of man. For you, it's Harvard Law School. It is that which holds you, obliges you, so that, as the song says, *When temptation calls, [you] just look away. Good boy.*

Like the rest of us, Brian was stunned:

"Damn, Dynamo. All along I thought hair shirt was a cool way of saying pussy."

That's the way it always went. From base revelry, to profundity, and back to debauchery, without transition. That's what Harvard Law School will always mean to me. Edgar was dizzy. But he didn't shut us out of his existence, and he didn't try to keep up by pretending to be someone he was not. Throughout the entire ride, he was himself. Finally, I had to ask him:

"What burned you?"

"Beg your pardon?"

"When we got our grades, you said you'd been burned before. What was it?"

I expected any number of nonspecific responses from Edgar—ranging from a litany of stereotypical snubs to simply not remembering. Instead, I got:

"Niccola. She was my first. I met her in my senior year."

"Of high school?" I asked.

"Harvard."

The Dynamo started to snicker, but The Kankoos silenced him with a glance and asked: "So how'd you meet her, Edgar?"

"My senior year. I used to hang out quite a bit with my kid sister and her best friend in the Square. That's where we met. It must have been love at first sight. She just came right up to me. We were in bed within the hour. You know, the kind of thing that always happened to somebody else."

"Never happened to me," The Kankoos said.

"Yeah, well, the next thing I knew, I was smoking pot on her stoop, sleeping past all of my classes, and drinking the governor's booze in his office after hours..."

"Governor's office?" asked The Dynamo.

"She was some sort of political operative. I blew off half my classes that year, and I didn't even care. It was the best time of my life. Then, it all went as fast and strange as it came. I got my first two B's, and I got a 167 on the LSAT, which was five points below my average during Kaplan. So I ended up in Wait List Hell at Harvard Law School. I made it in on the second try. But I promised never to put that kind of shit ahead of my goals again. Of course Niccola dumped me, too."

"What made her leave?" Brian asked.

"I don't really know. She just bolted. I always figured her punk-rocker speechwriting colleague had something to do with it. Turned out she had been sleeping with him at least part of the time we were together. What's worse, he was supposed to be my sister's boyfriend!"

"What a dick!" The Dynamo said. Everyone nodded, except The Kankoos, who was simply silent.

Fifteen minutes later, we were waiting in the hotel valet line and "Good Boy" was spinning for the fifth time in a row. The Kankoos turned to me and said:

"This song's about you too, Marquart."

"What are you talking about?"

"You look away when temptation calls. You paid for five of Edgar's lap dances last night, but you didn't so much as put one dollar in a G-string yourself."

"I've got a girlfriend, Kankoos!"

"So that just ends the discussion?"

"That's all there is to say."

"There's a lot more to say, Jaime. I could care less whether you like that sort of thing or not. Truth be told, I could do without it. But something about your reasons says you're not being honest with yourself. You're afraid of something."

"OK, Fucko, what am I afraid of?"

"I could be wrong. But most people who stick with the very first person they lay are afraid of quite a lot. Here . . . "

He reached into the ripped army bag that served as his luggage, pulled out a book, and handed it to me. The cover read *Human, All Too Human*. Nietzsche.

"When you get some downtime."

The valet attendant opened The Kankoos's door before he could continue. I handed him back the book. We never finished the discussion.

Atlantic City held an allure that Foxwoods couldn't—vast options. The next morning, the speciously infinite selection of casinos was revealed to be only twelve, and I saw the city for the poverty-stricken, dirty place it was. But that first night, I was enraptured.

Each of us Comchecked a grand and hit the tables. Edgar winced over the exorbitant Comcheck fees (about $50 for a grand), but he was in the game. We all sat down at the same table, a table that happened to see more dealer busts than usual. The Kankoos, Brian, The Dynamo, and I all turned one thousand into two. Even Edgar turned his grand into twelve hundred. Edgar looked a little confused at the disparity between our stack and his as we colored up. The Dynamo explained, "It's Bonetti's Law, Edgar: The less you bet, the more you lose when you win."

We spent the next couple days giving most of our winnings back. A classic case of winning too soon. It's not like anyone was going to stop gambling. There is nothing else to do in Atlantic City. Actually, there are a few other things to do in Atlantic City, and we did a lot of them. Our days were filled with seafood buffets and gambling; our nights with strippers, hard liquor, a pill or two, and more gambling. By the third day, you couldn't tell Edgar from any of the rest of us, though he tended to drink a little less and gamble slightly smaller amounts. We crashed at 3:00 A.M. on the third night with our bankrolls where they were when we started, and two more days to go.

As usual, I woke up at 7:00 the next day. I can never sleep more than four hours around a casino. Edgar was already awake. He was sitting cross-legged on the floor, hunched over, reading.

"What you looking at Edgar?" I asked.

"Property."

"*Whose* property?"

"Property Law. I've got a flight home in an hour. I can still make Property today."

"OK, Edgar. Who did you talk to?"

"What do you mean?"

"Who did you *call*? You obviously called someone. That's the only thing that would explain why you've lost your fucking mind, why you're taking off two days early."

"If you must know, I spoke with Tom O'Toule. I ran into him just as I was heading to my room to pack, and he offered to keep me up on what I missed while I was gone."

"Sure he did. O'Toule doesn't give two shits about you. He wants you to fail."

"You're paranoid, Marquart. O'Toule and I go all the way back to freshman year at Harvard. We shared an entry in Wigglesworth. He actually encouraged me to go on this trip. Thought a break would be good for me."

"Then why is he busting his ass while you're in Atlantic City? He's happy to see you blowing off class, because it makes him feel like he's getting ahead. And I'll bet my left nut he just told you you missed a whole bunch of property law while you were gone."

Edgar's blank face told me I'd accurately described his phone conversation with O'Toule. I was no longer focused on Edgar, though. The Kankoos was awake now, and pissed off. It was the second time in a couple of months he'd been awakened by my attempts to calm a desperate soul in the middle of everyone's sleep.

"I don't get the whole betting-your-left-nut thing, Marquart. Why do you think your left nut is worth so much anyway? And why your *left* nut? Just *please* go ahead and tell Edgar your theory so we can all get some sleep."

I explained the whole Zero Summer/Cold Stover view of law school to Edgar, ending with O'Toule's pleasure at Edgar's screwing off. Edgar responded with a confused, incredulous stare. I went on:

"Last night, Edgar, I watched you while we played blackjack. The first time you drew a fifteen against the dealer's ten, The Dynamo told you to take another card. You busted. You followed his advice one more time and busted again. So the third time you had a fifteen against the dealer's ten, what did you do?"

"I stayed."

"Why did you stay? You knew The Dynamo had the odds right."

"I was tired of busting. I wanted to see if the dealer would bust."

"Exactly! You were so burned by your earlier busting that you ignored the odds. You got to hold your hand a little longer than if you had busted. But you lost something greater—the chance of improving your hand by taking another card. Classic Cold Stover behavior."

"How much difference could it make anyway?" Edgar snipped.

"Quite a bit, as it turns out. Did you know the House makes three times as much on a player who never busts as one who goes by the book?"

"That much?"

"That much. And the metaphor goes a lot deeper than that. It also explains why you're leaving two days early."

"How's that?"

"I'll tell it to you like my grandfather would, with a story. Wednesday night of exam week, I went to Foxwoods with The Kankoos. That night I had my weirdest gambling experience yet. Within minutes of arriving, I had lost a grand, but that wasn't the odd part. For whatever reason, the dealer took pity on me. When she dealt me a fifteen against her ten for the fifth time in the shoe, she decided to make my night. I didn't know it at the time, but she had been peeking at her undercard as she dealt, so that she knew what her total was before I played my hand. Some of them do that out of nothing more than boredom. This one did it out of altruism. As I was about to add another card to my fifteen—like I was supposed to—she gave me a little shake of the head. I stayed. Turned out, she had a five underneath her ten. She busted. For an hour, she signaled me when to hit and when to stand. It was like she was dealing both cards face up. I couldn't lose."

"Great story," Edgar said. "But what does it have to do with me leaving Atlantic City early?"

"Imagine that same situation with three players at the table. The dealer's got a ten showing and a five underneath. She's trying to tell the players not to hit. Two of the players understand her signals. They basically 'see' the undercard. The other is just concentrating on not busting. The first informed player tries to let the ignorant player know he shouldn't hit. The second informed player not only refuses to share what he knows, but makes comments before and after playing his hand to suggest he's a freaking psychic. He won't give away his secret, because he wants to be the only good player at the table. The less everybody else knows, the more they lose, the more important he feels."

"Alright, I see where this is going. Tell me who's who."

"Of course, you are the ignorant player who never busts—the Cold Stover, overwhelmed by the notion of Harvard's rigor, entranced by the ten it's been showing for the past three centuries. Even after someone who's been there tells you there's nothing to be afraid of, you won't listen. The first informed player is your friend—me, The Kankoos. We want you to know what we know—that Harvard's got nothing but a five underneath. The second informed player is Tom O'Toule, the Zero Summer. He knows there's a five underneath too. But instead of helping you, he leverages your ignorance into esteem for himself. And you call him a friend."

"O'Toule's not my friend. Look, maybe you're right. But I am what I am. With one glaring exception in my life, I'm the guy who buys a girl a drink and spills it on her before she can say thank you; who dances in the street and gets ticketed for jaywalking; who has spontaneous outdoor sex in a poison ivy patch. If I stood on fifteen when I knew the dealer had fifteen, she'd probably draw a six. I'm no Kankoos. Just give me a plain girl, a loyal dog, and a patio barbecue on Sundays. And a Camaro. I always wanted a Camaro. Thank you, really. I had an incredible time. But I gotta go."

Edgar grabbed his bag, which was already packed, and left.

Edgar's early departure left us all with a tinge of gloom that lasted at least a minute and a half. Not insignificant under the circumstances.

There were tasks at hand. First among them, make something happen. Two days later, something had happened: the money was gone.

On the ride back to Harvard, sitting behind the wheel of the rental, I turned Big Picture, and the events of the past six months began to sink in. I had renounced my fears and traveled thousands of miles from anything familiar. I had confronted my spiritual doubts and emerged a free man. And I had challenged one of the oldest and strongest academic myths in the world and come out on the other side unscathed, so far at least. The worst should have been over. Yet, I felt as though it was just beginning. Was this the typical anticlimax that follows the end of any big accomplishment? Or was it Elise? We had grown in different directions, and I was more anxious than excited about living with her again that coming summer. The summer—maybe that was it. I was all set to work as a summer associate back in Dallas, and there was always the possibility, albeit slim, that my ignorance of the law would be exposed. I looked over at The Kankoos, who was staring into the Nietzsche book he'd tried to give me. His expression was the same as mine. I shifted the focus to him.

"What's wrong, Kankoos?"

"Nothing."

"Oh. You look like something's bothering you."

"I didn't mean 'nothing' in the sense that nothing is wrong. I meant, nothing is what's wrong."

He stared ahead in silence for two more minutes, then asked:

"What matters to you, Marquart?"

I rarely entertained nihilistic pondering about what "matters." I hadn't scratched and clawed my way over and beyond the poverty line by wondering what the point of it all was. Still, The Kankoos's question and mood deserved reflection. I thought about all of the possible answers. We had already been over religion. And Harvard, the law, and career were quickly becoming a joke. Elise? A passable answer, but likely to restart the conversation we had started when we pulled up in Atlantic City. Friendship? That would have been my choice, but it was far too Hallmark for The Kankoos. Money, fame, recognition? Of course, but those choices ignored the breadth of the question. I chose the best of the lot:

"Elise."

He laughed.

"What's so fucking funny about Elise?"

"*Nothing,*" he said, leaving me to wonder in what sense he used the word.

We returned to a world that had been reconfigured. In the aftermath of grades, social institutions were reshaped as One Ls gradually but ungracefully realigned their study groups and social circles to match those of comparable stock. Cold Stovers wouldn't possibly deviate from their usual course and flirt with failure, especially now that their risk aversion had been validated. As for the Zero Summers, the competition had only begun. Those who did more poorly than they expected took additional strides to improve—they briefed every case, lifted ideas from *Law Review* articles that weren't assigned, and hogged professors' office hours trying to draw a bead on that semester's exam questions. Those who did better than they expected made every effort to convince others that any efforts at improvement were futile.

As for The Parlour's regulars, the unanimous reaction to getting away with a moderate level of laziness was to entirely ditch classes, casebooks, and the urgent strides. We replaced them with credit cards, altered states, and perpetual vacations. I saw Montreal for the first time, learned to ski in Vail, and did New York City the right way. The first six months of law school, I missed a handful of classes, read 90 percent of everything assigned, and blew off studying for one final. After that, I *went* to a handful of classes, read basically nothing, and crammed for every test the day before.

The second-semester exam period itself was a predictable nonevent. Edgar continued to over-study and obsess over rumors of guys who knew guys who knew guys whom Professor Kennedy failed in 1992. Tom O'Toule and Vicky Sentence continued to linger in the student commons and broadcast obscure resolutions to difficult issues in prior exams. Brian, The Dynamo, The Kankoos, and I spent the day before each of our three exams in a coffee shop deep in Harvard Square. Torts, Property Law, and International Law (an elective I chose because it had a paper instead of a test) all came and went without event. I left my nihilistic dialogue with

The Kankoos somewhere between Atlantic City and Boston. Brushing aside any sense of conflict, my thoughts turned to the summer—being a summer associate, maybe not law school's biggest scam, but definitely its most widespread. And, at last, Elise.

CHAPTER 18 | LET'S BUY STUFF

The second semester came off the tracks around its three-quarter point. Standard stuff: money problems, girl problem. There was also a looming disciplinary action, the meeting with the dean that Tim Apparel and I had finally been forced to schedule, for the semester's very last day.

The money issue scotched my plan to be a San Francisco bike messenger during the summer. Not only had I drained the Wells Fargo card down (to under $1,000), but minimum debt service on the Discover and MasterCards was getting steep, nearly $500 per month. Being a bike messenger wouldn't cover that plus San Francisco rent. Each San Francisco trip during the second semester had involved a maximum ATM withdrawal by both me and Tim Apparel. Most of our cash found its way either to Paris or into the San Francisco rave scene economy. There were also the usual expenses that hit everyone but were novelties for me: car insurance, paying for liquor and gasoline. I had fallen into the trap of spending like a lawyer while I was still a law student. The only solution was the lawyerly one. There was no advantage in bankruptcy, because I'd still be in it for the student loans. For the first time, I'd have to do something just for the money. Tim Apparel had the solution:

"Be a summer associate at Young & Mathers. In L.A. You can dress like a bike messenger there. And make an assload of money."

A superb idea. All true, too. Young & Mathers was a relatively new Los Angeles firm that had absolutely no dress code. Earrings, tattoos, tank tops, baggy shorts, skullcaps, shock-dyed hair, spandex bike gear. Anything goes at Young & Mathers. I had found my law firm. It made no difference to me if Young & Mathers specialized in underwater treasure law or defending Nazi art hoarders. In the short run I was looking for a little sartorial freedom and a chewy paycheck. Young & Mathers also inspired some hope about life after law school. I imagined it as the Amsterdam of law firms: profitable, efficient, all that; but dedicated to keeping life's fire alive despite the necessity of a job.

So I took becoming a summer associate at Young & Mathers seriously, bothering to find out that it is a litigation-only firm, a "boutique" according to Stanford's Office of Career Services. I signed up and prepared myself for a Monday interview with the simple pitch that my destiny was in both Los Angeles and litigation. I had been inside the Los Angeles airport on at least two occasions, and I had of course seen the city in movies and on television shows. Litigation was less familiar. The summer at Young & Mathers would acquaint me with both.

With the money problem in line to be solved, the girl problem hit. It was six o'clock, a Sunday morning, the day before Young & Mathers was coming to Stanford to interview for summer jobs. In that pocket of tranquility cooking at Breakers, I cranked the music and made a sprawling *huevos rancheros*. I was mixing and folding a potato blintz appetizer and grooving to a Replacements bootleg when Francine Lewis appeared next to Breakers' industrial-sized galvanized steel mixing bowl:

"You fucking told me you were fucking studying last night which I knew was a complete fucking lie because you never fucking study but stupid asshole that I am I tell my fucking friends that you aren't with me at the *Law Review* dinner because you're supposedly fucking studying and they look at me like I'm a complete fucking dipshit and tell me they heard you and that fucking cretin Tim Apparel are at some rave up in fucking Oakland."

"Berkeley."

Tim Apparel and I had been at a rave, but in Berkeley, not Oakland. Francine Lewis was right, though, when she came around to the "this isn't working" part. Then she asked:

"So, do you have anything to fucking say?"

"Not fucking really."

After I finished at Breakers, Tim Apparel and I went for a mountain bike ride that left me spongy tired. Back at Leland we trued our wheels outside and worked through a Jim Beam flask. Staying up all night Saturday, Sunday's romantic conflagration, a heavy meal, the sun, liquor, and riding all combined to throw me into an enchanted sleep at 7:00 P.M. I didn't wake until the next day, Monday, sometime long after noon.

I'd slept through the Young & Mathers interview.

The workday was still on back east, so I rang up Niccola, who put me in touch with Blaine McKisco, who had worked for a Boston law firm, Long, White & Borren LLP, prior to taking a job in Weld's legal office. I told Blaine that Long, White & Borren LLP was, to my mind, a first-notch firm; summer associate would be a fitting way to launch my career there. Could Blaine McKisco put a word in?

Three Mondays after sleeping through the Young & Mathers interview, a phone call came telling me I was set up to be a summer associate at one of Boston's oldest and most esteemed law firms. They would pay me $1,400 a week (now it's at least $2,400). While I was on the phone, I heard Tim Apparel's cross-hall rustling, by this point a signal that he would soon appear at my door.

"The City?"

We arrived at the corner of Haight and Fillmore, found Clara, who took a ten to watch the Beetle. Then we found Paris, who said:

"You're college boys?"

"Basically."

"Bringing some back to school for the ladies?"

"Not the ladies we hang with."

"I tell you this. The white women, they love the rock."

"You don't say."

"Yes they do."

"You wouldn't have another twenty on you?"

"Matter of fact I do."

We headed to PoMo, bathroom.

Why do it? A lot of people, especially junkies, will give you some line of crap about how their favorite drug puts them "beyond ordinary human experience." Then they'll proceed to burn several hours of your time explaining the inexplicable. They'll balance it with proper regret in the form of a few stories from the dark side, generally involving vomit, abusing domestic privileges offered by a concerned friend, or inadvertently exposing a child to their practice. I'll be quick, and just tell you that my own favorite drug is rooted in the ordinary. There are the drawbacks (poor quality, erratic supply, guns, cops, being white in a predominantly black scene, as well as the arrhythmic Elvis-thump your heart does). On the better side, it's a brush with pure pleasure. It reminds you that pleasure is at its maximum in anticipation rather than at execution. The high is not so much like a first kiss itself, but like the first kiss's imminence, the confirmatory flicker of time when desire goes mutual. That flicker is the weightless anticipation of knowing you're about to be supremely happy. With rock, the flicker lasts two, sometimes ten, minutes. A short high? Yes. As drug highs go. But it is an unnaturally long time to feel the pleasure spikes that usually happen in moments too short to measure. That there is an urge to keep the flicker going is often mistaken for instantaneous physical addiction. But unlike heroin or nicotine, your body does let you walk away. Your mind will tell you to keep doing it, though, unless you have other things to do. Paris didn't have fuck-all else to do. After a week in San Francisco, Tim Apparel and I did.

Final exams.

First, I transcribed my Constitutional Law notes into an outline. Then I read through half a dozen Property outlines from years past. For Law and Social Science, I held to the original plan. I spent the morning of the day the paper was due writing it, twenty-five pages. The paper was an attempt to locate some sociological constants among those who attend law school. The thesis was a simple one: a buffed-up version of the Dullard exposition Tim Apparel and I had during that first PoMo visit. I thought it best to duplicate the original creative conditions, so I wrote the paper in the PoMo bathroom, and then roared back to the Law School in the Beetle. As a piece of scholarship, the paper was horrendous. I handed it in as the two-week exam period began. On the same trip to the Law School to hand in the paper, I picked up the Modern American Legal Thought exam. It was a two-week take-home, as advertised. The task was to answer two questions:

1. How has politics influenced American legal thought?

2. Discuss the tension between clarity and principle in American legal thought.

After reading the questions, I let answers simmer in my mind over the next two weeks, when I had the two ordinary, in-class exams: Constitutional Law and Property.

Early, early on the morning of the Constitutional Law exam, there was a snap-snap-snap knock at my door. Davis Mund. With him: Bobby Boylan and The Barrister. Bobby made the plea:

"*Byrnesie!* We need you. Word is you're the Con Law stud."

To this day I have never been in a school or had a job that didn't surprise me with a few screw-offs in far deeper shit than me. Davis, Bobby, and The Barrister had cut all but a couple of Constitutional Law classes. The Barrister was obviously extracting another good deed from me; Tim Apparel and I were due before the dean of students in two weeks. Davis and Bobby had done me favors (contracts outline, orgy arrangement). So we found an empty room in Leland and settled in for a three-hour tutorial. They all began the session knowing less constitutional law than my high school social studies teacher, who guessed the Supreme Court had "something like twenty" justices. Bobby, Davis, and The Barrister were in passing range by the end of the first hour. By the end of the second hour, they were in the game to hit the mean, B+, or better. Diminishing, even negative, returns set in as I burdened them with nuance in hour three. We called it done at four hours. I gave them all copies of my outline, a "bloody good" outline, The Barrister remarked, that you're also welcome to have.[8]

As I took the Constitutional Law exam that morning, I glanced occasionally at Davis, Bobby, and The Barrister for signs of distress. They were always smiley. I guessed they would all do no worse than B's, which was irrelevant, anyway, because they were all taking the class pass-fail. They beat me to the exit on this one, making golf-swing gestures on the way out. I used all of the allotted four hours.

For the Property exam, I stayed with the semester-long practice. I got high, took the test, and left believing any grade, except for a stunningly bad one or a stunningly good one, was possible.

---

8. Get it at www.brushwiththelaw.com.

All that remained was the Modern American Legal Thought exam, strictly limited to ten pages, double-spaced; two weeks to finish it. For two weeks: write a page, read a bit, bike ride, get fucked up, write another couple of pages, review and revise, head to The City, PoMo, come back, run the spell check, and make my answers a few lines shy of ten pages. As I narrowed the margins and hit Print...at that very instant, there was a rumble. It was like the familiar rumbles of passing trucks or heavy construction, but also distinct. It was notable in the same way that a coyote looks just like a domestic dog, but you know it's something different, closer to nature and more ominous. There was a knock at my door. Tim Apparel.

"You feel that?"

"First one for me."

The rumble had been an earthquake. A small one. But a real earthquake.

"Little reminder that nature wins in the end. Best to live fast now," Tim Apparel said. "Bike ride?"

Tim Apparel chose his newest road bike, which was in fact my old road bike, the one I'd assumed demolished in the minivan crash. We first stopped by the Law School, where I handed in the Modern American Legal Thought exam, and then headed out of and away from Stanford, west, toward the hills, then up.

We push on to Old La Honda Road, forty-five minutes of up, and not a foot of flat, sprinting into false summits, breaking into a cloud layer. The ride goes cold, damp, shitty; all mist, road, mica flecks in the pavement and redwoods high above us, extending down equally far, into the canyon. I'm cursed with pricks of excess *awareness*. The sting in my ankle has a different bite from the pain in my thigh, which is different from the desire to quit, a spiritual ache. Tim Apparel's audible breathing annoys me. Then there's a taunting road sign. Upenuf Rd. *Upenuf?* Not up enough, not yet. I want to commit mayhem on the sign. A mica fleck embedded in the tar becomes brilliant, then fades, then another and another roll past. I glance back, uselessly, for a lower gear, then do it again, and once more.... Then, the redwoods thin and higher-altitude trees appear, and we break through the clouds, into sunlight, riding side by side, the grade levels, and there's the Pacific, down the other side, the Bay behind us. Right next to us, another road sign: Skyline Boulevard.

Flicker, flicker.

The only ride from Skyline is down, fast; forty, fifty. We go along the ridge, my front tire three inches behind Tim Apparel's back tire, drafting, eyes fixed to see any movement in his brake pads. He goes, I go. And then we cut a left for, now... seven miles of sweet, smooth down, on Page Mill Road, grabbing corners, blasting back into and out of the cloud layer, our two bikes combining to make a *whurrrrr* that sounds exactly like grace and power. At the bottom, we hit Palo Alto's residential fringe. The new billionaires have sliced trees and poured concrete. We roll back onto Stanford's campus, the mountain ridge we just climbed so distant it is only silhouette, all detail and texture lost, Skyline hidden by conifers. Helmets off, bikes rolling, side by side again, hands at our thighs, no words spoken, Tim Apparel and I are feeling the same. At Leland we stop. He says:

"Let's buy stuff!"

Law school's first year was almost over. There was one last obligation. Tim Apparel and I still had to commit an act of contrition with the dean of students. He spoke first:

"First of all, I want to assure you both that your being here only concerns the *Law Review* letter and the photograph. Nothing else."

Was he saying that we were not there on account of orgies, class cutting, or crack smoking? And I'd forgotten about "the photograph." In front of him, the dean had a printout of www.timapparel.com, with its shirtless Barrister photo. He had circled and annotated with an exclamation mark Tim Apparel's preposterously inflated hit counter: **You are visitor number 12,337,192.**

"Burley Mahnmeets assures me you all have made amends regarding the two of you revealing the contents of his private letter from the *Law Review*. I do understand that anonymous e-mail is protected speech. But assuming another's identity and publishing private information are not protected. So I trust we have seen the last 'Barrister' e-mail. The only remaining issue is the very wide publication of this equally private photograph," the dean said, holding up the fatso Barrister photo, "on Tim's Internet page."

"I've been meaning to delete that picture," Tim Apparel said.

With summer associate jobs in place and a free day before my flight back east, Tim Apparel and I went to Armani in San Francisco to get work clothes. Even as a child, I took suits to be symbolic of conscription in a crummy life. Around the time I saw *The Paper Chase*, I asked my mother:

"What's the point of ties?"

"That's just how things are done."

"Do you think it will be the same when I grow up?"

She took my second question to be nonsensical. *Just how things are done* implied timelessness. And twenty years after my first panic about them, I was buying suits and ties, with money yet to be earned at a job that required suits and ties be worn. Still lodged in my mind was that Los Angeles firm where you could wear whatever the hell you wanted. I hoped these would be the last suits I'd ever buy. (And they were.) I figured, though, why not make an extravagance of necessity? Between us, Tim Apparel and I dropped $6,286.59 at Armani. From there, he took me to the San Francisco airport. I was going to Boston, first class. Tim Apparel headed back to Palo Alto to make $2,000 a week at a Silicon Valley firm.

When I got to Boston, my grades were available through the Law School's Web site. I came in a shade above Stanford's B+, 3.2 mandatory mean:

FIRST SEMESTER

Course	Letter Grade	Numerical Grade
Criminal Law	B	3.1
Torts	A–	3.7
Civil Procedure	B+	3.2
Contracts	K (A–)	(3.8)

SECOND SEMESTER

Course	Letter Grade	Numerical Grade
Property	B	3.0
Constitutional Law	A–	3.7
Modern Legal Thought	A–	3.7
Law and Social Science	Incomplete	—
Legal Research and Writing	KM	—

That was that. First-year grades are what law students travel into the job world with. Mine put me in a position to get probably 95 percent of the available law firm jobs. I was in the middle, which at Stanford Law School meant an abundance of job security for life, if that's what you wanted. And I'd get around the suit-wearing problem the next summer. These grades were more than good enough for Young & Mathers.

There was also some bad news embedded in the grades; the Incomplete in Law and Social Science, for instance. An Incomplete meant the paper I'd written in a morning at PoMo was so poor it hadn't merited receiving a grade, not even a failing grade. I would investigate the Incomplete later, sometime during the summer in Boston. (I should also point out that the A–/3.8 in Contracts was a tree falling in the wilderness. Remember, I took Contracts pass-fail. So my actual, recorded Contracts grade was just a pass, K, credit.) Some good news: I had passed the Legal Research and Writing class (KM = pass in a class that is mandatory pass-fail) despite only going twice and knowing as little about the topic as the day I arrived at Stanford. The plan was to learn legal research and writing on the fly, at a law firm, during the summer in Boston.

My mood soured as I put on a suit and knotted a necktie for the first day of work as a summer associate at Long, White & Borren LLP. It was hot, "muggy," as they say in Boston. Before I made it to the subway, my scrotum had pasted itself to my thigh. I passed an artsy girl with blue hair. She looked straight through me. I was too common to even burn a little punker contempt on. Slacking in its most primitive and passive forms— overspending, oversleeping—had sent me back to Boston, wearing a suit.

As I walked into Long, White & Borren LLP, I had a single ambition: *don't sleep through the Young & Mathers interview next time.*

PART 8 | **SUMMER AFTER FIRST YEAR**

CHAPTER 19 | **RUSH**

Working two jobs in college to make ends meet, I was always too poor or preoccupied to join a fraternity. In the summer of 1996, I got my chance all over again, at a law firm in Dallas. Working as a summer associate in a law firm is just like rushing for a fraternity or sorority, except they pay their rushees $20,000 for the summer.

The summer at a law firm is one big lie, and everyone knows it. Obviously, the firms don't stay in business by throwing parties for their employees. Still, it's easier than you think to believe the hype. And the lie goes a lot deeper than you might imagine. Lawyers are essentially paid to take summer associates to baseball games, watch movies with them, dance with them at nightclubs, and pretend they like them. It's prostitution. Lawyers even hide their work from associates. Those who are especially busy or surly are left off the short list of regular lunch and dinner attendees.

Of course, there *is* some work involved in being a summer associate— usually researching an obscure area of the law that doesn't matter or writing a legal brief that probably won't be used. The best strategy for a summer associate is to accept as little work as possible, but do that work well. It's not about proving yourself; it's about not giving them a reason to eliminate you. Most summer associates arrive with a presumptive full-time, post–law school offer and try not to do anything to lose it. My first summer, I didn't do anything to lose mine.

With work presenting little more than the occasional distraction, I turned again to Elise. She and I were living together for the first time since I'd left for law school and she'd flown off to Spain. On the surface, things were as they had been in the past. We laughed, we fought, we made up, we screwed. Still, a reality loomed that we were unwilling to admit. Ours was the most stereotypical of all romantic outcomes, so stereotypical that you forget it can actually happen to you. We had grown apart. The hardest thing of all was, I liked the person she had become. And I liked the person I had become. They just didn't seem to like each other. So I had to pretend *not* to like the person she had become in order to protect the person I had become. Of course, liking the new her and the new me were not mutually exclusive, and doing both might have made me happy. But I didn't want to be happy, I wanted to win. Romances are all too often zero sum. We hadn't invested the last five years of our lives, though, just to give up so easily. We held on tightly, sometimes painfully, often resentfully.

To my surprise, I did like a lot of the people I hung out with at work during that summer, especially the older ones. The skittishness and caginess I'd come to expect at Harvard had been purged from their personalities with time and perspective. That said, Zero Summers and Cold Stovers were everywhere. I always imagined law firm life as a separate realm. It had never fully occurred to me that lawyers were made up of the same type of people I went to law school with. Yet, unlike law school, I could not just fly away from it all on a whim. Consequently or coincidentally, most days I just shut my door and gambled on sports.

One day in the middle of the summer, as I was riding that week's paycheck on a baseball Over/Under, I got a timely call from The Kankoos, who was in Washington, D.C., for the summer.

"Question for you, Marquart. What's with this whole '*I was like*' phenomenon? I'm having a conversation with this guy the other day, who's bitching about his boss and telling me how he gave the guy a real ass-thrashing. But, he keeps prefacing everything he says with the words 'I was like . . . ' He says, 'And then, I was like, fuck you dude, you can take those motions *in limine* and shove them up your ass.' So, I ask him, 'Did you literally ask him to shove them up his ass?' And he says he didn't use *those exact words,* but he *did* tell the guy that he couldn't finish the motions. But those exact words are the only thing that make the story worth telling."

"Hey, Kankoos."

"Yeah, hey. So anyway, I finally figured it out. Every time someone says 'I was like . . . ,' what they're really saying is, 'I said something similar to what I'm about to tell you but not nearly as cool, which is what I really wanted to say but didn't have the balls to say, but which is close enough in spirit to be like what I really said that I don't feel like I'm lying to you right now, because I *did* technically disclose that it was only *like* what I really said.' So, how's things in Dallas?"

"Same, I think. The people are cool enough, but every conversation has at least two different layers—the surface layer of what the speaker is literally saying, and the bottom layer of what he really means. Everyone seems to know about the bottom layer, but you've really fucked up if you call attention to it. And I can't stand Casual Fridays. It's as if it's OK to be comfortable, so long as it's only for 20 percent of the week. There are just as many clients around on Fridays as there are Monday through Thursday. But when I asked a partner why they don't just dress casually all the time, his answer was: 'Because the clients would never accept it.' So, I was like, 'You're all a bunch of pussies and your clients know it.' But what I really said was: 'So let me get this straight, clients don't care if you wear blue jeans on Fridays, but they *do* care the rest of the week?' 'That's right,' he said. 'And why do they care, again?' I asked. He said: 'The dress preserves a degree of professionalism and establishes confidence in our work.' So I asked him: 'You save the professional work for Monday through Thursday?' And he was like, 'Blow me,' but he actually just left. I'm dying for an honest conversation."

"Why don't you try to start an honest conversation?"

"Can't be done. Round here, honesty ends conversations, it doesn't start them."

"I think I've got your answer, Marquart. Young & Mathers. It's a law firm in California. Founded a few years ago by some dude in one of New York's oldest and stodgiest firms. One day, he just got tired of all the suits and the bullshit. He said California is the place he ought to be, so he loaded up the jet and he flew to L.A. And the best thing is, no dress code at all. Fuck business casual. You can do anything but show up naked there, and I heard they even do that sometimes."

"There's only one problem, Kankoos. It's in California!"

"Since when is that a problem? You're not gonna find a cooler firm anywhere. It's not like I said New Hampshire. By the way, did you get your grades in the mail yet?"

"Yeah. Three B+'s, one better than last time. And you?"

"Same. Fucking joke. Gotta go."

"See ya."

The Kankoos was right—why not California? I asked some of the Cold Stover and Zero Summer summer associates in Dallas about Young & Mathers, and their unanimous disdain for the joint sealed it. The Cold Stovers had never heard of Young & Mathers, and thus found it lacking prestige; unknown, and, therefore, risky. The Zero Summers dismissed Young & Mathers as illusory. An anomalous, iconoclastic law firm could only short-circuit their calculus. With an offer from a tolerable Texas firm already in hand, I made it a goal to spend my second summer in L.A., at Young & Mathers.

CHAPTER 20 | STRIDE OF THE SUMMONED

As I arrived for my first day at Long, White & Borren LLP, the summer associate orientation talk had already begun. At the front of the room, a full-time associate was wrapping up. He was a young lawyer, two years out of law school, and his voice had assumed a perky, summary crescendo as he gave pointers on "casual fridays":

"...the thing is, you don't want to be so far out there that you call attention to yourself. Be professional. You guys know what that means. You wouldn't be here if you didn't. In fact, that's my advice not only in deciding what to wear on Fridays but for conducting yourselves throughout the summer. Be professional. Which isn't to say don't have a good time.... You guys will have a *great* time this summer! I promise you that."

Next came Archibald Long, the firm's partner in charge of recruitment and hiring. Archibald Long was irresistibly likable. He looked to be around fifty. He had used his years not to slouch into decrepitude but rather to fashion a depth of character that could never have been built on quirk or specious eccentricity. He told us:

"In the twenty-odd years since I was sitting where you are today I have made a mess of my life. Though I earn an excellent living, my wife also earns an excellent living and is more distinguished in her field than I will ever be. I have six children, spanning in age from third-grade to college sophomore. By our most recent household pet census I counted two dogs, a cat, a rabbit, and some manner of desert reptile that frightens me too much to make a close examination. I take on more work here than I should because I am burdened by a peculiar affection for intellectual property law. Call me strange, but thoughts of retirement only fill me with sadness. I often fritter half my day away chatting with colleagues who always teach me something new. Like many of you I have recently discovered the Internet can consume the other half of the day. . . ."

As a piece of rhetoric, Archibald Long's remarks were worthy of Reagan: simple yet compelling. You knew where he was going, but still craved to hear the resolution:

"I cannot imagine a happier chaos."

Archibald Long was a finished person. He also possessed the recruiting partner's single essential trait: an appealingly busy life. A lawyer recruiting fresh bodies for his firm has to cop to being busy. Archibald Long cast his frenetic life as energizing rather than dispiriting. The subliminal message was: *Do it right, and you could end up like me, Archibald Long.* The more deeply coded message was that the multiply divorced, secretary-banging, liquor-soaked, lard-ass law firm lifers, even if they were in the majority, represented a failure of will. With a disciplined mind and a vision for your life, you could be Archibald Long, who next set out his vision for being a summer associate:

"This is a time for all of you to learn; who we are; what we do. My hope is that you'll juggle. Take on a lot of assignments; spend two hours at lunch getting to know us; come with us to the symphony in the evening; have that extra cocktail; discover a passion in an unexpected practice area. And if you fall asleep as happily worn out as I do each night, you will forever be at peace with having chosen to attend law school. Needless to say, my sincere hope is that you will also choose Long, White & Borren."

I fought an unwanted wave of admiration for Archibald Long. Long, White & Borren LLP would certainly be his Last Place. *What about making Long, White & Borren my own Last Place?* Sitting with me in that conference room were thirty-seven other summer associates. As they introduced themselves—name, law school, what they did for fun—I imagined a possible future. Among the thirty-eight entering summer associates, chances were good that all thirty-eight of us would receive offers at the end of the summer. Probably thirty would accept the offers and begin work at Long, White & Borren after graduating from law school. Attrition would be steepest in the first few years. By year five the entering class might be cut by half, to around fifteen. Several might eventually make partner. Thus somewhere in that conference room were six or eight people destined to spend more time with each other than they would with their spouse or kids, more hours at this law firm than sleeping or watching television. Somewhere among the thirty-eight were future rivalries, marriages, late-night blow jobs, divorces, friends for life.

Near the end of the summer associate introductions Archibald Long left the conference room, and I could peripherally see that he had to shuffle by a still later-arriving summer associate, just as I spoke:

"Robert Byrnes. Stanford Law School. I like to play darts."

That task fulfilled, I regained my true bearings. I was wearing a suit. By my own indolence, I had been shipped back to my past, to Boston. There was zero likelihood of my being among those who would grow old at Long, White & Borren, LLP. It would never be my Last Place. I wouldn't even work there again after this summer. Every law firm has an Archibald Long. A year later, I'd be listening to the same sort of talk from J. Mark Mathers, the recruiting and hiring partner at Young & Mathers. Young & Mathers, Los Angeles—that might be my Last Place. Not Boston. This summer would be nothing but a time-kill, a money injection. The introductions wound down. From behind me:

"Augustus Mahnmeets. Stanford Law School. By way of Harvard College and the U.K., where I will be clerking for the second half of the summer."

Augustus? *The Barrister!* He had mentioned working in Boston to Tim Apparel and me. Whatever firm he'd named I instantly forgot, under the assumption they're all the same.

The final three introductions were a pretty-girl cluster:

"Victoria Sentence. From sunny California. I go to HLS. I am hoping to clerk for a federal judge before beginning full-time as an associate."

"Jenny Cavataio. Columbia. I unapologetically confess to liking Neil Diamond."

Jenny drew a real laugh and, with so few words, engendered some quick admiration. She comported herself with extreme self-knowledge

and comfort—a younger, female Archibald Long. Then, the last introduction:

"Lauren Leaven. Victoria and I are in law school together at Harvard.
And I also love to play darts."

Of course Lauren Leaven looked straight at me as she said *darts*.
Though it felt more jokey-friendly than amorous, I knew that before long
I'd be playing darts with Lauren Leaven. I was less certain that this was anything more than the repeatedly fruitless search for a Helen replacement. As
I often had before, I again made the error of converting irrelevant coincidence into romantic destiny. Flipping through the summer associate pro-
files I discovered that Lauren, Helen, and I had all been in the same class
at Dartmouth (before I transferred); and yet none of us had met there.
B.F.D.—that's what Tim Apparel would have said. But I was on my own.

I settled into my windowless office and further discovered that Lauren
Leaven was sharing an office with Jenny Cavataio and Victoria Sentence,
on the nineteenth floor. I began compiling reasons to wander purposefully
on the nineteenth floor—checking out the firm library, dropping in to see
my chum The Barrister... and then my phone rang:

"Robert Byrnes? Dirk Pussinger here. I see that you put down on your
questionnaire that you have an interest in bankruptcy law. If you don't have
too much on your plate, I have a work assignment that might be right up
your alley."

A "full plate" would have been impossible on day one. I walked down
the hall to meet with Dirk Pussinger, a younger and considerably less
appealing figure than Archibald Long. Dirk Pussinger shook my hand,
hard, and claimed what appeared to be permanent social advantage, not
on the basis of either his equity position in the firm or superior legal acu-
men, but because he was more of a square-jawed manly man than me. He
also fixed his eyes on my earlobes, the vacated earring holes, as if to say:
homo. I disliked him just as reflexively.

Dirk Pussinger handed me a stack of papers filed in regard to a donut
chain's bankruptcy and said:

"I'll c.c. you updates and new filings as they come in. Just monitor it
over the summer. Give me a heads-up if anything jumps out at you. That's
the assignment. Clear?"

He obviously never wanted to see me again. I returned to my office and put the bankruptcy papers on a shelf. Then, the phone rang again. This time I looked at the display screen: Dirk Pussinger.

"Me again, Bob. You come back down here real quick?"

I suppose it would make a more gripping story to say I had some sort of dread on the way to see Dirk Pussinger, but I didn't. All else equal I just preferred not to put myself in settings of mutual contempt. When I got to Dirk Pussinger's office, though, he was smiling, elated by some unexpected discovery. Dirk was flicking his rubbery wrist, packing a tin of Copenhagen. The chewing tobacco container had fallen out of my suit-coat pocket on the prior visit. He spoke first:

"You dip?"

"Tin a day. Baseball habit."

"No shit. Me too. Mind if I grab a lippa'?"

For the next hour, Dirk Pussinger and I pinched snuff; he talked. Each Dirk Pussinger story was preceded by the preamble: "I really shouldn't say this, but . . . " On more than one occasion, Dirk had crapped himself at orgasm. Dirk had also been praised on the basis of that heretofore underlauded virtue: "nice balls." Dirk was a fairly dumb guy. Even so, Dirk's exceptional lawyer skills were among the most repeated firm legends, second only to his prodigious sexual achievements. A lot of brainy associates resent partners like Dirk Pussinger. The whip-smart ones are disheartened to discover their mind power is better suited to solving Rubik's Cubes and acrostics than the ordinary day-to-day in a law firm.

On that first day of uninterrupted braggadocio, I pulled back from telling Dirk my own orgy tale, law school Halloween, excusing myself to a made-up appointment "down on nineteen." I didn't want to wind up at a Red Sox game with Dirk Pussinger, chugging four-dollar beers and clamming into a peanut bag. One hour was enough.

Feeling filmy, I set off on my true summer mission. I went to the nineteenth floor, in search of Lauren Leaven. As I approached her office, I sketched out how it might go. After picking up on Lauren's darts comment, I'd be left dry for conversation. I needed material. So I made a quick compilation. Yes, Dirk Pussinger had nuzzled himself—"motor-boating" he called it—between the "most asymmetric pair of melons on God's green earth." If presented with just the right distance and disapproval on my part, I could play that and other of Dirk's observations to sympathetic advantage. My objective was twofold: to make a dart-playing appointment with Lauren Leaven and confirm myself as a right-minded person, setting myself in clear opposition to all the world's Dirk Pussingers.

It turned out that Lauren Leaven wasn't in her office. Jenny Cavataio and Victoria Sentence were, however, so I launched the prepared routine in the hope that they would report favorably to Lauren Leaven. I spoke entirely with Jenny, as Victoria fixedly squeaked a yellow highlighter across her legal research.

"...Then Dirk looks up at me, with this big wad of chew, and says 'Mark my words, this firm has more choice beaver than any in Boston.' And then he..."

Jenny found it all unremarkable. She didn't go in for fashionable outrage over things that aren't so outrageous. So I steered the conversation toward the *what did you do before law school?* angle. This was Boston, home court advantage for me. I was playing the Weld card like a stuck-in-the-past pro quarterback who's now selling aluminum siding. I let Jenny know I could still get past the State House security detail and punch the code to the door that led to the corner office. I also attempted to slide in a carefully edited précis of my time in law school. The amended objective: that Jenny Cavataio tell Lauren Leaven I was enigmatic, dangerous, appealingly restive, dark, and cerebral, yet passionate, and still well-connected to the most powerful people in Massachusetts. Jenny previewed her assessment of me, *to* me:

"So let me get this straight. You're the jaded political poet dragged into this soulless world because he's so devilishly intelligent. Even though you get laid constantly yourself, you don't boast about it the way troglodytes like Dirk Pussinger do. To take the edge off a cruel world that doesn't understand your passion for bike riding, you do some unnamed but serious drugs while nevertheless breezing through America's most elite universities where, despite your craving for solitude, you are simply not left alone. And if I'm not mistaken, you'd like to screw my officemate on the governor's desk."

Jenny Cavataio detected and dismantled all my affect. The attempt to cast myself as a combination of Jack Kerouac and George Stephanopoulos had been hopelessly transparent. There was only one response: enlightened surrender. There was nothing to say. That I was committed to putting Jenny's critique to good use centimetered me up, I think, in her estimation. I imagined she might not torpedo me with Lauren Leaven.

The first-day socializing had gone poorly, so I headed back to my office. The voice-mail light was on: another work assignment. This time I met with Mackenzie Tanner, a third-year associate. Mackenzie Tanner asked me to research whether the results of polls and surveys are admissible in federal court.

"At the end of the day, we win this case if the judge allows our survey evidence," Mackenzie said.

"Where would I start on that?" I asked.

"Well, I'd try *Moore's* first. Then Westlaw."

Westlaw, I knew, was an on-line research service. It worked like an Internet search: type in key words and responsive cases turn up. But what the hell was Moore's?

"Moore's?"

"Yeah. Try *Moore's* first. It is more cost-effective for the client if you begin your research with the books. It narrows the Westlaw search."

"Moore's is a book."

"Good one. Could you get me a memo in, say, two weeks."

Mackenzie Tanner spoke with a frostiness that told me she suspected that my not knowing *Moore's* was a book had been genuine ignorance, not a "good one." Her hope, for the moment, was that I had just missed the day in my Legal Research and Writing class when I would have learned what *Moore's Federal Practice and Procedure* is, and how to use it.

With law school laxity on my mind, I went back to my office and checked again to confirm that my grades were as I had first seen them. They were. I had indeed passed, even Legal Research and Writing. But I was reminded that even if I hadn't failed anything, I hadn't passed everything either. The Law and Social Science professor had given me that Incomplete. I checked my Stanford e-mail. There was a two-sentence message from the Law and Social Science professor: "Your paper puzzled me. Please call." I did make the call—five months later, in November. For the summer I put it out of my mind. It was 4:00 P.M., and I headed for the elevator, past nineteen, then all the way down and out the door.

"Keeping banker's hours, Byrnes?" The Barrister asked, on the way back from getting his late afternoon coffee. With him was a throng of other summer associates, including Lauren Leaven.

I gave the obligatory chuckle and went to the subway. I ended that first day as a summer associate playing darts, peacefully alone, at an empty Drumlins Pub in Cambridge.

It wasn't until the summer's third week that I played darts with Lauren Leaven. We had been at one of the firm-sponsored outings, the dominant objective being to get drunk. Past midnight, I'd had enough. We were at a pool joint. It was turning loud, and the guys were starting to break out cigars and call for Scotch older than themselves. A circle of suspendered and tie-loosened summer associates stood fielding Dirk Pussinger's queries (e.g., *Who's your favorite 'supermodel'?*). I was wearing the same green Armani suit as I had on the first day. It drove my behavior. Green's a good color for me. I'd thought it would be an edge with Lauren Leaven, but there wasn't a nibble. She'd spent the night cloistered with her officemates and, eventually, The Barrister. Lauren appeared improbably engaged. My imagination? Jenny Cavataio breezed by me and then bent back in my direction to say:

"You better get moving. She's developing a thing for The Barrister. Says he 'looks good on paper.'"

I joined the group. The conversation was about breasts. The unspoken purpose was for everyone to demonstrate that they could engage a taboo subject with educated focus. Lauren had just said that her own breasts, although smallish, satisfied her in their shape and proportion. I guessed that The Barrister hadn't spoken for a long time, yet also wanted to quickly assert his dominion over the just-arrived me. I could practically see the huddle in his brain, which made a very wrong call. He said:

"Like any bloke, when I'm down there, in between them you know, I just don't want to come eye-to-mam with a couple of ski jumps. Or bananas. Know what I mean. Aesthetics is what it is. Can't be thinking of grandma's saggers."

Silence.

It was the old lead balloon, fart in church; a case of bad-joke leprosy. Tough luck, Barrister. Grandma's saggers put him out of the game with Lauren Leaven. Yet I felt no compensating vibe coming my way. Lauren,

Jenny, and Victoria edged into a vacant corner for some female-only sequestration after The Barrister's flameout. I set myself toward leaving. I wanted the suit off. And I wanted it not to smell like cigar smoke. So I headed out, taking in the snappy sea air, savoring an ideal pitch of drunkenness. I was almost leapingly excited at the prospect of going home alone.

Right behind me, though, was Lauren Leaven.

"Sneaking off to play darts?"

"How the hell did you know?"

"Maybe we just think alike."

Though there was this lusty start to things with Lauren Leaven, our romance assumed a rational mission. Lauren Leaven had accumulated the usual romantic disasters and near misses. That first night she said:

"I haven't the slightest idea if you and I are compatible. But you look good on paper. I'm attracted to you."

I'd been held to the same screening standard as The Barrister. I took no pains, therefore, to carve out a unique realm for Lauren Leaven. I told her that I'd spent five years trying to find the next Helen; maybe she would be it. We reached a concord. Lauren Leaven and I made the very adult decision to go sexual and see where it went.

Back at work, we neither publicized nor concealed our status. I spent the better part of my days in Lauren's office, talking with her, Jenny Cavataio, and, as needed, Victoria Sentence. With her heavy sighs and crinkled forehead, Victoria seemed always on the edge of telling us to piss off and go talk somewhere else. For Victoria, relief came whenever her phone rang. The ringing phone meant a chance to travel to a different office and be assigned more work. Victoria spoke in the hurried, panting way of a hunched-over serf. As she gathered a writing tablet and pen to go off to wherever she was going, Victoria seemed genuinely zealous about capturing that eighth-of-a-second she saved, cumulatively, by doing small things very fast: rustling for a spare pen, forcefully hanging up the phone, briskly rising from her seat, looking at the time, looking at the time again. She even turned her head and blinked her eyes more quickly than the ordinary, unconscious way. With all her necessary materials gathered, Victoria would set out on her journey by activating the Stride of the Summoned—the most red-alert, high-crisis gait of all, and seemingly the favored walking style in a law firm. Victoria walked with a message: *I am off to do something very important.* Walking protocol reflected law firm hierarchy. While the partners also walked fast, theirs was a higher-caste professional dressage, with longer strides and heads aloft rather than to the ground.

Jenny had gotten us going on the Stride of the Summoned by doing an imitation of Victoria. Lauren, in turn, did a perfect take on Dirk Pussinger's walk—feudal lord crossed with professional athlete pretending there aren't 40,000 people staring at him (which is a form of arrogance that's easily excused if 40,000 people are in fact staring at you. No one was staring at Dirk Pussinger). With another Victoria impression (chirpy phone voice), Jenny put us all into a communal laughter fit I hadn't known since Halloween. Victoria returned, and it seemed that she could smell the residue of having been made fun of.

"I've just come from Mackenzie Tanner's office," Victoria said. "She asked me if you were out ill."

"Me?" I said.

"You. She has apparently left several voice-mail messages. She'd like to see you in her office."

Victoria had happened on an official way to boot me. I assumed that Mackenzie Tanner needed, or at least wanted, the memo on the admissibility of polls and surveys in federal court. It had been more than a month since we first met about it. I did my best to be breathless and disheveled when I arrived at her office. Mackenzie Tanner looked up and asked:

"The evidence memo?"

"Done. I've been tied up all day with a bankruptcy thing for Dirk Pussinger . . . juggling, you know . . . I'd like to just go over the memo . . . tighten it up . . . I could give it to you now and then come by with the polished draft in the morning . . ."

"The morning is fine. I don't want to have two versions of the same document floating around."

Of course the memo didn't exist. I stayed late that night, past eight, researched and wrote the memo, and then sent it by interoffice mail to Mackenzie Tanner. I ate dinner, on the firm, and took a taxi, also on the firm, to Lauren Leaven's Harvard Square apartment, where I spent the night for the first time. I rolled in the next morning long past noon, reward for the late night and job well done. I hoped and believed I might never see Mackenzie Tanner again. I figured the best insurance toward that outcome would be to ring her and close the circle on the memo.

"Just calling to see that you got the . . . "

"Quite frankly, I don't know where to begin," she said.

"So you got it?"

"Well, yes. FYI, firm style is Courier twelve-point. And you used the external memo macro."

"Right, right . . . I was so swamped with Dirk Pussinger's bankruptcy thing . . . "

"By the way, did you Shepherdize all the cases you cited?"

Shepherdize? Funny word. "Shepherdizing" was another part of the craft of law practice that had been taught in Legal Research and Writing. To Shepherdize a case is basically to look it up in a book, called Shepherd's Something or Other, and check to see that it hasn't been overruled—an undeniably useful precaution. My plan to learn the mechanics of the job on the job, apprenticelike, was not being well received. Shepherdize?

"I actually don't know what that is."

And that was the truth.

"OK. You know what. Never mind. I have this brief due c.o.b. tomorrow. I'm going to go ahead and find someone else to do this research. Good-bye."

I never did see or speak with Mackenzie Tanner again. That deck cleared, I continued to "monitor" the bankruptcy filings Dirk Pussinger sent my way. Every morning I arrived to find the latest installment. I did attempt to read the papers. Bankruptcy is one of those areas of the law that has a magic-dust quality to it. Crank up the MasterCard, then tell your creditors to bugger off, with a duly deputized federal court throwing stiff-arms for you. In the corporate setting I imagined bigger drama—entrepreneurial dreams gone awry, and then the attempt to salvage something from the failure. Not Dirk Pussinger's bankruptcy case. The papers lacked story. They were an interminable series of letters; bickering over whether a creditor meeting would happen in Trenton or Columbus; during the first or second week of August; and whether one lawyer could participate "telephonically." At least seven law firms were involved, and for each letter the identical version that had gone to law firm one through seven was in my stack—seven copies of the same letter. The only variations were the address and salutation lines.

So I spent workdays during the middle part of the summer putting the bankruptcy documents into a burgeoning pile, breaking even on e*trade, reading reviews of Paul Westerberg's tour, loafing in Lauren Leaven's office, and taking the firm up on all its offerings. The lunches truly never were shorter than two hours. At night, no one ever did say *no more liquor.* I'd close the days out over at Lauren Leaven's. At this point our destiny was uncertain. We hadn't fallen into either magnificent passion or intractable conflict.

One afternoon as I lounged in Lauren's office with her and Jenny Cavataio, a call came for Lauren. It was effectively a call for me.

"Archibald Long wants to see you in his office," Lauren told me.

This couldn't be good; sent to the office, high school redux. When I got to Archibald Long's office, he said:

"So do you think your old boss has a shot at the Senate seat?"

Then again, maybe this wasn't a bad turn. Weld talk. Archibald Long just wanted to bullshit. His question caused me to recognize that I had been more immersed in Lauren Leaven than I had previously acknowledged. I hadn't seen Niccola at all during the summer, and I hadn't given Weld's chances in his Senate race against John Kerry real thought. I had read the polls, though.

"No. Kerry looks strong."

"Robert, the reason I asked you in here is to get and give a sense of how things are going for you. You came highly recommended by Blaine McKisco. I'm wondering if there is any difficulty in your personal life?"

"Everything's good."

"Well, then, let me give you a sense of what happens at the end of the summer—when it comes time to decide whether we are going to extend a particular summer associate an offer of permanent employment. As you know, it is relatively rare that we don't make an offer. Generally, one of two factors is at work. Either the summer associate has produced exceedingly poor work product. Or there is not a good personality fit between the summer associate and the firm . . . "

The Mackenzie Tanner incident had obviously bubbled its way up to Archibald Long.

" . . . Shitty work or shitty person, if you will. What is uncommon is that a summer associate will be at risk of not receiving an offer for *both* of these reasons. Now, I am certainly not saying this is something that can't be undone. The summer still has a good month remaining. No decisions have been made. As a courtesy, though, I thought you should know that there is an issue. That's all, just an issue."

An issue? Shitty person + shitty work= two issues. From Archibald Long's office, I went straight to the elevator, down, then out, against the after-lunch return wave. I walked the short distance to the State House, dropped into my old corner store at the base of Beacon Hill and bought a half-pint of Jim Beam. Bill Weld had introduced me to Jack Daniel's. Tim Apparel converted me to Jim Beam. There I was, back on Massachusetts soil, opting for the new, the future. I threw back the Jim Beam, hard, an homage to Tim Apparel and California. Then I boarded the Orange Line, a subway route I had never, during all my time in Boston, been on. It took me to Roxbury, Boston's ghetto. I had been to Roxbury before, with a state police security detail, and with Weld, when he delivered an economic revitalization speech. Roxbury was looking just as unrevitalized as it had on that prior visit. The same merchants were on the streets. Tax breaks and speeches hadn't brought legitimate business in. I was looking to transact illegitimate business. I did up a rock and a half in a doorway, and then took the subway back downtown, switched to the Red Line, and headed to Lauren Leaven's place. It was getting late, eleven or so, and Lauren was just rolling back from work. We flipped the television on and found saturation coverage. TWA Flight 800, JFK to Paris, had crashed, exploded apparently, in Long Island Sound.

Lauren and I stayed up late the night TWA 800 crashed, and laid still in the postsexual, midsummer heat. The plane crash, on top of Archibald Long's setting me up for a no-offer, had given the day a mood of peril and instability. Lauren Leaven, asleep in my arms, represented the possibilities of safety and stability. And isn't that how people end up married? You grab a little tighter in a weak time; she does the same; no one ever lets go; you sleep, together, forever. If I had fallen asleep right then, who knows. I stayed awake, though, and considered how she and I would come to this embrace. Lauren Leaven and I would begin in a regular fashion, but usually just inched away into ourselves—parallel, side by side, simultaneous masturbation—touching toes or ears to keep up the illusion of two-person sex. Once she asked:

"The sex with Helen, how was it?"

The sex with Helen? Those nuclear collider fuck-blasts where we'd smash a bed frame?

"Not bad," I said.

We headed into work together the next morning. I got out of the elevator on nineteen, with Lauren. Victoria Sentence was standing outside the elevator. She was crying. *Crying?* A sullen collection of other summer associates stood outside the conference room. Victoria said:

"You guys are the last to get here. Archibald Long wants to talk to all the summer associates in the conference room."

I already had this one figured out. One of the partners had been on the TWA Paris flight. The sorry punter had bitten the dust. Whatever. We'd have to spend the rest of the day feigning grief for some contemptible fuck none of us knew.

Wrong. This time there would be no feigning, gaming, or scamming. There would be no cheeky commentary or above-it-allness. It was Jenny Cavataio. Jenny Cavataio was dead. Just dead. That was it. Archibald Long told us. I couldn't bear the specifics. I drifted away, to Lauren's office. Time passed, and then Lauren returned, with Victoria Sentence and The Barrister. Victoria was still crying, hard; I was medium; Lauren not at all. Same feeling, different expressions. Even The Barrister was puff-ruddy around the eyes. His face had settled into an unguarded innocence, vestiges of childhood, a time before The Barrister became a generally regarded oaf.

"Cruel," The Barrister said. "What a cruel thing this is."

It had been an aneurysm, or an embolism; something that kills fast and without warning. Sparkling and sassy, Jenny Cavataio died the night before.

Archibald Long flew a group of Jenny's close summer friends to her funeral in the Midwest. The rest of us stayed behind in a funk. After the funeral, there was to be a memorial service at Long, White & Borren. On the morning of Jenny's memorial service, I rode in the elevator with Archibald Long, who had just returned from the funeral. None of the initial sadness had lifted. Archibald Long looked punished, weary, yet he also stood tall, unvanquished. It had been left to him to be the paternal figure to the thirty-seven remaining summer associates. Archibald Long was like my own father, Ed Byrnes, the most generous person I have ever known or am likely ever to know. The more they took on others' pains and burdens the lighter their own bearing became. Generosity levitates them. How was it that Archibald Long and I spontaneously hugged that morning as the elevator door opened and then shut on our floor? Even your basic American law firm couldn't suppress its hidden humanity. Archibald Long and I talked of how the true loss fell on those who had known Jenny for the previous twenty-five years—the parents, the boyfriend who I gathered had become or would soon have become Jenny's fiancé. Yet among the summer associates there was genuine hurt. It cut away the summer's carnival atmosphere, but also undid the workplace stiffness that now looked especially silly. The Stride of the Summoned had slowed to a plaintive, authentic crawl.

"We were the ones who would have seen the most of her over the next twenty-five years," I said to Archibald Long before we parted, outside the elevator.

And that was how he began Jenny's memorial service, with the observation that a piece of a shared future had been lost. There had to be other reasons it hit hard. I, for one, had never intended to share in that future. The same was true for other summer associates who had no plans of returning to Long, White & Borren. In fact, there was considerable doubt that I would even be given an offer to share in that shared future. Still, Jenny's death laid me out, for what reason or reasons, who knew, who knows. As Archibald Long spoke, I stopped bending my mind for theories and answers. A person I slightly knew and vastly liked had died.

The summer at Long, White & Borren ended with a final paycheck, and then three days to pack and kick back before returning to California. As I sat in my apartment watching Weld (still stuck far behind John Kerry) speak on television, a phone call came. It was Lauren Leaven. The plan had been for her to fly to San Francisco over Columbus Day weekend. We were launching a long-distance thing. Her call was to ditch all that. It was the same call I would have been too lazy to make myself until Columbus Day weekend was drawing nearer. We parted with a laugh about our sexual fiasco. Friends. I turned the TV off and sparked a joint, peacefully alone but already churning with anticipation about meeting Tim Apparel at the San Francisco airport and then heading straight to Skyline. The phone rang again. It was Archibald Long. I'd gotten an offer.

Flying back for the second year of law school, there was clarity. Wherever I worked the next summer could be my Last Place, where I spent most of my remaining life. I tend to engage a lot of drunken resolution-making on airplanes. This time the plan was to reach into my past, in a last attempt to give some shape to the future. To the point, when I got back to Stanford I would send two e-mails. One would be to Helen. The second e-mail I'd send to Dawn, the Weld work-study assistant I couldn't shake from my memory, though I'd barely known her. Helen was love lost, Dawn love untold. I planted within myself the vague hope that something permanent might arise from one of the e-mails.

Jenny's death occasioned a broader choice, as well. That "dying is mellow" revelation from the minivan crash now seemed vain, arrogant. Death was only a theory for me. Jenny died without trying. I crashed a bike semi-on-purpose and wound up with cuts and a chipped tooth. That was looking small in hindsight. I wasn't feeling so fearless anymore. But I wasn't sold on a dull life of perfect caution where any untempted fate— pancreatic blob, cranial explosion—strikes you dead in your boredom. When I got back to school, I would either:

(a) slow down and be careful; or,

(b) live fast, like I'm going to die anyway.

I was leaning toward careful, (a). Tim Apparel, the virulent (b) factor, would be picking me up at the airport. I would tell him about Jenny. He'd understand all that implied. Careful. Slow. Prudent. Or...

...as the plane rolled up to the San Francisco gate I fell back into indecision.

PART 9 | **SECOND YEAR**

CHAPTER 21 | **THE SYSTEM**

I returned to Harvard for my second year of law school with replenished bankroll and renewed spirit. I had netted $10,000 over the summer, after gambling losses, added a couple of preapproved Gold cards to my cache, and maxed-out my student loans. I would be living with The Kankoos in the second coming of The Parlour, a two-bedroom, one-bath suite in Wyeth Hall, a significant step up from the cramped Gropius Complex.

The day I reported for registration, I strolled through Harvard Yard sporting a smile that must have looked like the one I wore during my first walk through the Yard a year earlier. It was different, though. Harvard was neither the intimidating nor the glorious place it had been when I arrived from Eagle Lake. My smile was now a complex smirk. I laughed at the reflexive awe I'd felt toward frauds like O'Toule, and I was finally confident on the big stage. On the other hand, I couldn't help but feel a little let down. It was like The Kankoos said, *same shit since grade school*. Only this time, that fact didn't sit as well. Along with the promise of Harvard's rigor, I had lost my faith in the Bigger Things. And I returned to Elise after my first year of school with an uneasiness that the summer had not erased. I recalled the dark conversation I had had with The Kankoos on the way back from Atlantic City, just after grades had come out. I remembered thinking then that I had never had the luxury or the inclination to entertain nihilistic thoughts about what, if anything, mattered. Now, one thing was clear: I would have nothing but time. Time to figure out what purpose remained in my life, if any. Just in time, a new hope had emerged.

I approached my second year with two goals: one, take classes that required the least amount of work and the least amount of attendance, and, two, work at Young & Mathers the next summer.

To accomplish my first goal, I devised The System, a short instruction manual on the principles behind selecting and ditching law school classes. The System's goal was to fuck off as much as possible, with few if any consequences. The System's goal was not to pick interesting courses with interesting teachers. People tended to show up for interesting courses with interesting professors, so those who blew them off stood at a disadvantage when exams came. Instead, mind-numbing subjects with old, apathetic, dull professors who most people ended up hating were The System's ideal courses. This point was reason enough for many of my friends to opt out of The System. They had come to law school with a higher purpose in mind. So had I to some extent. But I chose to approach my circumstances with a little more honesty in light of what I'd already seen. What were the chances—of all the interesting things I could do with no financial or time constraints over two years—that I'd pick a Harvard Law School course? Sometimes that happened. When it did (like Alan Dershowitz's class on ethics), I went. But I was no longer willing to ascribe nonexistent purpose to my law school classes. In a way, I had reached the same conclusion that several others before me had reached. Their reaction was to bitch and moan about how hard or heartless the place was. Mine was to take the opportunity to go out and experience life.

The System's application is not limited to Harvard Law School, or even law school for that matter. It will work in just about any academic setting, and its spirit extends to all of life. It goes like this:

Will Need
Course evaluations (available through Harvard), past exams (available at the Harvard Law Library), course schedule (available through Harvard), exam schedule for the current semester (available

through the Harvard Registrar), outline bank (available at Harvard Student Copy Center, on-line, or lifted from *Harvard Law Review*'s private stash).

One: Review of Course Evaluations
Students fill out course evaluations during the last lecture of the semester. They contain the usual information, about whether the professor was friendly, responsive to student concerns, and an effective communicator. A ditcher is generally not concerned with these traits, at least not in the traditional sense. That said, professors who score poorly in these categories or elicit negative comments about their teaching style usually best suit the The System's purposes. Comments in a course evaluation like, "This professor couldn't teach a schnauzer to hump his shin," are just what a ditcher is looking for.

Two: Calculating a Ditch Ratio
A few days before registering for second-year courses, I was checking over my short list of Harvard's worst classes to make sure I was not taking any small classes (it is a lot harder to be inconspicuously absent from a 14-person class than a 100-person class). Then I realized that, in addition to the number of students enrolled in a class, the course evaluations disclosed another seemingly inconsequential statistic—the percentage of students completing a particular course evaluation. The intended purpose of this number was to judge the evaluations' statistical reliability. But I saw a better use. Because evaluations are filled out the last day of class, this is one of the most highly attended days, because the professor will often give a summary of the course or talk about the exam. And nearly everyone who attends the last class fills out the course evaluation. Still, some of the classes had a huge disparity between the number of students enrolled and the number of completed evaluations. Within this disparity was the key to what I was looking for: *a direct measure of how many people had blown off a class in the past.* I named the ratio of enrolled students to completed evaluation forms the Ditch Ratio (DR). Here's how it worked: in a class of 150 students, with 120 students submitting evaluations, the DR would be 1.25 (150 divided by 120); if only 30 evaluations were submitted the DR

would be 5. The higher the DR, the better the class was to blow off. The DR is the most important factor in deciding which classes to take. In Step Two, our ditcher isolates the twenty classes with the highest DR and ranks them in order, from highest to lowest.

Three: Review Exam Schedule for Take-Homes
Harvard has three types of exams: in-class, eight-hour take-homes, and long take-homes (turned in two weeks or more after they are handed out). Take-home exams are preferable to in-class exams. Long take-home exams are preferable to eight-hour take-home exams. Take-home exams have a leveling effect, making the ditcher's test less distinguishable from the hard worker. When you've got only three hours it helps to be able to recall some law on demand. Over two weeks, anyone can look up anything. At this stage, our ditcher highlights every class that offers a long take-home exam and underlines those with eight-hour take-home exams.

Four: Make Sure Outlines Exist for Each Class
Step Four is self-explanatory. Don't get stuck in a class that has no student outlines from past years. Ever.

Five: Select Classes
Take the list of classes with the highest DRs (see Step Two). Cross through all that do not have long take-home exams. If there aren't enough classes left to fill a schedule, select classes with eight-hour take-home exams. If you're still short of classes, you've got some priorities to set. I would recommend keeping the DR as high as possible, even if it means an in-class exam. The System's core premise is that skipping class is both a means and an end. It's all about free time, not getting good grades.

Six: Make Sure the Classes Don't Meet at the Same Time
This is an easy step to overlook. I have forgotten it myself. After all, you're not going to be attending any of these classes. Unfortunately, the Registrar requires that you be able to attend—technically at least—each of your classes. The Registrar takes the hard-to-dispute position that you can't be in two places at once.

Six (a): Make Sure Exams (If In-Class) Don't Happen at the Same Time
Again, self-explanatory. See Step Six above.

Seven: Miscellany
Usually, you will find an abundance of courses with high DRs and easy exams. If you find more classes than necessary, you can allow yourself other luxuries, like trying to get better grades. If this is a concern, one good move is to look for instructors who are skipped often but are still rated fairly highly. Students like them, they like students, they give higher grades. Another trick specific to Harvard was to look for classes beginning with "Law and" or ending with "and the Law." These classes were notoriously easy. Examples included Law and Economics; Law and Medicine; Psychiatry and the Law; Law and Politics; and Sexuality, Gender, and the Law. Over the next two years I would take them all, with not-so-bad results: A, A–, A–, A–, B+.

And that was it. With The System activated, I could focus on my second goal, Young & Mathers. In this respect, I was not alone. For everyone, the second year of law school is all about one thing: landing a job.

CHAPTER 22 | **ALL THIS**
USELESS BUTANE

"The City?"

"And just how do you propose we do that?"

Tim Apparel had met me at the San Francisco airport on a new, black BMW motorcycle. I had flown with the usual luggage bulk.

"You rent a car. Meet me around PoMo."

In my rented Mustang convertible, I found Tim Apparel sitting astride his motorcycle, just off Fillmore, under a sign: WARNING: DRUG-FREE SCHOOL ZONE! ENHANCED CRIMINAL PENALTIES.

As I fed the meter, I slid Clara a ten-dollar bill, from which she would keep the meter current and use the remainder as compensation for protecting the car and its contents.

"Where you been all summer?" Clara asked.

"Back east."

"I'll take care of it for you, honey," she said.

Tim Apparel and I found Paris, standing in an apartment doorway. He wasn't alone. On her knees, in front of Paris, was a loud, unreliable dealer known in the area as Angry Woman. Angry Woman appeared to be settling up with her wholesaler, Paris, who wagged the sort of rangy cock you imagine drug dealers have. Angry Woman finished off Paris and offered the same service to me and Tim Apparel. Guys complain about "toothy" blow jobs—not a problem with Angry Woman. We declined her offer with the flimsy lie that we were "in a hurry," and then transacted a smooth deal, splitting our business between Paris and Angry Woman, scoring her a quick turnaround profit on her just acquired supply. We went to the PoMo bathroom to get juiced up, torching three rocks before returning to Paris.

"How'd that treat you boys?"

"We could use another big one for the road," Tim Apparel said.

"Hundred?"

"Better make it two."

"I'll do you sweet justice for three hundred," Paris said. "Bulk discount."

"Five hundred," I said.

Paris handed over the thirty rocks, one by one and with all deliberate speed, the last several coming from under his tongue (a concealment device, but also a shortcut authenticity test because crack isn't saliva soluble). Paris filed his new cash flow in the hundreds section of a money roll that was the shape and size of a filet mignon. Paris was soliciting inquiries about his prosperity. Tim Apparel asked:

"Business good?"

"That. And I got me some gate money. Just finished three months in county."

Paris had spent the summer in jail, the same just-ended summer that Tim Apparel had worked in Silicon Valley and I had been in Boston at Long, White & Borren, LLP.

"Po-po," Paris said. *"Po-po."*

A star-on-the-door San Francisco cruiser was approaching. Paris's always-sharp cop radar had just gotten the two-strikes upgrade. Though he was working off peripheral vision and we were looking toward the police car, Paris saw it first.

"As your lawyer I advise you to get the fuck out of here," Tim Apparel said.

We spread in three directions.

———————————————

Tim Apparel and I rolled back to Stanford, downtown Palo Alto actually, where we'd be living in a house that would sell for a million bucks after we were gone. Tim Apparel drove his motorcycle straight into the house and parked it in the living room. The BMW was the house's lone fixture. It was time to go shopping.

We took the Beetle, which had barely churned to life after sitting dormant in summer storage. First stop: cash-preferred Costco, where we bought family-sized everything. The dominant item was Jim Beam, handle-grip jugs. Quantity: 30. Costco ran us $1,000. Tim Apparel laid out ten hundreds. We shared expenses. He'd pay, then I'd pay, and maybe I'd pay the next time, like young two-income spouses. Next stop: Cambridge Soundworks (two stereos, two and a half grand each). Then: Fry's Electronics for some TVs and a microwave. Next: Puff's, a headshop on El Camino that insisted we refer to bongs as "water pipes." We bought a handful of glass straight pipes, a low-end bong, an easy-on-the thumb butane torch, and eight boxes of two-dozen nitrous cartridges (plus a brass nitrous cracker and a gross of balloons). The charge at Puff's: $237.43, which wouldn't have to be paid out until November, charged as it was to my never-a-balance MasterCard. From Puff's, we went straight to the Stanford bursar's office. After a lot of line-waiting, we paid our tuition with borrowed money, checks received at Bursar Window 2, then paid out at Bursar Window 4, an archaic formality in the middle of Silicon Valley. By the time we closed out the day's errands at the Wells Fargo ATM, we each still had a stack of checks (remainder of three separate student loans, less tuition, plus the last of the summer associate paydays). The checks gave the illusion of positive cash flow when in fact we had no real cash flow. At least I didn't. Still, my Wells Fargo balance stood at an anxiety-free $14,223.27 as the semester began. On the way home, there was a motorcycle for sale next to Stanford Stadium. Yamaha two-stroke, lacking a throttle. $100. I bought it. We returned to the house.

I went straight to my room to write two e-mails: one to Helen, the other to Dawn, as I had resolved to do, back on the airplane from Boston when I was still shaken by Jenny's death. The Helen e-mail amounted to little more than a disingenuously regretful summary of the Weld years and my time in law school. I abandoned it. Helen wouldn't have bitten on anything short of a St. Augustine–scale confession. And what was there to say in the Dawn e-mail? *though we barely knew each other when you were an intern for weld, it occurs to me now that you are my last chance at connection and salvation . . . .* Instead, I figured I'd start out simple: *What's up? I'm still in law school. Where are you?* Where indeed was Dawn? New York, Columbia Writing Program, last I knew. I needed her e-mail address. No e-mail address for Dawn Ebert. No Dawn Ebert anywhere. Maybe she wasn't called Dawn Ebert anymore. I gave up the e-mail project altogether, poured a Jim Beam, packed the bong, and sat silently on the porch with Tim Apparel. Classes began the next morning.

The next morning, early, Tim Apparel woke me by starting his motorcycle in the living room. He was wearing a suit, tie, and a full-face helmet.

"Where the fuck are you going?" I asked.

"Work."

"Work. Of course. How silly of me."

"Night ride later? Skyline?" he asked.

Tim Apparel didn't wait for an answer. He gunned the BMW and was out the door.

I headed over to the Law School, the Office of Career Services. Posted about were sign-up sheets for law firm interviews. I put my name down for a late afternoon slot in October with Young & Mathers. Standing to my left were Lucy Faar and Celia Shackles. Francine Lewis stood to my right. She spoke:

"Young & Mathers. Isn't that the place in Seattle where you can wear shorts?"

"It's in L.A. I need some classes."

"Tax, Civ. Pro. II, Business Associations," Francine Lewis said. "That's what I'm taking. All very ditchable."

"What about this paper class, National 'X' Racial Formation. I thought you might be in that one. More theory than law. Good for an aspiring academic."

"You're obviously thinking about someone else you fucked."

With that, Francine Lewis left. Lucy and Celia remained, signing up for interviews. It was Lucy who wanted to teach. Lucy spoke to me, the first time since we'd gone to see *Clockers* with Becky Klamm, almost a year before:

"I'm taking that paper class. Any idea what National 'X' Racial Formation means?"

"None."

"Maybe I'll see you there."

"Maybe."

"We should hang out sometime. Been a while."

"Maybe head up to The City."

"Maybe, yeah."

Lucy and Celia left. On her way past me, Celia gripped my arm, affectionately it seemed.

Next, I was off to the registrar's office. I signed up for my classes: Taxation, Business Associations, Civil Procedure II, and National 'X' Racial Formation. Then, I signed up to take all but the last one pass-fail. In this, I was with the mainstream. Standing around the job interview sign-ups I had caught the drift that large numbers of second-year students would be taking all their classes pass-fail to relieve some of the crunch associated with job interviews. Finally, I asked the registrar whether the Law and Social Science professor, who had given me an Incomplete the prior semester, had submitted a grade. He had not. The registrar told me:

"I suggest you contact the professor directly."

I left a note at the professor's office, passed the afternoon with two fat rocks in a lockable library bathroom stall, and then headed to the house. Tim Apparel was there, on the porch, still in his suit and doing double nitrous hits out of a balloon. He asked:

"Night ride? Skyline?"

"Mountain bikes. And what's with the suit?"

"Meeting with investment bankers up in The City. Bankers still wear suits."

We rode our bikes along Sand Hill Road, reputed to be the world's venture capital Mecca, toward the trailhead. Tim Apparel explained that he would be working throughout his third year at the Silicon Valley law firm where he'd worked as a summer associate.

"I pop out thirty or forty hours a week, at sixty bucks an hour, and I'm pulling down a four-grand paycheck every couple of weeks. Not bad for a starving student scraping by on loans. Let's go. . . . "

We shot onto the trail and up to Skyline—on mountain bikes for the first time. Three coyotes watched us watch the sun go down. San Francisco came to light beyond the peninsula's tip. Tim Apparel stood pissing next to a newly planted tree. There was a hand-painted sign tied to the tree: *Please water me, so I can grow up to be, a splendid tree, for thee.* Tim Apparel regarded the tree and the sign for a long time. Then he took off his water pack and emptied all his water at the tree's base. The sun dipped into the ocean. Before leading the ride down, Tim Apparel switched his headlight on and reached down to disconnect his brakes. I did the same. We each pedaled the initial thrust, then gave over to momentum. Riding at night, you see only where the headlight shines in front of you. There's no peripheral vision, which, Tim Apparel later explained to me, is a good thing because the inability to see any more than you need to makes you bolder, ride faster, without the side blur. Hardened horseshoe imprints mark the trail, so bumpy that simply being thrown from the bike is the ride's most likely conclusion, and yet we pass that bumpiest stretch, catch air on a lip at the smoothest and steepest segment, and come to the point of just holding on, all speed and sensation. The drama is the crash—when and how. I'm listening to Morphine, *I propose a toast/to my self-control,* when Tim Apparel's front wheel locks and he shoots over his handlebars. My bike crashes into his bike and I'm deposited in a smooth, painless fall next to Tim Apparel. We sprawl out giggly in the mud and spark a bowl.

"Clean living," Tim Apparel said.

Tim Apparel and I settled in during September and October, living off the bounty in our well-stocked house. Out of bed we went straight to Skyline, by either road or trail. We returned home to the ever-present glass pipe and nighttime conversations that lasted until tumblers of Jim Beam dimmed our lights and drove us into sleep. Sixty miles a day on the bikes left us believing our bodies were indestructible. With all the grinding climbs and downhill blasts, it felt as if we were massively outpacing decay. Bobby Boylan, once lean, had gone fat. Not us. Whatever the nighttime abuse, we always woke fresh and ready to ride again. We never went to class. Tim Apparel had only one ordinary class to ditch; I had four. He loaded up on examless "directed research," a version of independent study in which his papers regularly maxed-out the grading scale, getting 4.3 or A+. Always in the air were the entertainment staples: Howard Stern in the morning, *Beavis and Butthead* and *LoveLine* at night. On the stereos, my Orbital fought with Tim Apparel's Dave Matthews Band. Francine Lewis and I started up again, then we stopped, though she kept hanging out with us at the house. I confess now to a quick fling with Becky Klamm, who wasn't so horrid with a bong hit in her. I further confess to being not quite able to invite violin-clutching Celia Shackles in when she would pause for a quick chat on the way to her string quartet practice somewhere in our neighborhood. For a time I fell in with a Stanford undergraduate, a finely tuned athlete who could stay with us on mountain bikes. She also liked to dance in the moonlight on the patch of grass between the Law School and the Bike Shop. A friend of hers once found us there and said to me, "dude, you're old." I played in a dart league and won consistently. Tim Apparel crashed his motorcycle. I read and reread a Young & Mathers brochure. Niccola phoned from Boston most nights, gradually spending more time speaking with Tim Apparel, whom she had never met, than me; two friends of mine making their own connection.

Though I recall it as a fast and zesty time, I see now that the details were unextraordinary.

It felt like an achievement.

By mid-October, home supplies were thin. One morning I woke to find Tim Apparel in my bedroom with his cheek to the floor. I asked:

"Are you looking for something?"

"As a matter of fact I am."

Tim Apparel showed me his fingertip. On it was what appeared to be 30 percent carpet lint, 30 percent crack break-off, and 40 percent miscellaneous floor whatnot. He smoked it.

"We're out."

"Good time to quit?"

"Running out isn't quitting."

"The City?"

"I just got back," Tim Apparel said. "Seems that Paris is lying low. Could have something to do with the thirty police motorcycles lined up at Haight and Fillmore. We'll have to do it the way the old settlers did. Make our own. Punch up that recipe."

An Internet recipe for crystal methamphetamine:

The ingredients and necessary materials—extensive, occasionally exotic: One (1) gram of purified ephedrine, pseudoephedrine, or phenylpropanolamine. Glacial acetic acid, a lot. Concentrated muriatic acid, one

(1) jug. Anhydrous HCl gas source pH-indicating paper. Copper sulfide, quantity unspecified. Naphtha, 500 ml. Permeable, lamb-membrane condoms. Lead or graphite electrode, 1/2-inch wide by five inches long. Six one-inch alligator clips. Several feet of 16- to 20-gauge insulated copper wire. Phlogiston, seven (7) cubic decameters. Ammeter capable of measuring up to three amps, with resolution to 1/10 of an amp. Voltmeter (optional). One (1) troy ounce ingot of palladium.

The process: maddeningly complex. Making crystal meth takes longer and is harder to do than a law school exam.

We set out to acquire the necessary materials. There were no one-stop efficiencies. We toured Silicon Valley's old economy. Pharmacy (pseudoephedrine, rubbers). Wal-Mart (naphtha). Hobby shop (chemistry set). Hardware store (muriatic acid, electrode, ammeter, protective goggles, apron, face mask, gloves cut to the elbow). Target (cooking pots, never to be used again; more expensive than Wal-Mart, but we were spreading out the purchases). Photo shop (copper sulfide).

"Copper sulfide? That hasn't been used in photography since, oh, World War II," the photo shop's owner said.

"We're old-school," Tim Apparel said.

"Unfortunately *we* are not. It's all copper nitrate these days, fellas."

"Then copper nitrate it is," Tim Apparel said.

"I take it you'll be paying with cash."

The disapproving yet accommodating photo shop was our final stop. We arrived back at the house, and Tim Apparel began cooking. I asked:

"Palladium ingot?"

"I'm thinking the commodity exchanges are shut for the day. So fuck the palladium ingot."

Over the next fourteen hours, we were reintroduced to ions, isotopes, coulombs, moles, Avagadro numbers, meniscus curves, Brownian motion, Bunsen burners, Erlenmeyer and Florence flasks. The result was the same as it had been for me in high school chemistry: failure. A liquid that looked as if it had undergone chemical slam-dance did drip out of the condoms. The liquid did crystallize. Street value? Zero. It was green. Crystal meth isn't green. Only pot is green, happy and organic green. This was Superfund-site green. And though it was plainly toxic, we did give the green crystal a smoke. Our bodies revolted. I felt several months of life expectancy sweeping out of me as developing fluids and driveway cleaner made a home in my lungs.

"Must have needed the palladium."

"Next," Tim Apparel said.

The next recipe: a dextromethorphan (DXM) extraction. DXM is the active ingredient in cough syrup.

"Screw it," Tim Apparel said.

We took an Incomplete. Tim Apparel untied his Mylar apron, tossed away the goggles, crumpled the face mask, and let the gloves fall to the floor. He cracked open a Robitussin bottle and drank it in a succession of gulps, then a second bottle, and then a third. I did the same. For three days we had Robo Trips, which are called poor-man's acid trips for good reason. At its thirtieth hour, the Robo Trip gave commendable visual, auditory, and tactile sensations: stop-action piss, rubberized asphalt, Aphex Twin bending around our heads. Boner and bike riding impossible. From hour forty to forty-five, I took the same five steps forward, then five steps back, then forward again. Francine Lewis dropped by and thought I was faking. Coming off the Robo Trip, and with two hours of sleep over the previous five days, I fell into a true sleep, the afternoon before my Young & Mathers interview.

The next day marked two law school firsts. It was the first and only time I had set an alarm to wake up. It was also the first and only time I sized up the competition. I arrived outside the classroom that was hosting Young & Mathers early enough to read the interview schedule taped to the door, behind which J. Mark Mathers was conducting interviews. None of the notorious gunners had signed up. Not Celia Shackles. Not Lucy Faar. No Davis Mund on the list, either. They were all heading for law school teaching careers or New York City law firms. That sealed it. Of the twelve people interviewing with Young & Mathers, between four and six would be flown to Los Angeles for a further round of interviews. My slightly above-average grades meant the trip to L.A. was mine to blunder away. The Robo Trip's lingering fog left me slow-witted and taciturn, not susceptible to a verbal gaffe. The door opened.

"Ahh, Mr. Byrnes... You look like just the sort of freak who'll fit right in at Young & Mathers..."

The interview was merely a conversation—a test of minimal social competence. At the end, Mathers said:

"Why don't you plan to come interview down at our office in L.A. Make a point to meet Bob Young. He's a biker, too."

A week later, I flew to L.A., stayed at the Ritz-Carlton Pasadena, took a limousine to Young & Mathers's offices—all expenses for which Young & Mathers would reimburse me.

Los Angeles: I'd never seen ugly and beautiful in such overlapping proximity. Muscular hills, far taller than the Skyline ridge, abutted heinously awful "gated communities." Downtown, where Young & Mathers is, stands lifelessly, a business-only district. Young & Mathers, though, snapped with a more entrepreneurial than bureaucratic beat. I did my interviews with five lawyers, some shoeless, most shaveless, all suitless, and one woman whose ass filled out a pair of frayed, red-tab Levi's just the right way. By noon I had a letter, signed by J. Mark Mathers, confirming that I had been offered a position as a summer associate "at a salary commensurate with other leading Los Angeles firms." As I walked out of Mark Mathers's office, his next interview was on the way in.

"Rob, this is Jaime Marquart. From Harvard by way of Texas."

That was it. My Last Place loomed seven months down the line. Young & Mathers—the but-for cause of all future friends, failures, triumphs, and romances.

I'd always chased and then fled from institutional tradition—Ivy League, politics, New England. Young & Mathers promised newness, individuality, a sense of justice. By appearance you couldn't tell its partners from its paralegals. But I had none of the comfort that certainty is supposed to afford. If the established order's principal drawback is proven though stultifying efficiency, the alternative order's main frailty is that places like Young & Mathers too often overpromise as they regress toward convention. Like Starbucks, they start out hip, but time dulls their edges.

I bolted straight from Young & Mathers to LAX to the San Jose airport to the house. There, Tim Apparel sat cross-legged, in the living room, surrounded by stacks of law books. There was no music in the air, only a droning audiocassette law outline. *The Court will apply strict scrutiny when core political speech is regulated, blah, blah, blah . . .*

I asked, "What the . . . ?"

Tim Apparel explained: "Well, this morning I went to my mailbox and there was a note from Kathleen Sullivan. She pretty firmly suggested that I begin attending her First Amendment class or else she'd flunk me. Then the *Law Review* rang me up and said I had to do this edit, or they'd sack me too. All in all, not a good day."

"The City?"

"I'm afraid that's not possible."

"Dullard."

"Gargle my bag."

Getting to San Francisco this time was more complicated than usual. Tim Apparel rose early the next morning and established a presence in Kathleen Sullivan's First Amendment class. Then he quit the *Stanford Law Review*, handing his resignation letter to The Barrister who, along with around 50 other Two Ls, had just joined. Finally, after Tim Apparel billed a few hours at his law firm, we were off. We took the Beetle to San Francisco. On the way Tim Apparel said:

"When I quit, our old friend The Barrister told me the *Law Review* would 'inform my future employer.'"

"Sounds like a bluff."

"By the time I got to work, The Barrister had already called."

"And?"

"The partner said 'I told the *Stanford Law Review* we don't give a fat crap.'"

Tim Apparel and I shifted from our Palo Alto pattern to the San Francisco rotation: Paris to the PoMo bathroom to Paris, back to the PoMo bathroom and then, propelled by crack's fellow-feelingness, into the night with a new (and never to be seen again) circle of friends gathered from PoMo. Each day ended at dawn in the apartment of one of those new friends, with us throwing back some over-the-counter sleepers for the comedown. Wedged within it all was the writing of my National 'X' Racial Formation paper. All the writing happened in the PoMo bathroom, on my laptop. This, our longest continuous time in San Francisco, occasioned what I took to be a fresh and enduring revelation: there is no need to attach to anything permanent when you can make a new world, serially, night after night. It was in fact a recycled revelation, the same one I'd had back in Boston, before it went sour. That it was Tim Apparel instead of Niccola; a law school paper instead of speeches; and rock instead of powder suggested novelty, but obscured that my life hadn't evolved a great deal since I left Boston looking for drugless solitude and change.

On the morning of day eleven, Tim Apparel nudged me awake: "Need to get back. Sullivan's class. Work."

We drove straight to the Law School. I spent the day popping in to see that my classes weren't branching into unoutlined territory. Then I went to the National 'X' Racial Formation seminar and tested out some of the ideas that were going into the paper that was the lone requirement for that class. After the seminar, I would have gone back to the house had the past not unexpectedly revisited me.

"The City?"

It was Lucy. She told me she still went up from time to time, just to eat, walk, be somewhere else. It had been a year since the San Francisco trip during which I'd told Lucy and the others about the Halloween orgy. Since then, Lucy and I had each established ourselves in our own law school realms sufficiently that we could now step outside them. We decided to meet at a pizza place. I suggested the one next to PoMo, and that we go in separate cars.

"I might hang out there for a few days, finish my paper."

"Jesus! I don't even have a topic. I feel like an idiot," Lucy said.

"You're still nine smarter than me."

I beat Lucy to San Francisco, found Paris, and went to the PoMo bathroom to knock out the last bits of the paper. With only a concluding paragraph to write, I went next door and found Lucy. She'd already gotten me a slice of pizza. She said:

"I love that seminar. Just like college. No law. So, your paper?"

I was feeling talkative. The comedown hadn't arrived.

"It's about the cultural identity of the Wampanoag Indians. They wanted to build a casino in Massachusetts. They struck a deal with the governor. He announced it and, in the same speech, introduced the Wampanoag to Massachusetts. So their identity was basically represented through someone else's voice, a non-Indian voice. Mine, really, since I wrote the speech and didn't know a thing about them. All I could do was write about how 'noble' and 'proud' they are."

"The point being?"

"That people have an interest in being represented by their true details, telling their own stories."

"Otherwise all you get is cliché and gossip."

"Right."

"Did one of the summer associates you worked with in Boston really die?"

Lucy's question elicited the conversation about Jenny's death that had never happened with Tim Apparel. After telling her about Jenny, I felt re-engaged with the normal, functioning world. I resolved, at that moment, to turn my life about, to set things straight, put myself on a definite course. The push to quit is never mightier than at the apex of a good hit. A sum-mary vow coated my mind: to go clean, attend all my classes, forswear all vices. With crazy zeal, I engaged this new mode. I told Lucy I'd be right back. I went to PoMo, to write the concluding paragraph to my National 'X' Racial Formation paper. Then, back to Lucy. I put my laptop beside her pizza. Next, I left Lucy again, ostensibly to load the parking meter, but in fact to find Paris, to score my last hit. Then, back to Lucy, where I ate half a slice of pizza—not because I was hungry, but to eat, because that's what people do—before telling her that I had to retrieve a nonexistent casebook "next door." I did go next door. The last hit went down so splendidly that I found Paris, for the last, last hit. Paris told me he needed food. I gave him a ten. He needed me to buy the food for him. The nearby supermarket wouldn't let him in. Before making the supermarket run, I went back to Lucy and told her the truth: I was off to buy food for a friend who lived on the street. I left Lucy and, before returning to Paris, stepped into the PoMo bathroom and torched the last, last hit. Then, I found Paris. We went to the supermarket. Lots of political signs. Election Day, 1996.

"This one can't come in," the supermarket's security guard said.

"I'm his lawyer and I say he can."

We went in. As we waited for Paris's deli meats to be sliced, Paris asked:

"That lawyer thing bullshit?"

"Sort of."

"Look," Paris said.

A man stood near us. He was in a nowhere zone—too far from the deli counter, the bread island out of reach. He wore a White Sox cap that was fashion-dead yet weirdly new, its brim stiff, uncontoured. He appeared to be staring at my feet, then Paris's. Paris and I slid a few yards. He moved too. Paris and I met eyes: *undercover.* Paris headed out. The suspicious guy lingered, then drifted out of my sight. I grabbed the turkey, gave the appear-ance of a regular shopping trip, roaming several aisles and then making a quick keep-the-change bolt through the express line. I found Paris at the Haight and Fillmore bus stop.

"Lost him," Paris said. "Here."

He gave me another rock. I handed over his food. I ran back to the pizza joint, told Lucy I would be right back, went into PoMo, real quick, then back to the pizza joint.

Lucy wasn't there. My laptop was gone. I sat and waited, ten minutes, a half hour.

Then, from the counter: "Is this yours? She left. Said to give it to you."

So ended the clean living vow. After torching the pipe for residue, I sat in PoMo's main area. Over the previous weeks, Tim Apparel and I had just sat there and waited for a small community to germinate around us; new friends, disposable and regenerating. This night, though, something wasn't right. Rather than being drawn to me, the others passed by with quick glances of curious repulsion. The inner comedown must have been showing outwardly. I found Paris again, did another hour in the bathroom, and resettled in PoMo. Same result. Same looks. I went back to the bathroom, to look into the mirror that I'd never before looked into. I was expecting the usual story line: the drugged-out, alien face that used to be me. It was nothing of the sort. I looked healthy, together—unappealingly so. My hair was parted—*parted, why?*—my shirt tucked in—*why?* again. The laptop was under my arm along with three university press books. It was as if my appearance shifted to maximum disadvantage. Lucy had seen the drugged-out desperado. PoMo's bohemians saw the Dullard.

It was time to go back to the house. I still had a friend. I wanted to be where my friend was. Before leaving, I gave a quick look for Paris, couldn't find him, and so I scored five rocks from Angry Woman. Stocked up and heading home in the Beetle, I was settling back into calm. When I hit Palo Alto, I sparked one of the rocks which, like the other four, turned out to be a chunk of nothing. It feels like getting whacked in the stock market, an assumed comfort whisked away from you; makes you frantic and discomfited at having stupidly assumed you had something you didn't really have. You resign yourself to inferior substitutes: liquor, tobacco. When I got to the house, the front door was open. Tim Apparel's motorcycle ticked from a recent ride. I chugged some Jim Beam, went to sleep, and woke up the next day, late, and only then due to a ringing phone. Niccola. Weld lost the Senate election. We hung up, and Tim Apparel's phone rang. Niccola calling him now. They talked, not about politics. I'm quite certain Tim Apparel couldn't name a single U.S. senator. I called the registrar's office. Still no grade from the Law and Social Science professor. I called the professor. No answer. I left a message. I called the registrar again. Then, there was a call-waiting click. On the other line: J. Mark Mathers. He said:

"Rob, just calling to see if you're foolish enough not to join us here at Young & Mathers for the summer."

CHAPTER 23 | **GET A JOB**

Every October, law firms from all over the country come to Harvard to interview second- and third-year students. Getting one of those on-campus interviews is as simple as signing up. In that first interview, the goal is to get invited to visit a firm for a second and final "flyback" interview. After getting to the flyback interview stage, the job is yours to lose.

For everyone at Harvard, getting a good job is just a numbers game. The most socially inept students might score one flyback interview from ten on-campus interviews. So they just signed up for forty or fifty interviews and got their four or five flybacks, which landed them three or four offers. On the other hand, even the best students rarely had a success rate of higher than 70 percent. And for popular firms like Young & Mathers, the odds were less than 50 percent. So although I already had eight flyback interviews in my bag and a 60 percent rate of success going into my Young & Mathers interview, I approached it with a fairly realistic sense of uncertainty.

Before the interview, I made one more pass through Harvard's binder of firm brochures. A lot of firms promised "business casual" attire and early responsibility. Young & Mathers promised something like this:

Want to make a whole lot of money practicing litigation with high-profile clients, and do it all in shorts and T-shirts? Not afraid to go to a place where you are judged by your abilities, not how long you've been here or what your last name is? If so, Young & Mathers is your place. Our motto: Be the very best at what matters, and forget the rest...

It was the best thing going, at least. But what would it think of me? I was not some pierced, tattooed genius. I was, and am, damn ordinary.

My Young & Mathers on-campus interview happened on the last day of interviews. That was good for two reasons. One, I had all of my fallbacks in place. And two, Young & Mathers had one of the shittiest interview slots at Harvard. Most people cancel their last few interviews after they get enough flybacks.

I showed up early for my interview at Lincoln's Inn, Harvard's coed drinking club ($250 a year got you twenty-four-hour access to the fully stocked bar, pool table, big screen, and foosball). Most law firms held their interviews in vacant Harvard offices or nearby hotels, but Young & Mathers always held their interviews at Lincoln's Inn. My interviewer was the hiring partner, J. Mark Mathers. He appeared to be working on his third or fourth pint when I caught up with him. He offered me an Anchor Steam, which I changed to a Maker's Mark, and we went into the poolroom.

"Nice suit, Mr. Marquart," he said sarcastically. "Don't you know that ass-kissing doesn't work on me?"

"I figured the kiss-ass move was ripped jeans and T-shirt. Everyone's read the brochure. You wear those jeans to court?"

"Fair enough. It doesn't matter either way. So how does it feel to get a bunch of B's for the first time in your life? Finally hit a wall you couldn't climb?"

"It was easier to walk around it. You know, your motto—figuring out what matters and ignoring the rest. B+'s are good enough for my purposes, and law school's my last chance to be unemployed with spending money and a good excuse. Turns out, I'd rather be at Foxwoods than the library."

"Where in Hell is Eagle Lake anyway?"

"Middle of nowhere."

"So your old man owns a bunch of land and a handful of oil wells and collects six figures a year in wheat subsidies?"

"The crop's rice. I spent a few fourteen-hour days in those fields, but nobody I'm related to ever owned 'em. I was on the unspoken end of that poor farmer propaganda—the one who gets half minimum wage cuz they let 'em pay by the day. No oil wells in the family either, far as I know. My dad and mom were divorced when I was eight, and my mom, my brother, and I lived at the poverty line ever since."

"Is that right? I like a little hard work. Then again, we've hired our share of rich kids, too. By the way, I like all of this math and science on your résumé. Shows you're not some intellectual lightweight hiding behind a bunch of philosophical puzzles with no right answers. There *are* right and wrong answers at Young & Mathers. And there *are* good and bad lawyers. I hope you don't expect me to give you a break just because you're some poor kid from the sticks."

I had no idea whether I was making any impression at all and, if I was, whether I was challenging him or pissing him off. But he was challenging me, so I rolled with it.

"You won't have to give me a break. You'd be better off worrying about those little rich kids you've hired. Speaking of which, I did some reading between the lines in your write-up, and I've got a question for you. How do I know Young & Mathers isn't just a sweatshop in biker's clothing?"

With that question, Mathers's veneer cracked, then shattered into laughter.

"Funny you should ask that, Jaime. We just had one of our best associates quit the other day. When I asked her why, she told me the same thing when she left. You're right about those rich kids, too. Bunch of wussies. I tell you what, Jaime. I want you to fly back to our firm to get a look at the place. Just do me a favor and don't tell anyone else for a couple of days; some of them will still be waiting to hear from us. Now rack 'em up, I've still got ten minutes until the next schmuck."

I walked out of my interview triumphantly and poured another drink to celebrate. I had a flyback in my pocket; I knew that a summer job offer was damn near definite. And, more important, Mathers was everything I had hoped. He took shit as well as he dished it, and he wasn't afraid to be honest. He was Papaw with a law degree.

Flyback Week came a few weeks after my on-campus Young & Mathers interview, in early November. During Flyback Week, Harvard stops classes for Two Ls and Three Ls so they can travel to law firms. Even though classes are suspended for only a week, flyback interviews can span over two or three weeks. It was also pretty common to use flyback interviews as a chance for a free plane ticket and hotel room in a cool city. I've heard it called a "bad-faith flyback." The Kankoos recommended arranging several. For the next few weeks, Parlour representatives took their mixed motives to every desirable part of the country—Chicago, New York, Los Angeles, San Francisco, San Diego, Dallas, Atlanta, and Charlotte. My plans were linear: a few days in Austin, then on to L.A. and Young & Mathers, before finishing up with another interview in Austin. The last interview in Austin was intentionally saved until the end to allow for a couple more days with Elise on the firms' dole.

During my second year of law school, Elise was living and going to medical school in San Antonio, an eighty-five-minute drive down I-35 from Austin, where I would be interviewing. I decided not to bother with any form of cover for the law firms that funded our rendezvous. I flew straight to San Antonio. After a short, quiet ride from the airport, back in Elise's apartment, at 3:00 P.M. on a Sunday afternoon, an otherwise insignificant moment occurred that now tops my list of Things I Best Not Rehash But Always Do. I was curled up on the couch, reading. Elise was twenty feet across the room at the table, reading a medical school book. Or maybe she was painting. Maybe music was playing. I had nothing to say. Elise had nothing to say. I remember getting the idea that I should just walk on over, embrace her, and tell her I loved her. In saying it, maybe she would say it back, maybe we would believe it again, maybe we would want to try. But I didn't. I just rolled over, put my book down, and closed my eyes. I wasn't taking a stand. I wasn't pissed. I wasn't scared of what she'd say or do in return. I just didn't have the momentum to go over and do it. We would revisit that moment often during my second year of law school—the vast distance between us reduced to twenty unpassable feet. On bad days, I think those twenty feet were all that separated emptiness from fulfillment. I'm sorry, Elise. But it was only twenty feet for you, too.

On the job side, Austin was not memorable—two interviews, two summer offers. On Wednesday, I said good-bye to Elise and headed west. I checked into my hotel room in L.A. at 5:00 P.M. My financial future was more secure than ever. I had $500 loose in my front pocket, and a bottomless tab in room service, courtesy of Young & Mathers. I went straight to my room, tossed down my bag, ordered the twenty-four-hour noon-to-noon special on the pay-per-view, and reached for the phone to order my first fifth of something good. The message light was on. Elise was the only person I told where I'd be staying. I dialed the operator and got this message:

"Hey Marquart. Kankoos. Change of plans. Interviewing in L.A. tomorrow. Called Young & Mathers and got your number. Call me when you're done at Y&M. I'll save you the cab ride and buy you a six-dollar beer."

I got to Young & Mathers the next day, an overenthusiastic thirty minutes ahead of schedule. The recruiting coordinator met me in the waiting area and took me to my first stop, J. Mark Mathers's office. As we walked up to his door, it opened and Mathers emerged laughing, his arm around another recruit he had just finished up with. The recruit was my first taste of the Young & Mathers of my generation, the people I could be spending the majority of my next ten years with. I captured a quick video still for future reference.

Fashion: Head-to-Toe Crazy
Up top, a thrift-store-chic, burnt umber button-up with orange embroidery on the pocket and sleeves. Below, Diesel jeans with a bike chain dangling from the pocket where a watch chain might have hung in days past. Aside from the three-inch soles, his shoes had the shape and shine of formality, but were a rainbow of burgundy, navy, olive, and black. Tattoos and hair that defied brush and comb complemented the rest.

Presence: Ambiguous
My impressions alternated between genuine shy guy and aloof misanthrope. Overall, though, his demeanor was more encouraging than intimidating or off-putting. He confirmed my romantic image of the place as one of comfortable eccentricity.

Mathers interrupted what could have become an awkward silence: "Marquart! Meet the competition. This is Robert Byrnes."

"Hey."

"Hey."

"Come on in, Marquart! How the hell are things in the rice fields . . . "

As I moved around the office from interviewer to interviewer, I revisited my initial impressions of Gropius (the man and the Complex). Young & Mathers's office was high function in its most irreverent and beautiful form—Bauhaus meets Blutarsky. It had no ceilings, only exposed bare pipe and shaft. Its offices were sparsely decorated with clean lines. The dress code was nonexistent, as promised. The occasional peer through a half-cracked office door revealed a guy changing from shorts to Armani, just in time for a court appearance. Bob Young himself wore shorts and a bike-racing shirt. He had not shaved in three days. Yet, several others were just as comfortable in Dockers and Arrow oxfords. Meanwhile, as much as it was evident what did not matter to Young & Mathers, it was also clear what did. People were busting their asses left and right, so intensely that they were oblivious to my presence. It stood in contrast to the show that a lot of firms put on during Flyback Week. I loved it. And it loved me, at least enough for J. Mark Mathers to give me a summer job offer on the spot. I did not accept it on the spot. Now that Young & Mathers was a real possibility, I had to bring to bear the rest of my reality. Elise had three more years of medical school in Texas after this one. In less than twenty-four hours, I would be back in San Antonio with a lot to talk about.

I checked out of the Biltmore and camped out near the cab line, where I was supposed to meet The Kankoos. Ten minutes later, he pulled up in a black convertible Mercedes.

"Nice Benz. What the hell are you doin' in L.A.?"

"Booked a last-minute interview in L.A. after I finished up in San Fran. I wanted to see California the right way—just me, a convertible, and three hundred miles of coast. I'm sold. What about you, Marquart?"

"Not sure yet. I have some things to sort out."

Ten minutes later, we were heading south on the 110. The Kankoos broke the silence as we sat in bumper-to-bumper traffic under a highway sign that read I-10 ¾ MILES.

"You know the best thing about L.A.? It's only a four-hour drive from Vegas. Ever been?"

"No."

"Me neither. Wanna go?"

We were about to pass the I-10 exit as The Kankoos's words settled in. Eight miles west was LAX, and then San Antonio. Two hundred and ninety miles east was Las Vegas. I looked at The Kankoos and smiled for the first time in four days. I dialed the Benz's car phone as The Kankoos swerved into the east-most exit lane of I-10.

"Hello?"

"Elise?"

"Hey."

"Something's come up. I had to cancel that last Austin interview. I'm not gonna make it back down this time."

I waited for the worst, preparing a more detailed lie—a car wreck, a glitch in the system. I didn't need it.

"No problem. I'm swamped anyway."

"Cool! I'll see you in a couple of weeks then, I guess."

"OK."

"OK."

I was far too blinded by my own self-interest to make note of Elise's insanely understanding reaction to my sudden change of plans. Vegas was four hours away.

Just outside of Barstow two hours and change from Las Vegas, The Kankoos reached into his bag and gave me a gift, Edward Thorpe's *Beat the Dealer*, the card counter's one Great Book, the one that started it all.

"Maybe you can make some sense of this. Made my head spin."

"Thanks. What is this, more philosophy?"

"Nah. At best, it's a way to turn the tables on the casino. At worst, it's a damn good rationalization for gambling more. But don't thank me, I've got my own ass in mind. Only one of us has to understand that nonsense for both of us to make a lot of cash."

I digested most of Thorpe's statistical charts and counting strategies by the time we hit the city limits. The Kankoos's instincts were right. I got it. But understanding card counting and practicing it are two different things. In the end, it seemed like too much work for too little gain. I put *Beat the Dealer* down for the moment and concentrated on Vegas.

I didn't sleep for the next thirty hours. I did, however, manage to lose a crapload of money. Only a couple thousand dollars, actually, but that was still a decent amount of money my second year gambling. Unlike Atlantic City, Vegas actually did offer attractions other than gambling. But who among us would be able to lounge by the pool, ride a goddamned roller coaster, go to a water park, visit the Liberace Museum, play a round of golf, or watch a movie when he just dropped a grand at the tables? OK, so I might have had a problem. But the only answer for me was to borrow some money, Comcheck, and give Thorpe's con game a try.

I borrowed $1,000 from The Kankoos, who was flush with cash from who knows where, Comchecked another grand, and went to a lower-end casino with rules favorable to counting cards. They used two, intead of six, decks, which put the odds more in my favor. It took a little while to get the hang of it, but before long I was confident I was onto something. Being onto something in card counting only means you have a 1 to 2 percent edge over the casino, even with the best rules. You've got to gamble thousands of hands before you are pretty much guaranteed of winning. But even if you don't do that, you've still got a better chance of winning than the House. They usually don't like that.

Once you put the sophisticated statistics and necessary mental discipline aside, the strategy for counting cards is simple. At certain times during a blackjack game, there are more tens and aces in the deck relative to the lower cards, and the odds are actually in the player's favor. Only a card counter knows when this is and is not the case. To make money, a counter bets the lowest amount possible when the odds are against him and bets the big bucks when they are in his favor. The only problem is that any card counter can usually spot another of his kind from all the way over in the Keno lounge. And casinos don't even require such long-range vision. It's all right there on camera. To deal with the fact that a casino can easily spot card counters, Thorpe devised a number of "cover" strategies, meant to disguise the fact that a card counter is counting. I had ignored the section on cover strategies, figuring Thorpe for a wacko conspiracy theorist.

I didn't play the thousands of hands needed to guarantee victory, but I won that day. I recouped my couple thousand and added a couple more to the kitty. Then, the telephone rang in the pit. The pit boss answered, took a quick glance my way, and hung up. I shook it off as Thorpe-induced paranoia and played on. A few minutes later, the count was sweetly in my favor. I upped my bet from $25 to $125, a modest five-times increase. As soon as I did, a 300-pound Italian in a double-breasted blend suit walked over from the pit, stopped the dealer in the middle of the game, shoved my bet back at me, and stated as matter-of-factly as warranted:

"You're done with twenty-one here. Cash out."

The rest of the table, even the dealer, was frozen with shock. I did not argue. The Harvard lawyer in me might have wanted to talk about my rights (and I would have been wrong anyway); but the street-smart poor kid in me said leave quietly, with your wallet in your front pocket and your attention over your shoulder. Another case of nothing-comes-for-free. Maybe, but this marked the beginning, not the end, of my days as a hustler. I went back to the hotel, reopened *Beat the Dealer*, and read about cover strategy.

The next day, The Kankoos and I drove back to L.A. and were on a plane back to Harvard, jobs in tow. Exams were in a month.

| CHAPTER 24 | **CHOOSE A CAREER** |

I flipped back from the Young & Mathers phone call to the other line, the Law School registrar:

"I handed in my paper on time. The professor gave me an Incomplete. His only explanation was that the paper 'puzzled' him. That was five months ago. Since then I've left notes and phone messages. He's never responded. Could you ask him either to fail me or give me a grade? I have to go."

Back to the Young & Mathers call:

"Yes, I'm pretty set on coming there for the summer."

As I said this, Tim Apparel (still on his own phone line with Niccola) walked into my room and placed his cheek to the floor. I continued with the Young & Mathers call:

"Can't imagine working anywhere else. I have..." Then there was another call-waiting click. "...an allergic reaction to wearing suits. Can you hold a second...?"

On the other line: Celia Shackles. She heard I went "up to San Francisco a good deal" and wondered if I might give her a ride there and back.

"Quite possibly, Celia. Can you hold on...?"

Back to Young & Mathers. Mark Mathers hadn't been silently holding, but talking on. I picked up the last part of what he was saying and
responded:

"No, no. I don't have an actual allergy to suit fabrics. Why don't you
just put me down as coming this summer. I'm in. Very excited. Only law
firm I'd ever work at."

"Good choice!" Mark Mathers said.

"Got it!" Tim Apparel shouted, now done talking to Niccola. He
dropped a recovered pebble into the glass pipe. I switched my phone back
to Celia:

"Celia, can you hold on?"

Tim Apparel triggered the butane torch. This little pebble just burned
like worldly material, though. It gave off a limp streak of unsweet smoke.
Smelled like regular stuff burning. Tim Apparel took it in.

"A booger," Tim Apparel said. "I smoked a booger."

Back on the phone:

"Actually Celia, my roommate and I were just about to head up to
The City."

Celia came to San Francisco with me and Tim Apparel. We dropped
her off on Union Street, a shopping district. Tim Apparel and I rolled
over to Haight and Fillmore, found Paris, and sealed ourselves in the
PoMo bathroom until it was time to retrieve Celia. We torched up on
the way, until Celia came into view. Tim Apparel crawled to the rear
seat. Before Celia bent into the Beetle, I slid the just-used glass pipe into
my sock.

The Beetle sputtered as we made our way out of The City. The car was
behaving as if it wouldn't make it back. I was feeling the same. It's a short
high. The comedown started to hit not long after we picked up Celia. Tim
Apparel suggested "getting gas," a detour that included a bathroom rendezvous, after which I slid the pipe back into my sock, feeling the singe.

Back in the Beetle, Tim Apparel and I zoned out, half-listening as
Celia spoke, her head angled high:

"So what's up with you two?"

"Byrnes chose a career today," Tim Apparel said.

Career? Right. Young & Mathers. I told Celia. She said:

"Shorts in the workplace. Peculiar."

The pipe was biting into my shin. Celia continued speaking and her gaze remained aloft, averted. I reached down, removed the still-hot pipe, and put it in the change well, above the gearshift. The Beetle was still gagging on gas. Topping off the tank hadn't solved the problem. More than that: dense black smoke was coming out the dual tailpipes. I kept it to myself. The comedown was creeping on us again. The engine let out an explosive backfire. Then the high snapped out, off, gone, coating me with panic: *the Beetle will die, I need a hit, we won't make it back, I can't speak my fear, answer my craving.* Celia talked on, just noise. Tim Apparel fidgeted, scratched himself, though he had no itch. He adjusted his seating position, readjusted, then readjusted again. I reached for the pipe and slid it, low, between the front seats, to Tim Apparel, who put both the pipe and an American Spirit in his mouth, lit them both, let the pipe tumble to the floorboard, and retained the cigarette. He gave a relieved exhale, lost his posture, and flopped deeper into the seat, until his shoulder blades came to rest where his ass had been. He stayed motionless the rest of the way. His cigarette burned into a long cold ash. Celia cracked her window open and continued talking, about law firms, appropriate attire, long hours, benefits, partnership chances, 401Ks, city versus suburb, buying versus renting, law as a learned profession. Then: STANFORD UNIVERSITY, NEXT EXIT. Safe zone. Back home. My relief.

I dropped Tim Apparel off at the house, popping in for a quick hit, and then took Celia to Leland. She asked me in, poured some Scotch. There was the whiff of a potential sexual encounter—night, late, liquor—so I steered the conversation to sex's natural predecessor, candor:

"Celia, why are you the way you are?"

"You mean formal and stilted?"

"I'd say formal and elegant."

"Why are you the way *you* are?"

Though Celia always angled her head upward, she also caught the action closer to the ground. I told her:

"I have fun. Nothing better to do. No reason."

"Your depth psychology is a tabula rasa?"

"It seems that I'm unmotivated except by immediate and fleeting pleasures. If that's what you mean."

"We all have some motivating phantom. A piece of the past that eats at us."

"You too?"

"No doubt. Unfortunately, I am unable to identify mine. Which leaves me unable to say why I am the way I am."

She then looked straight at me, the first time ever. Celia Shackles's eyes had all the gentleness her hard-reasoned classroom words lacked. She said:

"I do know this. Whatever my phantom is, I will not be finding, much less slaying it, while I am working in a fucking law firm. By then it will be too late. I suspect we are quite alike in that regard."

"Good theory. But I'm pretty phantomless. A simple person when you get right to it."

"Of all the immediate and fleeting pleasures in the world, do you ever wonder why you choose the ones you do? Blowing off law school. Orgies. Crashing bikes. Whatever you and Tim Apparel do up in The City."

"Just passing time with a friend."

"No need to connect with anything. You don't require praise or affirmation. Disapproval doesn't affect you. I get it. But you know what Dr. Drew would say?"

"*LoveLine?*"

"Our secret."

"What would he say?"

"That what you do today is all about what happened yesterday. That hopelessness isn't some original condition. It is a species of lost hope. That the self-destructive ones love being alive more than all the rest. That lost hope is the phantom—lost but still alive. You either go out and try to recover it or pack your life with distractions."

Celia closed her eyes. We sat leg-to-leg against her bed. The day had been the usual succession of distractions. For nearly five years since walking away from Helen and into the speechwriting job I'd always opted for the next sensation. Just fun. No reasons. No point asking why. Too many ways to answer the same question. Nothing at stake.

I stood, and ran my fingers through Celia's hair. Whether I woke her or she hadn't been sleeping, I didn't know, don't know. Her eyes opened.

"Celia, I'm heading home."

CHAPTER 25   A GLITCH

The System tested out perfectly. Grades, first semester, second year: A–, A–, B+, B+. The big uncertainty was where I would work that next summer. I wavered, because I could. Through January, I held open offers in Austin, Dallas, and Los Angeles. Except for that one loose end, I looked forward to a leisurely rest of my second year. Then, as usual, I hit a bump in the road. Law school was back.

The System's first glitch came during our winter session. For Two Ls and Three Ls, Harvard replaces the long winter break with a four-week session in which students take one course, kind of like summer school. Brian, The Dynamo, The Kankoos, and I all signed up for Professor Stern's Evidence course. Stern was a brilliant, eccentric guy with a multimedia fetish. Reliable rumor had it that he once gave all but one person in his class A's. Rumor also had it that attendance was optional. The Ditch Ratio was enticingly high, going several years back. But if either of those facts was once true, neither was true anymore. Stern had taught his Evidence class the same way for several years, but this year he changed things. The class was to organize itself in groups of ten or twelve, and each group picked a project. In addition to the "project" straight out of a high school Social

Studies class, Stern revised his grading policy to more closely resemble the typical Harvard Law curve. He also instituted a traditional exam and a peer grading system.

Of course, we didn't find out about Stern's new policies until halfway through the first week of class, too late to switch courses. Having heard about the group requirement late in the game, we were among the last students to form a group. There were two types of people who had yet to find a group: those who had also planned to blow off the class and those who were so neurotically zero sum or cold stove that no other group would have them. Our group was composed equally of both types. On our side were a couple of otherwise diligent guys who had priorities other than law school and realized law school was all bullshit by that point. One of them was an Orthodox rabbi with a full house; the other a Mormon who was expecting his first baby during winter session. We weren't going to be making trips to The Foxy Lady with those two, but they were damn good guys, and on the same ditcher page for their own reasons. On the neurotic side were Franklin Hughes, Emerson Fitzgerald, and Anne Connely.

Franklin was equal parts Zero Summer and Cold Stover. He had bothered to transfer from Duke to Harvard during his second year of law school. His only friend, if you could call him that, was Emerson Fitzgerald, a rich kid who went to Harvard undergrad. Emerson was 80 percent Zero Summer, 20 percent Cold Stover—more competitive than neurotic. Rounding out the neuros was Anne Connely. Anne was 90 percent Cold Stover and 10 percent psychopath. She shed a handful of roommates in two years, a couple of whom she claimed were "stalking" her. During one group session, Anne was brought to tears over the issue of whether we should buy a laser printer from Circuit City and return it after we were done with the group project. Later, when we had to make a Web site for the group, she asked that I withhold her name. She was afraid that one of our research subjects might find out where she lived. I suspected she was a virgin. I was kind of attracted to her.

The advent of a group project had the Franklin/Emerson/Anne triumvirate more nervous than any of us. None of them fared well in groups. Each of them loathed the unfamiliar. Sensing the rest of the group's ambivalence only drew them closer to apoplexy. From the get-go, they used Stern's peer review system (upon which our group grades were partly determined) and the threat of exposing our slacking to make sure that everyone in the group behaved as neurotically as they did. In third grade, they were tattletales. At Harvard, they were the schoolyard bullies.

Worse, our assignment was the most challenging in the class. The other groups had the freedom to do whatever they chose—cheesy home movies, skits, songs. But because we had taken so long to form our group, Stern "suggested" our assignment. He had already promised the assignment to a lawyer friend of his, and no other group volunteered. It was a "real-life" assignment involving a film student, Kyle Epstein, who was arrested and charged with attempted arson. The D.A. claimed Kyle tried to burn down an apartment building while walking home from a late-night party. Kyle claimed it was a case of mistaken identity. The only witness was an ex-con transvestite who apparently saw a guy in bright green jogging shorts near the scene. Kyle was a half mile away from the scene when the cops stopped him. He was on a path that followed a straight route from the party to his home, a route that did not include the scene of the crime. Kyle was also nervous when the police stopped him. He had been drinking heavily and was only twenty years old. He was wearing army green shorts that night, and he was one of only a couple people on the streets at 4:00 A.M. That was enough for the police to arrest him and the D.A. to charge him with arson. Our assignment was to help Kyle's lawyer persuade the D.A. to drop the charges. Kyle was fucked, but he hadn't even begun to understand the gravity of his situation. Half of his supposed saviors hadn't attended a full set of classes among them over the last two years. We knew less criminal law than your average COPS devotee.

The first plain lesson to be taken from this: The System was fallible. That said, there is always a way to do less than expected of you, at Harvard Law School or anywhere else. Stern's Evidence class was no exception. We approached the class with two newly developed principles in mind, borrowed from Young & Mathers's do-only-what-matters-and-do-it-well motto. First, most "requirements" are not actually required. Second, if effort actually is required, make it count toward as many requirements as possible.

The first principle told us that attending class was not truly required. Groups met right after class ended. So we eased in the backdoor right after Stern finished class and joined our group as if we had been there all along. Most days, we sent only one representative from the four of us, along with a story about why the other three couldn't make it. That took care of the group attendance requirement. As for the group project, real effort was required. It seemed like Kyle might be innocent. That's when the second principle came in: make any effort count as much as possible. Fortunately, our group was made up of some of the most technologically inept people in academia. The Kankoos and I saw opportunity. He proposed, and the group agreed, that he and I create a Web site dedicated to making Kyle Epstein's case. The first day, we worked up the Web site in a couple hours. For ten more days, we complained to the group about how laborious it was. On the twelfth day, we showed the group the Web site. They were impressed. We were done. But we weren't yet done with that second principle. Professor Stern was so pleased with the Web site that he agreed to let us make it, along with a ten-page supplement about the Internet, our required third-year thesis paper. Other students' papers were 100 pages long and took an entire year to finish. With that one effort, The Kankoos and I had solved our group assignment problem and taken care of both of our thesis papers; a few hours of work, and we had each knocked off two classes.

We handled Stern's new exam with the same spirit. As in previous years, the exam was in-class. The difference was that Stern added an essay question to what was, in past years, just a multiple-choice exam. In typical Stern fashion, he leaked the gist of the question before the exam. It was expectedly broad—something like "Show me the essence of evidence."

The Kankoos and I rolled in from Foxwoods at 6:00 P.M. the day before the exam, and started getting our essay answers in order. Counting on Stern's kindred eccentricity, The Kankoos settled on comparing the law of evidence to blackjack. I decided to write my essay from five different first-person narratives (Stern loved perspective). In the middle of sketching out my essay answer, the phone rang. It was Elise, calling from San Antonio. I was in midsentence, but I told her I had ten good minutes.

What followed was a classic long-distance moment, where everything's great for the first nine minutes of a self-mandated ten-minute call; then somebody says something that comes out wrong; then the other (instead of saying she's probably misunderstood what was last said and is a little hurt by it) decides to make the speaker feel the same sting she felt through a completely different and usually more direct approach; then the speaker gets pissed and asks where the hell the other gets off saying whatever; then the other finally admits that she was hurt by the earlier statement; then they both find out it was all a big misunderstanding. But by then the ten minutes have long expired and no one feels like hanging up on such a bad note, so they talk for forty minutes more until each can hang up with a smiling "I love you." Then each smile diminishes within seconds as awful thoughts creep into each of their heads and then sometimes they call back and sometimes they don't. Suffice it to say you're not going to be real productive for the first few hours after one of those.

I was just hanging up and my smile was about to fade when The Kankoos, who was finishing up his essay in the next room, popped his head out:

"She loves you out of weakness."

"Are you trying to piss me off?"

"Not at all, Marquart. I've been there. Five years ago, I was damn serious about a girl. Her name was Amber."

Not in the mood for his lost love tale, I preempted him:

"What do you mean, 'out of weakness'?"

"Think back to a time when Elise was on top of her game—got all A's, won some contest, lost some weight, whatever. . . . Got an example?"

"Yeah."

"Alright. Now, try to be honest here. Was she more or less into you during those moments? Was she excited to celebrate the accomplishment with you, or was she a little more withdrawn? Were you more or less secure?"

With all of my zero sum and cold stove depth psychology, I'd never thought about Elise and me that way. But The Kankoos was right. The time Elise landed a new job, the time she got into good medical schools, especially when she went off to Spain—each time there was definitely a withdrawal. And I was less secure.

"You're right," I breathed.

"It's OK, Marquart. The truth is, every relationship occurs out of weakness to some extent or another."

"Yeah . . . So anyway, tell me about this Amber. Pretty hard to imagine The Kankoos in love."

"I cheated on her. She found out. She ditched me. Then I realized I loved her. Then she got married. And then I stopped caring."

"Whoa. Well, she loved you out of weakness anyway."

"I never said *she* loved *me* out of weakness. I just said I'd been there."

And so had I. I looked at the clock. It was 8:00 P.M., 5:00 P.M. in Los Angeles. I picked up the phone and made a call I no longer needed to put off:

"Mr. Mathers? It's Jaime Marquart. I'll be there this summer."

The next day, The Kankoos and I both got A's on Stern's exam. We finished an hour and a half early and headed back to The Parlour to celebrate. Five minutes into my first beer, the phone rang again.

"I'm not here," I said.

The Kankoos picked up the phone.

"Hello . . . yeah . . . yeah . . . thanks."

He shrugged, hung up the phone, and grabbed another beer.

"Who was it, Kankoos?"

"Kyle Epstein's lawyer. Channel Five ran a story on his case the other night. They showed our Web site and a bunch of people e-mailed the D.A. They just dropped the case. Pass me the Monsignor. This beer blows."

And that was the effective end of second year. From there on out, every day was like Sunday. There were no more glitches in The System. Second semester, second-year grades: B+, B, B+. And, my summer at Young & Mathers was settled. I would spend the first half of the summer with Elise, to try and get things right one last time, and the second half in L.A. Money was coming in from all sides and all of my options were open. Things could not have been better. And I was becoming profoundly unhappy.

CHAPTER 26 | **GOING HOME**

Pummeling El Niño rains started in December. That meant no biking. Our bodies were starved for thrill. So Tim Apparel and I moved into San Francisco hotel rooms, walking distance from PoMo. I don't recall eating, though I'm sure I did. We spent loads of money, but emerged with no durable goods. We began to smell bad, but in a way that we believed suggested vitality rather then destitution.

Law school pulled us back.

In mid-December, exams: Business Associations, Tax, and Civil Procedure II. I also handed in my "National 'X' Racial Formation" paper, still not knowing what the title of the course meant, but feeling good about the Wampanoag Indian paper, which I had an inkling would get an A. I took regular exams in the other classes, all pass-fail. I passed, which is to say I woke, ate, crapped, breathed. I did in fact get an A– on the paper, a 3.8 to be ridiculously exact, which put my grade point average somewhere above 3.4 at law school's midpoint, three semesters done, three to finish. My transcript was acquiring both bulk and solidity, and then lost its conspicuous gap, the Incomplete in Law and Social Science. In the middle of exams, I got an e-mail from the registrar. The Law and Social Science professor had caved, without explanation, and given me a grade; a K, credit, pass.

Law school was going swimmingly, so my concerns were elsewhere. The rain persisted throughout December. Like me, Tim Apparel was still writhing with a biking jones. He packed up his bikes and made the loose plan to hop airplanes between "warm dry places with hills" for the month between the end of exams and the beginning of the next semester. He'd amassed fifteen grand doing law firm work during the semester and was committed to blowing it all during the break. I didn't have that kind of cash. This meant a long month of solitude for me. Add to that the fact that the dense black smoke coming from the Beetle's tailpipes was indeed a harbinger of a moribund engine. Alone and immobile, I could feel one of Celia Shackles's phantoms knocking around inside me. It just rattled from within, like the bizarre noises from the apartment above you that have no obvious source, thereby converting mere annoyance into insoluble rage.

The rage started taking hold right after exams ended. I had driven Tim Apparel to the airport with the intention of heading to PoMo afterward. The Beetle's engine croaked curbside as Tim Apparel sprinted for his flight. I struggled to restart the Beetle. Each cylinder gasp was fainter than the previous one. Getting back to Stanford would be a drag without a car. Getting into San Francisco by taxi would cost a good chunk of my dwindling cash store. Screw it. I was at an airport. I still had credit card space. One of those officious airport traffic guys would have the Beetle towed and safely stored, probably before I made it through the ticket line and figured out where I was going.

Where was I going? Home, the deep, original home—New Hampshire. I flew to Boston first class ($1,875 one way), a relative bargain next to barbaric, jammed-to-the-edge "full-fare" coach ($1,000). Aboard the flight I slouched into a six-hour superiority complex, watching the soon-to-be-curtained-off wobble themselves back to row 38, seat E. In first class everyone emanated haughty relaxation, life without phantoms or middle seats.

The landing snapped me back among the masses, on the lower end at that, owing to my $153.17 cash balance at the ATM. Living loan check to loan check as I was, that would have to stretch four weeks, until the next semester began. The emergency credit cards had gotten me halfway through law school, back to Boston in comfort, and they would take me the rest of the way. At the Hertz desk, I rented a Mustang convertible, then headed north, toward New Hampshire, with the roof down and the heat at full blast. Midway to New Hampshire, at Kappy's Liquors, I charged a $3.50 half-pint of Jim Beam and put the roof up, both for concealment and because I was becoming reacquainted with wind chill. I rolled into my hometown at midnight, searching for revelation, and got it.

Durham, New Hampshire... *Look there!*... the field where I first smoked pot, and where I smoked pot again, many years later, with the wife of a prominent conservative pundit. *And there*... the tree I crashed my first car into; the basement where I first touched a boob; the high school that suggested I complete my education elsewhere; the planetarium we'd broken into and dropped acid in during a school dance; the police station where I'd sat handcuffed, waiting for Aimee to bail me out, after I'd committed a disorderly conduct act of conscience during a summer between years at Brown. Sweet memories, mostly, and yet... *fuck this place* with its stick-up-the-butt intelligentsia, always sneering if you didn't go to the Right College. These people's own kids, polite and compliant if not so bright, were off at Syracuse and Denison, worse than no college at all, doing tap sucks in the Beta House or sucking dick in the Boom Boom Lodge, getting the last bits of life out of themselves before firming their handshake and starting a career in brand managing.

When Durham gave me the push, I ignored my secret passion: ditch high school, head to California, and try to revive my career as a magician. My brother had done something like that—punt college, head to California, get into the music business. I admired his grit; lacked his courage, though. I took the Dullard route and became a valedictorian. Through it all, I suppose I cared about having left Durham as a consensus ne'er-do-well and aimed to return one day with all the right hardware. Dartmouth, Brown, Harvard—not just getting in and going, but landing awards there; then consorting with a rising political star, a Republican whom even university professors could love and who was beamed into the New Hampshire media market with me standing near him before I headed off to Stanford Law School.

Why law school? My hometown made me do it.

Flailing away and blaming, I turned the blame inward or, more to the point, shut it off and listened for what was really roiling me—my future. What were my plans? California, that piece I knew. The specifics were sketchy, though; full of the unknown. A solitary, loveless, drugged-out Road to Nowhere? Or perhaps the all-too-knowable (law firm, family, death)? Maybe the unknown and the all-too-knowable weren't so different. There in my First Place, some Last Place was drawing nearer. Time, again, to get out of town.

I headed back to California. Which would first mean driving to Boston and pissing another couple of grand to fly to where I had been less than ten hours ago, at the San Francisco airport, short of cash, and with a busted car, now no doubt impounded. As I approached the Boston airport exit, though, I had what seemed a mystical, possessed moment. Or at least I played it that way to myself. *Here's wishing you vision.* I drove past the exit and continued south on 95. To New Haven. Where Yale is and, getting right to it, where Helen lived. I was returning to Helen's apartment precisely five years from the day—December 21, 1991—that I had been alone there and gotten that phone call about writing speeches for Bill Weld.

What was happening here is easily explained. I was going back to the last certain future I'd held and tossed away. No, that's not entirely right. In fact, there had been other certain futures since Helen. I could have had some sort of not-so-miserable life working in politics or with either Lauren Leaven or Francine Lewis, those ersatz Helens who had turned up during law school. But Helen was looking like the Best Gig of All, and I was facing the tough truth that the Best Gig of All doesn't necessarily come last. With Helen, there had been a *good* certainty—smart conversation, reliably overwhelming sex, which about covered it all, I was starting to think. So I parked the Mustang in front of Helen's place, which had been my place for a time.

And just what was my objective? This: to reconstruct the past in its setting and on its anniversary, and figure out why I had so suddenly and remorselessly excised Helen from all my future visions. There was also the real possibility of a face-to-face with Helen. I imagined, and believe I hoped, it would go something like this: *I knock. The door opens. There is a wave of heart-thumping consternation. Memories are revived. Passions resurrected. Reluctance gives way. Letting go and forgiveness rule the day. Silence and tears. I stand again in the apartment Helen and I shared, see the television we watched together, the shower curtain that had originally been mine, in graduate school, where we met, and the dress that most captured Helen's essence hanging in the closet. . . . Calm sets in and I roam the apartment as I once did. I take a leak in the bathroom with the door closed, a habit five years dormant seamlessly revived, and then sit in the living room to contemplate where to go from here.*

I am the least prescient person I know. Invariably, I read the future exactly wrong. When I was a bike messenger, a temp worker told me about a breaking news item that to me sounded like a minor, one-day news story (Clarence Thomas and Anita Hill). This time, though, I had it right.

I stood outside the door to Helen's apartment and consciously recorded that this could be my life's last destiny-altering event. The door did open. It wasn't even locked. I did stand again among the familiar. I instantly spotted the television, the shower curtain, and the dress, because they were all that remained. My vision was accurate in its specifics, lacking only what it assumed. Helen. Helen was gone, freshly gone it seemed, but utterly gone. She had moved and left the shit she no longer wanted. I went to the bathroom, reflexively and uselessly closed the door, and then out to sit alone on the wood floor in the living room.

There was still time to catch the last flight to San Francisco, so I headed to the Mustang, not as spooked and dispirited as you might imagine at not only having failed to slay the phantom problem, but having compounded it by discovering what it was. At the curb next to the Mustang, there was a pile of garbage—not the smelly kind, but the kind that marks someone moving on. Somewhere in the middle was my graduate school thesis with a faded Chunky Monkey pint top stuck to its vinyl cover. There were also yellow receipts from an earlier spate of in-school credit card debt, times with Helen during graduate school—the Border Cafe in Cambridge, a western Massachusetts bed-and-breakfast (with a surcharge for a collapsed four-poster). Then, my Rosetta stone: a calendar, Helen's, for the current year at the time, 1996, with the usual jottings of appointments and notable dates. I scanned for an obvious boyfriend pattern (none discernible); reassurance (Zoë the cat, now five, going to regular vet appointments); and general signs of motion. It was in this last category—motion—that I found my answer. There was none. No motion. The calendar revealed the same nouns, tedious cycles, and dull colleagues for drinks from five years ago; the same sources of anxiety and disaffection that had fallen out of my nostalgic memory, but had made it possible not just to abandon Helen, but also to ignore her while I was working for Weld. All our stories have unique details, often held together by genuine affection and a few stunning coincidences that seem to make them worth telling. The thickest narrative thread, though, is often common, basically cliché. I truly had remembered only the good things.

Even so, why not track down Helen? I still had a month off school and plenty of credit card space. The search might have been full of motion and adventure. Perhaps finding and seeing Helen again would negate the whole stagnant calendar epiphany. And the calendar, I know, was soft confirmation that I had actually fled stasis. Helen might well have been full of undocumented activity those five years. I did give the calendar another look, chronologically, and found nothing, through November. Then, in December, the calendar's final written entry, for that very day, December 21, 1996, Helen had written:

Move to Chicago

I tossed the calendar back on the junk pile and got in the Mustang, driving, back on 95, north, a Big Audio Dynamite CD I had lifted from Helen's refuse, the same CD we'd fucked to, playing on the surprisingly fine factory stereo. *If I had my time again / I would do it all the same / And not change a single thing / Even when I was to blame . . .* going to California, this time for good, heading home.

At the San Francisco airport, I rented another Mustang. From there I was straight to Haight and Fillmore. Clara nodded my way. She'd watch the car. I went to the head shop first, because I needed all new gear, which amounted to three glass pipes, to account for breakage, and five disposable lighters. The first time, it seemed so exotic. Now crack smoking was looking like the fast food of drugs, which goes a long way toward explaining its popularity. A dumb move, loading myself with accouterments before the buy; usually we left the stuff in PoMo. I gathered my last hundred dollars cash, already converted to five twenties at the airport, folded them into separate one-inch squares, and put two in the right front pocket, one in the left back, one in the left front, and one in the little "change" pocket. I crossed Fillmore, into the Zone, where they knew me.

"You looking for Paris?"

"I guess so."

"Paris dead. He fall offa airplane."

Though the backstory to Paris's end (*off* an airplane? from where?) was nearly as intriguing as the payoff, I got to business with Hank, one of the most esteemed crack merchants in this part of San Francisco. He executed the move—pick the dropped bill off the pavement, drop a rock in its place. I headed to PoMo and bolted the bathroom shut. I set myself up yogalike, in a legs apart, back erect pose. For a day of so much dangling suspense and syn-chronicity, this turn of events had no dangle. I knew it was fake. Not by sight or feel, but by smell and sound. My lips never made it to the pipe. I'd bought a macadamia nut and transformed it into a charred lump. Back out to the street, then.

For the next buy, I forged deeper into the Zone, where the courage to go in is generally rewarded with real drugs at a reasonable price. I found my guy, more crunchy and Upper Haight than usual.

"Whaddaya need?"

"Four twenties."

He went to the drop. I crossed the street to wait. The rain slowed, then stopped. The dealer returned with a loaded handshake. I headed straight to the rental car, drove thirty feet, and came to a stop at the corner of Haight and Fillmore, a long red light. I pulled the four tiny, twisted balloon rubber pouches from my underwear band. I opened one. Not fake. Powder. Pow-der coke I could live with. This was powder smack. I stopped the rental in front of a driveway and flicked on the flashing hazards. I walked fast, like a worried person, like Victoria Sentence, back to the Zone and found the crunchy guy who, knowing he had sold me good stuff, also knew this wasn't an angry mission and, instinctively, that I wasn't a cop.

"What's up, my man?"

"Sorry, I meant rock."

"Not a problem. I'll fix you up."

And he did. Four of the chunkiest rocks I'd ever handled. I put three in my change pocket and rolled the remaining one in my fingers like a magician cascading a half-dollar. I had not a red cent, cash, for the next month, save for some stray change, yet I walked back to the car with a lilty gait. At the Haight-Fillmore bus stop, I put the last rock in my pocket, grabbed for coin, and unloaded all my change on Clara. She pocketed it.

Then: *screech*. Transmission thumps into Park. Lights. Doors click open. Doors slam shut. Long-stemmed flashlights held by their ends. Leather-metal utility belts crunch and rattle.

Po-Po.

"He sell you drugs?"

The question was to Clara. The person about to get fried, though, was the *he*—me? Two clear options, and only two. Run. Or, light a cigarette and do what someone who didn't in fact just sell drugs would do: don't run. Dealers run. Buyers toss. Citizens stay, don't run. And I hadn't sold Clara drugs. That I was loaded with rock, borderline dealing quantity at that, could diminish, in the eyes of the law, my being vouched for by someone they busted regularly on five-dollar doorway blow job raps. There was also the gear: a still-hot pipe sleeved in my sock and leaving a pearly ankle singe; the two spare pipes, plus the five lighters; and my pupils, too big for dusk. Clara walked into the street, then stopped. She appeared to be marshaling her thoughts, the way law students do when a professor calls on them. The cruiser blocked traffic in both directions. Onlookers looked on. I lit a cigarette and waited. The cops waited, too, for an answer. Unlike the minivan, this crash wasn't inevitable. Clara answered:

"No."

No was the only good answer. *Fuck you I don't do that shit,* possibly a richer and truer response, wouldn't have worked for me. Just *no.* The cops drove away. As did I, back toward Stanford, with an unabating case of the shakes, either because I felt "almost arrested" or because I was torching up, less than a block from where the almost arrest happened, out of a glass pipe, which looks nothing like a cigarette, a regular pipe, or a cigar, or anything but a crack pipe. I took the long way back, via Skyline, down the canyons, back up the canyons, then down to the ocean, where I slept, on the beach, at Half Moon Bay, until it started raining again.

I got back to the house the next morning. The front door was open. Every light, television, and stereo was on. We'd left two days before, in a rush, to get Tim Apparel to the airport. I checked my e-mail. School was out for a month and I'd been gone for less than two days, so I wasn't expecting the usual volume that greets a return home. I was hoping for a few stray e-mails, though, even a dreary solicitation that I could read, and affirm to myself some comprehension of and connection to the normal world.

I'd gotten two phone calls, one letter, and one e-mail while I was in Boston, New Hampshire, New Haven, and San Francisco.

Niccola had left a phone message, announcing a possible visit. She'd be in L.A. "sometime soon," staying with an actress friend, Claire, and was "considering a trip up north to finally meet the lovely Tim Apparel." The other phone message was from Francine Lewis: "I need a fucking moot court partner for next semester. Call if you're interested." There was also a piece of regular mail, from Young & Mathers, confirming I would be there as a summer associate, five months down the line. The e-mail was from Boston:

```
FROM: "Dawn E." <dawne@mfa.org>
TO: "Robert Byrnes" <rcbyrnes@leland.stanford.edu>
SUBJECT: you're a hard man to find

surprise!
do you even remember me? i hope so.
how goes it all?
ended up not going to new york. i'm at the museum of
fine arts, boston instead. law school might be some-
where in my future. advice?
do write soon.

dawn
```

Dawn. From Boston. Never thought she'd turn up again. I couldn't find her, yet she found me.

PART 10 | **END**

CHAPTER 27 | QUITE FRANKLY, QUITE FRANKLY

One morning in the middle of my second summer, as I hid in my Young & Mathers office with the door shut, the lights down and ESPN Gamecast on, begging for one more run from the Yanks in the bottom of the eighth, I got an unexpected phone call.

"Jaime Marquart. At last! I guess a good man *is* hard to find!" said an inviting, vaguely familiar female voice. An intense feeling of agitation was all that prevented the beginnings of a woody. The Yanks were down to their last out, and two more runs would really make my morning. Who the hell was calling me?

"It's Victoria!"

"."

"Victoria Sentence."

"."

"*Vicky* Sentence?"

"Oh yeah, Vicky. *Vicky Sentence?*" I asked.

"Yes, of course! I heard you were in town and thought I'd give you a ring. It's really been too long."

I was like, "not long enough." I would have said it had the Yanks not just put two runners in scoring position with a two-strike single. I suddenly felt playful.

"Yes, yes, too long, too long! How the hell are ya? Still bangin' around with that Supreme Court clerk? Wonder if he's tried on O'Connor's robe yet, *if you know what I mean.*"

"Actually, I haven't spoken to Ronald in some time. I was more interested in how you were doing." Vicky's pleasing tone was unrelenting.

"Job's great. People here care if they win. I work hard."

I was telling the truth, but I'd omitted that Elise and I were struggling to stay afloat, I was gambling about a thousand a day on the most impossible sport to handicap, and I was drinking myself to sleep most nights. "How *you* doin'?" I managed, as the next batter swung at strike two.

"I'm fine as well, thanks. I'm here at Meeger Talley this summer. Getting *great* work, too! Speaking of which, I just found out about a wonderful networking opportunity for you, and I just had to call. My firm's sponsoring a luncheon today on the status of the independent tort of spoliation and they've asked us to invite a few of our brightest friends to come along. Naturally, I thought of you."

"Naturally."

Ball three. Full count.

"Of course, it will also be a great opportunity to mix and mingle with some of Meeger Talley's rainmaker partners. You sound pretty happy at Young & Mathers, but it could be lucrative . . ."

Home run. Home-fucking-run! I had just made me a much needed three hundred dollars. Blood rushed back toward my jimmy. Vicky was still talking, her words now strangely sexual:

"I know it's late notice; it starts in a few hours in fact. I tried to call sooner and missed you, but it's just down the street at McCormick's a—"

"McCormick's? Isn't that the fancy seafood joint?"

"Yes, I think so. The keynote speaker is one of our most learned advocates of—"

"I'll be there."

"Great! I can't wait to see you there," she said. "Oh, by the way, love," she added in a tone I would have sworn was sexual had it not been Vicky Sentence on the other end of the line. "Could you do me a big favor and tell them Victoria sent you when you sign in? Couldn't hurt to let Meeger's brass know who's bringing in the talent."

Finally, the self-important motive was apparent. Still, it's hard to insult a guy with free crab legs and filet mignon. Besides, all pomposity aside, Meeger Talley was one of the oldest and most prestigious firms in the country, which meant the best-paying. Word had it they had just surprised their first-year lawyers with a "boom year" bonus of $25,000 on top of having the country's highest base salary. I was happy at Young & Mathers, at least as happy as I was going to be at the time. But an extra twenty-five grand or more a year was good enough to check out for a poor boy from Eagle Lake, Texas, who was clearly going to be very bad with money.

So I showed up early. But first I put the six hundred the Yanks had returned me into a two-team parlay that would make back last week's paycheck if I could pull off two more games in a row. A Dodgers win over the Astros and a San Fran win later that day would erase the entire last week's losses.

With the company predictably dull, the lawyer babble indecipherable, and the Dodgers about to throw the first pitch, I was eyeing the exit sign by my fifth king crab leg. Then a flicker of hope, or at least mild interest, appeared. Robert Byrnes, the enigmatic Young & Mathers recruit I'd met during interviews, had just sat down at the table of eight others I'd been eating with. He wore ripped shorts, an Alice in Chains T-shirt that revealed a band of tattoos around his right arm when he reached to grab a piece of bread, four visible piercings, and hideously fluorescent sneakers. I noted that he was a little older than most of the summer associates. He was conspicuously silent as the conversation bounced around our suddenly eclectic table. Whether his silence was due to poised independence or the simple ostracism of a suspected weirdo, I couldn't be sure. His only expression was a millisecond wince as Vicky Sentence returned from a round of mingling and took the seat next to me.

Jessica and Alan were also at the table, two talkative Zero Summer classmates of mine from Harvard. I hoped they would ultimately decide to work in a different city. They dominated the conversation. Over their shoulders, back in the bar, a television screen was tuned to the Dodgers' game, just under way.

"No way! You should totally not date someone from work," Jessica was saying.

"I agree. Quite frankly, it can only be detrimental to the working environment," Alan said. "I'm never one to dip my pen in the company ink, *if you catch my drift.*"

"So who *do* you date if you're at work most of your waking hours?" Jessica asked.

"Nobody!" Alan said.

There was laughter, which I awkwardly joined a little after the fact. The Dodgers had loaded the bases with no one out in the first.

Vicky Sentence whispered something into my ear about the partner seated at our table. I didn't hear her. All I caught was the phrase "book of business."

"Welcome to the real world!" Jess proclaimed with mock beleaguerment. "Actually, it is hard to balance a personal relationship with a professional lifestyle. You just have to *make* the time to get out and have a life."

"We hear you *made a little time* last weekend, Jess."

Jessica feigned embarrassment. "Alan, I can't believe you just said that in front of a *partner*. I must be beet red."

"If you guys want me to treat this as a confidential conversation in chambers, I will; or I can recuse myself to the lavatory," the partner said.

More laughter. The partner had made a law joke.

"So, Jess, tell us about your big weekend," Alan continued.

"Oh, it was nothing. Alan, I'm going to kill you when we get back."

"Don't look at me. Just something I heard."

"Well, OK—but it's *really* nothing. I can't believe I'm telling you this. Anyway. I was out in Santa Monica last Friday night and I was talking to this guy..."

An almost-collective "Oooooooohhhh..." redounded.

"Slut," Byrnes muttered sarcastically. I laughed. No one else seemed to have heard him.

"So can you make it?" Vicky whispered again to me.

Fuck! I almost yelled. The Astros had just blown the game open with a three-run double. That same team couldn't get a run across the day before, when I had two hundred on them. Today they were the world champs. I nodded my head in rhythm with Vicky's question, completely unaware of what she was asking.

Byrnes, meanwhile, appeared unengaged. He had refocused his efforts on separating the clam from his chowder.

Jessica continued to discuss her weekend encounter, and with exhaustive detail—address of the club ("just off Third"), prevailing music ("Flock of Seagulls, you know, early eighties cheese"), a "candid" assessment of her man ("He was handsome, but I have to admit a little dim"). She built to her story's climax, her initial reluctance either forgotten or dropped.

"So for like half the night this guy is going, 'I can't believe you're an attorney' and I'm like, 'Well, I *am* an attorney.' And so he goes, 'Let me see some proof.' So I show him my law school ID."

"Uh-oh. The H-bomb!"

"And he just went, 'Wow, I'm really surprised.' I was like, 'Get away from me.'"

Others confirmed that the guy was "*soo* rude." The Dodgers finally got out of the first inning, three runs in the hole. My parlay was in serious doubt after the first half hour of what was supposed to be seven more hours of entertainment. I gripped my napkin tightly and ground my teeth, making every effort to keep from slinging crab refuse across the room.

While others nodded and chuckled at usual intervals, Byrnes did neither. His manner might have appeared arrogant or dismissive to everyone but me. I was still uncertain about the source of his reticence.

I finally caught enough of Vicky's words to figure out what she had been whispering. I was one of a "select few" that Mr. Meeger had invited to join him at "The Club" after lunch, which I'd apparently already agreed to. The gist of it was that Meeger Talley—the same firm that wouldn't even give me an on-campus interview because my first-year grades were under their minimum—was now recruiting me, my grades nearing an A– average during my second year. Vicky stood to get a big money bonus, not to mention immeasurable "brownie points," for recruiting a fellow Harvard grad.

Alan took the conversational baton back from Jessica:

"Jess, remember that guy in our section who always talked about how his dream was to work at Meeger?"

"Mr. Inappropriate? Of course I remember him."

"My favorite Mr. Inappropriate story is how he spent his whole Meeger interview telling the partner how much he hated tax law. Well, come to find out the partner he was interviewing with was the *head of the tax department.*"

"Oh…my…God! That is *soo* unprofessional."

"Anyway, Mr. Inappropriate tried to salvage the interview by telling the partner about how his moot court brief was runner-up for best brief and…"

"And they dinged him anyway," Jessica finished.

More laughter.

"Never knew what hit him," said Alan.

"Unbelievable," said the partner.

The Dodgers got one run in the bottom of the first, but the Astros were threatening again in the second. I got up to leave. Then, his voice sluggish like a cold engine, still staring into his chowder, Byrnes spoke:

"My moot court partner and I actually had to tank it."

Alan's response to Byrnes, coming with a flat delivery and outside the usual response time that signals true interest, was obligatory, more suspicious and repellent than genuinely curious.

"Why is that?" Alan asked.

"Because we might have won if we didn't. And we had to lose."

I jerked away from the game to hear the rest. But that was it. The Byrnes moot court story ended there. His own curt and annoyingly cryptic response did nothing to allay the suspicion around the table that he was either being flippant or attempting to advertise an intelligence so keen that failure demanded effort. I had my own doubts, I admit. *Had* to lose moot court? *What did that mean?* Byrnes shrugged.

"With that, I'll bid adieu," Vicky said, rolling her eyes as they made contact with the partner's.

"Me too," said Jessica. "I've got a *ton* of work to get off my plate."

"Same here, lot to get out the door, lot to get out the door," said Alan, rushing after her.

Everyone except Byrnes got up to leave.

"Well, Jaime, we're pushing off," sighed Vicky. "Coming?"

I paused. Going meant an extra $25,000, or at least a chance to tell a bunch of stodgy old suits to go to hell when it meant something. And staying…actually, staying didn't mean a whole hell of a lot. Young & Mathers couldn't care less if I checked out another firm, and Byrnes certainly didn't look like he needed company. Out of the corner of my eye,

I caught a glimpse of more Astros rounding the bases. *I have to be some-place else*, I thought. Someplace where I can get piss drunk and yell at the screen. In shorts.

"No, thanks."

"Let me get this straight," Vicky sniffed, out of anyone else's earshot, "you're passing up an opportunity to make more money at a top-tier firm so you can hang out with a bunch of tattooed freaks in ripped T-shirts?"

"Pretty much."

They left. Byrnes looked up from his chowder.

"I need a Jim Beam," he said.

"I need five runs and a loan shark," I said.

"Let's roll."

On Byrnes's lead, we headed out of McCormick's and back toward Young & Mathers.

"Just curious, Byrnes. You *had* to lose moot court?"

Byrnes's expression, though generically a smile, was more exactly a look of concession coupled with delight; concession that he had been a bit dramatic by inviting further probing instead of just telling his damn moot court story; and delight, not only that I had picked up on his affectation, but that I had called him on it.

"It's actually about more than moot court. But it's a pretty good story."

And so Byrnes and I walked toward our office. He told me why he went to law school—to get a clean break and find solitude—and how he spent most of it haunted by his past. Byrnes and I were very different people. He was nine years older, much more the bohemian poet, and had enjoyed harder drugs and spicier sex than I had. But in his past, I saw my own. He and I shared an early reverence for Big Things—politics for him, religion and Harvard for me. We had both wanted to believe and we had each reluctantly separated ourselves from those institutions, to some degree. But none of the similarities could obscure the cold truth: I had a long way to go to be that free. So I wondered, *In Byrnes's past, might I also see my future? In his Helen, my Elise? In his fall, my own?*

As we stopped at a street crossing, a sign reading HANK'S AMER-ICAN BAR AND GRILL entered my peripheral vision, and I remembered the big bet that had oddly slipped my mind. Hank's was a gritty little dive with angry senior citizen patrons, but it had a TV. I'd spent a couple of days watching games there when the action got too suspenseful for Internet play-by-play. We were now just a few blocks away from Young & Mathers, and Byrnes had come to the midpoint of his second year in law school. He was out of money and had almost been arrested. There were still three months until the moot court story.

"Those three months are where all the action is. But it's a longer story than three blocks. I'll tell you the rest at the next lunch."

The street light changed.

"Fuck that," I said. "Tell me now."

We headed into Hank's, set up a tab, and Byrnes finished his story.

CHAPTER 28 | **LOSING MOOT COURT**

The January between semesters second year was my most barren, alone, and moneyless period in law school. There was nowhere to be, and fittingly so. I was going nowhere. The Beetle needed a new engine ($1,600) and would be in the shop until classes began, end of January, when the next round of loan checks came available. My motorcycle had no throttle, meaning it operated with a fixed gas flow and thus only at fifty miles per hour, no more, no less. Niccola had phoned to say that she would be in California "at the end of January." Tim Apparel would be returning around the same time. Until then: alone. Tim Apparel retrieved all the couch change before leaving on his world biking tour, so there would be no cash until loan checks. And there was no biking to be done. It rained all January, a stiffer, angrier rain than anything I had known in the East. All I saw of the outdoors was through windows and on TV, when the San Francisco stations covered flooding, the canoes-on-Main-Street kind, in downtown Palo Alto.

Eating was a binary rotation: once a day, before bed, torpor-inducing amounts of Domino's one night, then Chinese, then Domino's, Domino's again, Chinese, always on the never-a-balance MasterCard, which became a different kind of credit card as it crept near its $12,000 limit. The Jim

Beam, from that first Costco visit, a *glump-glump-glupp* before eating, a *splash-splop* after, made it an early-to-bed, late-to-rise regimen. Soon the Jim Beam was gone.

Out of liquor, homebound, and my sleeping time reduced, the days became longer, and I was burdened by the itch of mental clarity. One Tuesday I woke at six with resolve to do many things. Checking e-mail is a good step toward a productive day, so I did. Since returning from my Boston/New Hampshire/New Haven/San Francisco whirl and getting the e-mail from Dawn, she and I had established a regular back-and-forth, initially about law school and what she liked to call the "mirage" Los Angeles law firm, Young & Mathers, where I'd be working the coming summer. On this Tuesday, Dawn wrote:

```
FROM: Dawn
TO: Robert Byrnes
SUBJECT: law school


everyone i knew that went to law school loathed it
and went on to horrendous jobs carrying staggering
debt.
     it's funny you mention working at an L.A. law
firm. I'm finally ready to get off my world-weary ass
and move there, get into the movie business. it's a
mental health strategy. the best way to cope is to
always be making plans to be somewhere else.
     just occurred to me that after you left for law
school, i kept finding you, trying to find you, in
ghosted half-conscious reminders. seeing sunset
boulevard at the brattle (sassy william holden char-
acter, guess that makes you an incarnation of an
archetype); also, my hairdresser, your namesake — if
you had a gay, tad chunky twin also named robert,
he'd be doing my hair...actually, the first time i
went to him, he smacked me in the head — hard — with
the hairdryer, and it was love at first appointment.
```

Then I found another task: picking classes. Stanford requires that you take at least ten units per semester. I had taken fifteen units, four classes, the previous semester, so this coming semester I'd dip to the minimum and have no more than three exams—all of which would maximize spring biking and compensate for the January wash-out. I made my choices: Capital Markets and Securities Regulation, Family Law, Protection of Personality. 4+3+2 = 9 units. I needed one more. Problem: one-unit classes are both dull (e.g., Accounting) and their professors take attendance, likely a function of the dullness. So I looked at two-unit courses. Further problem: the only two-unit course was Moot Court. Moot Court had light work requirements, but you had to form a group of two. Francine Lewis had called looking for a moot court partner. No fucking way. She'd approach it like the invasion of Normandy. You could sign up for Moot Court singly, and then be paired with another who had done the same. But unless both members of a randomly arranged team share an identical vision for how difficult or how easy they intend to make Moot Court, it's a bad bargain. The drift of human nature is that it is the slacker who is compelled to adjust his output upward. I taped a note on Tim Apparel's door:

¿MOOT COURT?

With that, I put the course selection aside. Another unit or two would turn up. Having been awake for twenty minutes, I felt as if it was time to claim the reward for a productive day. There were still two rocks remaining from the almost arrest. I broke half of one into the pipe, enough to last an hour if sensibly rationed. This hit, though, was going to be lavish, festive, billowing, hyperbolic, absurdly delightful—irrationally rationed—a cloud of pleasure wasted in the air, dissipated, but appreciated nonetheless, for its beauty, the bodily pleasure both given and foregone. It was. The way a last hit should be. It's the only way to quit, feeling just the good side of an ultimately not good drug, and still having some left when you come down to stay. *Running out isn't quitting.* I quit. I taped the remaining rock and a half to the moot court note I'd left for Tim Apparel, finished his bedside Jim Beam, slept until it was dark, and woke up to consolidate that, on this Tuesday in January, I had gotten a lot done. I had chosen

(most of) my law school classes for the second semester of my second year
and knocked off crack cocaine forever.

Why quit? That question doesn't require multiple journeys into the past
or tracking down phantoms. I quit because I didn't want to go to jail—
deterrence. But for five minutes as part of a disorderly conduct scared-
straight "sentence," I hadn't been to jail. I hadn't really done time, but that's
one stove I didn't need to touch. I trusted movie images where jail is punishing
and squalid and had no reason to believe that jail would be starkly different from its on-screen portrayal. I fancied myself pretty hard in some
respects. I could take a good whack on my bike and push uphill endlessly
despite the pain. But I was also a person who found Dartmouth College too
rough-edged and mean-spirited. I'd suffer badly in jail, the way you're supposed to, and I'd never be able to transfer to the gentle Brown University
of jails. Quitting came at a cost. It was my first gesture of self-discipline since
I'd decided to become a superstar high school student, a long time ago. Forever, I'll fight back happy crack memories. And if they sold packets of
brand-name crack at the Rite Aid, legally, I'd buy a bundle every time I
went to get earplugs, shampoo, and various nicotine supplements that supposedly wean me away from the only drug that feels impossible to quit. But
crack isn't legal, it never will be legal, and someday I'd get arrested.
Someday I'd be sitting in county with the guys who deal rock and do lookout at Haight and Fillmore. So why quit? The law. One-step program.

. . . *Bababooey, Bababooey* . . . Tim Apparel's voice, not live but coming
from my laptop. Instead of the usual quack, eep, or beep, my laptop alerted
me with digitally recorded Tim Apparel saying *Bababooey*. It was a reminder,
too, that if Tim Apparel hadn't pirated me an Ethernet connection, I would
have no e-mail. *Bababooey.* I had new e-mail. From Dawn. Having exhausted
the law school topic, we filled in the two years since we'd seen each
other. She told me: working at the Museum of Fine Arts in Boston; dis-
solution with boyfriend; attending to dying grandmother instead of going
to New York. And then she moved backward through her life: working her
way through Harvard, growing up blue collar in Pittsburgh, raised by her
grandparents. I did the same. I told her everything you know, and then

some. It took three and a half weeks and a couple of hundred e-mails in each direction to bring us both into the present tense, which coincided with Tim Apparel's return at the end of January. He walked into my room as I hit Send.

```
FROM: Robert Byrnes
TO: Dawn
SUBJECT: recovered memory

just remembered the first girl in the world i ever
kissed was named dawn (summer after fifth grade).
```

"The City?" Tim Apparel asked.

"I quit."

"Quit law school?"

I tossed Tim Apparel the glass pipe. He left and I sat waiting for Dawn's e-mail reply. An hour later Tim Apparel returned to my room. Still no e-mail. He crawled under my bed, cheek-to-carpet and found what he was looking for this time.

Then: *Bababooey, Bababooey*. I punched up the e-mail:

```
FROM: Dawn
TO: Robert Byrnes
SUBJECT: recovered memory

what's that gal with the nifty name doing these days?
```

Tim Apparel dropped the stray rock into the pipe, torched it, and listened for a sizzle, the crack in crack. He continued holding fire to the pipe until all the residue was spent. He said:

"I quit, too. Let's do Moot Court. Two easy units. Mandatory pass-fail. Write a shitty brief. First round of oral arguments is April 14th. We lose, and we're out. Hit the trails all spring. Clean living. Let's go get loan checks. I'm out of money."

With me and Tim Apparel in chemical, academic, and financial alignment, I spent the next two months writing and receiving e-mails. Between January and April, 1,260 e-mails passed between me and Dawn; 110,880 words, longer than this book. There was a critical plot point:

FROM: Robert Byrnes
TO: Dawn
SUBJECT: recovered memory

niccola? she's still in boston.

FROM: Dawn
TO: Robert Byrnes
SUBJECT: recovered memory

right, niccola. at the time i had the hugest college
girl "thing" for you. i can finally relate this, much
to your amusement. it was ironic — i was an alterna-
gal and then you introduced me to niccola, who was
about as blonde and mainstream as they get, so i figured i was utterly not your type.

FROM: Robert Byrnes
TO: Dawn
SUBJECT: recovered memory

i remember everything but the "thing" for me.

FROM: Dawn
TO: Robert Byrnes
SUBJECT: recovered memory

how disappointing. you were supposed to tell me how
dark, intriguing, and utterly alluring i was.

FROM: Robert Byrnes
TO: Dawn
SUBJECT: recovered memory

i did think something like that — dark, alluring,
organically cool. those were hazy days for me, but the
day you met niccola is vivid; you were over near the
window in the gov's office, niccola and i were walking
out the door; the two of you exchanged some unsuccessful

banter about careers and connections then we left. i
had the impression you were unimpressed by me.

FROM: Dawn
TO: Robert Byrnes
SUBJECT: recovered memory

nice of you to remember my being by the window for
the introduction. i recall it being a black-cloud
day. i was sure that you'd pointedly made the introduction to your goddess girlfriend, niccola, to set
me straight of any 'seducing robert' aspirations i
might have had.

FROM: Robert Byrnes
TO: Dawn
SUBJECT: niccola

she actually claims to be visiting here this weekend. she and tim apparel have fallen into a phone
crush. niccola and I are post-sexual, but she's
arranging a fix-up with her actress friend, claire,
who has requested someone who will "rock her all
night long"; should i? can i?

FROM: Dawn
TO: Robert Byrnes
SUBJECT: niccola

do what you will and what you want!

FROM: Robert Byrnes
TO: Dawn
SUBJECT: the last true thing

it turns out that niccola's actress friend (claire)
is a true beauty; offspring of two princeton profs,
plenty of intell. inside; concert violinist.

late getting rolling saturday...i woke for good
at three after a wankie and restless day of what was
properly beauty sleep; i haven't much margin for
aesthetic error, you know.

i pick them up at the airport, crank the music,
roll down the windows; '73 beetle roars, new engine.

we get here, the house; would claire like a
drink? many, hold the water.

the fix is in. tim apparel is chatting with niccola; eight or so hours down the line, they'll be
screwing, and they'll have company.

claire comes to my room to examine my cds; she
finds satisfaction in van morrison, and i feign equal
passion.

time for a tour of my pictures, carefully
selected to show the evolution from uneasy adolescent
to cocksure chap, sporting just a soupçon of danger-
ousness, and most recently standing on the half moon
bay sands, sun striking the midriff, just so.

"do you still have that 'six-pack?'" claire asks.
i feign again: reticent, *what-are-you-talking-
about?* embarrassment.

away we go! to san francisco; claire and me in
the beetle; in another car: tim apparel, niccola,
and francine lewis — she, too, has taken a shine to
tim apparel, and seems ok with sharing.

claire insists that we listen, at maximum volume,
to haydn, #104, "london symphony," running time
approximately that of a hasteless car ride from palo
alto to san francisco; we drink a bike bottle of icy
vodka; our conversation moves like a fugue; she
bites her lip as crescendos relax; when they rise, i
witness extended air violin for the first time, and
it is good.

at pomo, things fall apart:

niccola wigs out from some brutal stew of pills
and liquor; claire and francine lewis erupt in

conflict over astrology; finally, claire wigs out
at niccola's having wigged out; turns out claire
is opposed to even a hint of insanity; the me
and claire thing goes all to shit. claire will
stay with her brother, san francisco resident,
rather than step into the night with me. she has
deemed me entirely resistible. i drive her to the
brother's place; we chat, smoke american spirits,
exchange numbers, part; see ya' . . . never . . .

tim apparel, niccola, and francine lewis all
came back here, started off in the car, i'm told,
before finishing on tim apparel's bed; i stayed in
the city, found paris, who is not in fact dead, to
prove to myself that i could say no, and i did: had
a beer at pomo, just a beer, me and paris, that was
that, because i might have found a truth worth holding
onto. i drove home at dawn with the replacements
blaring.

[and now a word from niccola, who is just emerging from tim apparel's bedroom]
Dear Dawn:
Excuse me, but I am very much in need of a new
friend. Someone dark, intriguing and utterly
alluring. I have high standards for best friends &
boyfriends . . . must be someone always making plans
to be somewhere else and who moves with stealth, as
if in possession of much secret knowledge. A puma.
Best,
Niccola

FROM: Dawn
TO: Robert Byrnes
SUBJECT: the last true thing

i'm still extracting the claws from my shoulder. i'm
either disappointed that niccola is less discerning
in her ability to pick up subtleties or that she's

so very protective of her darling robert. i, of
course, pose no threat, being much more the wolf
than the mountain lion.

FROM: Robert Byrnes
TO: Dawn
SUBJECT: the last true thing

you think you're disappointed? here i am, eyes
averted from the claire failure — with only some
wild urgency causing me to commit several true con-
fessions to your sole possession, and you are merely
disappointed.

FROM: Dawn
TO: Robert Byrnes
SUBJECT: the last true thing

you may consider me unappreciative of being the
recipient of some gang-bang authored drug-induced
snideness from your lost weekend.

FROM: Robert Byrnes
TO: Dawn
SUBJECT: the last true thing

is that to say you're upset?

FROM: Dawn
TO: Robert Byrnes
SUBJECT: the last true thing

is that to say that you're concerned?

FROM: Robert Byrnes
TO: Dawn
SUBJECT: the last true thing

in fact i am. and the last thing about the truth was
true.

FROM: Dawn
TO: Robert Byrnes
SUBJECT: the last true thing

some acknowledgment of nastiness would be nicely in
order. and i don't know what that last truth thing
was all about.

FROM: Robert Byrnes
TO: Dawn
SUBJECT: that last truth thing

around the time i first saw you, my vision was already
blurred by the kinetic swirl you seem to have heard
too much about; all the riotous excursions that i
assumed would end or slow down, not massively accel-
erate, in law school. it's the kind of motion that
draws you toward people with a mad passion but also
flings you into separateness.

   nastiness, you say; i hear the word but can connect it to no gesture, phrase, or thought, no sleepless sentiment recorded in the most candid 4am
state-of-being audit.

   you saw something i can't see.

   some things, though, i do know. if you have felt
hauled into a twisted stimulus-response experiment,
i would have to spill out the full inventory of my
thoughts and disembodied feelings to show you the
contrary, because i don't know where to go, what to
say. you already know everything i know about me.
you do make me try and think harder, though.

   so here it is: i repress voids, irretrievable
losses — like what it would have been had we worked
together in boston before i left for law school. had
it been you it would have been at least as grand, but
differently so. unknowably different, too. that's
life's rich pageant, again, and again, with all its
sparkle, all its colors of distress, green and grey,

all its clouds, love untold, imagined pasts, paths
overgrown, foregone, forgotten. and you do sparkle
for me, because i remember the sun shining that day
you were standing near the window.

FROM: Dawn
TO: Robert Byrnes
SUBJECT: that last truth thing

it appeared that you had joined with niccola and
focused sarcastic nastiness at my expense — whether
in a drugged-out giddiness or because you had talked
me up just a little too much to niccola and caused
some territoriality i don't know — but i respect the
great history there, and have no aspirations or
expectations to be another niccola in the book of
robert's journey. betrayal is something i am rarely
able to forgive. i find people in general inherently
disappointing. the diamonds among them that awake
the soul in unexpected ways are rare, worth culti-
vating at great effort.

I sat unable to compose a reply. I had been awake for three days, all e-
mails. Tim Apparel came to my door and said:

"Just downloaded a brief. Dumb it down a little and we're all set for
Moot Court. Bike ride?"

It was the only ride where Skyline failed to jolt me into fluid pleasure.
When we returned: *Bababooey.*

FROM: Dawn
TO: Robert Byrnes
SUBJECT: that last truth thing

what i mean is, you are a diamond in the canopy of
stars.

FROM: Robert Byrnes
TO: Dawn
SUBJECT: that last truth thing

with that, you've given me the sweet weight that
will finally hold me in sleep.

FROM: Dawn
TO: Robert Byrnes
SUBJECT: color me red...

and speechless... what's the occasion? i was just
minding my own business, not doing work...when suddenly, life (literally) becomes a bed of roses...

FROM: Robert Byrnes
TO: Dawn
SUBJECT: color me red...

do you know i had never before "sent roses"? it
seemed worse than owning a rider mower or going to
titty bars with the fellas from marketing.

FROM: Dawn
TO: Robert Byrnes
SUBJECT: !!!!

just because some cultural standards are subject to
mass consumption or veer into contrivance doesn't
mean that they are, in all situations, by nature, fraud-
ulent; put another way: things that go without saying
still gain something by being said from time to time.
      i thought one romantic gesture should beget
another:
      any free zones of time between now and summer? or
black-out dates, times that would just not be a good
time to visit (exams, etc.)?
      life is moving pretty fast, suddenly.

(and if you're lucky, maybe the last person in
the whole world you will ever want to kiss will also
be named dawn.)

FROM: Robert Byrnes
TO: Dawn
SUBJECT: ! ! ! !

all free zones, except the actual hours i have to be
in an actual exam, which would fall only at the end
of may, last week or so; even then, half of three
days; you could sleep while I take the exams. only
other binding commitment is april 14th — moot court
oral arguments.

so we'll drive down the coast, throw down the
roof, make sharp corners, take in the sights, let
the wind knot your hair.

FROM: Dawn
TO: Robert Byrnes
SUBJECT: so, come on, take my hand, let's go:

american airlines
BOSTON to SAN JOSE, 10 APRIL FLT129 arr 11:47
SAN JOSE to BOSTON, 21 APRIL FLT128 dep 1:00

Dawn did arrive in San Jose on April 10, 1997, a Thursday. I'd gotten
pulled over for speeding that morning on my bike. I was late; the gate
empty; no airplane. Flight 129 had arrived and gone. I bolted out of the
terminal, and there she was, the person I hadn't seen for two years, looking the same, better, beautiful. Then:

Last first kiss!

From the airport we go to Half Moon Bay and embrace on the
beach. Friday is a day of rest. On Saturday, we buy me a "dress shirt" that
I'll need for Moot Court oral arguments, and then go to eat, at Jack in the
Box where, during the drive-through wait, we make two joint resolutions,

each to be taken up sometime in the future, not just yet. First, we decide to stop eating meat, not for fat grams and staying svelte reasons, but for not killing animals reasons. Second, we decide to get married. And we make another decision bearing on the present: to drive south, down the coast to L.A.

We hit the road in the Beetle, up over Skyline, down to the Pacific Coast Highway. Saturday night we stay in Monterey, then, on Sunday, we continue south after buying estate jewelry. Sunday night we crash at Dawn's uncle's place in L.A. Her grandfather is there, too. Past eighty, his mind is full of youthful clarity; his disposition free of middle-aged complication and ceremony. He's the right person to tell about our wedding plans, too quickly assembled to inspire anything but words of caution from people our own age.

"So when you thinkin' of doin' it?" he asks.

During the drive south, Dawn and I'd loosely settled on a date.

"Thursday," Dawn says.

After a brief and unsatisfying descent into wedding politics—where? when? how? who's coming?—we veer into a *screw it let's just drive to Vegas* mind-set. We're dizzily tired, though. The guest list is expanding. The drive begins to look heinous. Thursday is starting to look unworkable. Uncle can't make it; mother's shocked; what about cousins, chums, siblings? Dawn's grandfather says:

"It's your thing. You two just go. That's what your grandmother and I did. I'll be around when you get back."

We decide to sleep on it.

April 14, 1997, Monday morning—early—there's a tap on my shoulder. Dawn says: "I bet you're dying to know what I'm thinking."

I already know. We drive the Beetle to the Burbank airport, get on a plane, then land. We take a cab downtown, to the Clark County Clerk's Office, then back to the Strip, the chapel at the New York–New York Hotel and Casino. After, outside the New York–New York, I call Tim Apparel and tell him.

"Ahhh, OK," Tim Apparel says. "You coming back for Moot Court?"

He thinks I'm joking. I think he's joking. Neither of us is. Dawn and I fly back, Las Vegas to San Jose. Tim Apparel picks us up at the airport. We have Moot Court oral arguments in three hours. Tim Apparel is topping out at a hundred. I unfold the Clark County certificate and hold it for him to see. The car's speed slows by half, and Tim Apparel drifts out of the passing lane. He says:

"Since I have a family on board, I guess it's time to start being careful."

We get back to the house. Moot Court oral arguments are in two hours. First we will argue the plaintiff's side, then the defendant's. Dawn sleeps as I read our brief for the first time. I wake her with a kiss, and we ride off to the Law School, Tim Apparel on his recently repaired motorcycle, Dawn and I on mine. Tim Apparel had installed a throttle while we were away.

Far from an opulent courtroom, Moot Court happens in a regular classroom, the same one I'd had Torts in. The operation is short-staffed, too, so Dawn keeps time; ten, maybe twenty, minutes for each side. Tim Apparel hands me an illegible half page of bullet-point notes. Then, Moot Court oral arguments begin:

"Hi...Robert Ebert Byrnes for plaintiff. As this Court has so eloquently stated, there can be no justice in a jurisprudence of doubt..."

Indifference becomes Tim Apparel and me. The Moot Court judges praise us for our relaxed manner and big-picture command of the case as plaintiffs. Our opponents are inept. There is now real danger that we will advance to the next round if we perform as well when we switch roles and argue the defendant's side. This can't happen. Dawn and I are leaving town tonight—our wedding night—immediately after Tim Apparel and I lose Moot Court. So we conspire to tank it. We get drunk at the campus burrito shop during the thirty-minute recess. As we argue the defendant's side, we replicate our opponents' execrable presentation in the first phase. We speak in a slow, glazed manner that accentuates the thin line between lawyerly precision and full-on retardedness. Then we commit obvious breaches of decorum while the other side is speaking. I let go an exaggerated facial response to every major legal point. Tim Apparel is in perpetual just-trying-to-position-his-ass agitation. He leans back in his chair, third-grade style, and makes a quick grab for the table to avoid tipping over. Our opponents locate the fatal flaw in our argument, rebut us thoroughly, eviscerate our logic. It seems we've neglected to mention the leading case on the issue. Tim Apparel attempts that annoying debater's pen flip, but the pen tumbles to the floor despite his lunge to catch it. I allow my laptop to speak: *Bababooey, Bababooey...*

The "judges" tell us: "Mr. Apparel and Mr. Byrnes, how you comport yourselves while opposing counsel is addressing the court is at least as important as the persuasiveness of your own legal position. This is a lesson in professional maturity well worth learning before you commence the practice of law."

We've successfully lost.

Dawn and I fly away, to Los Angeles.

Law School is over.

There was still law school's last year, but we lived in Los Angeles for my entire third year, at the base of the Hollywood Hills. Mulholland Drive, L.A.'s Skyline, is out our front door, then up. I'd fly to Stanford for finals that third year, showing up, then always returning home, the Last Place, my latest last chance, this time for good.

CHAPTER 29

THE PRINCIPAL DRAWBACK OF DITCHING

I stared into my beer, saying nothing for five minutes or more after Byrnes had finished his story. Finally, the silence went awkward. Byrnes took on an agitated, vulnerable look. "What?" he asked defensively. I shook my head incredulously, much the way that Edgar had when The Kankoos got a higher grade in Criminal Law, and answered:

"Your story has a happy ending."

He gave an understanding nod. I stared back into my beer and thought of Elise, my only hope left for a happy ending. As Byrnes himself had just said, there's no guarantee that the best thing comes around last. And Dawn herself was never more than a flickering interest to him for years. What if Elise was *my* real thing? But even the gambler in me had to realize that the chances for a happy ending to my law school days were slim. I felt more alone than ever.

I looked up from my beer and realized that I had completely ignored the last three hours of the game. The Dodgers were one out away from one of their biggest comebacks of the season. As the last Astro looked at strike three to end the game, a feeling unmistakably like jubilation pumped through me, my brooding a distant memory. Byrnes picked up on the mood shift and said:

"You need action. Motion. It's a good thing sometimes, bad thing other times. If you want steady and predictable, chase down Vicky Sentence."

I declined Byrnes's offer to rejoin Vicky and pals and headed back to Young & Mathers. I got back to the office a little after five. Byrnes had just ridden his bike home to Dawn. I shut the door to my office, pulled down the shades, and logged on. The last game of my parlay was a tight one. Tied at three in the fifth. I thought again about Elise and turned toward my phone. The red light was lit. Voice mail. A familiar feeling returned, less guilt than not wanting to be caught, watched. Or bothered. *You have one new message . . .*

My first reaction upon hearing Elise's voice on the message was relief—that no one at Young & Mathers had missed me—followed by hope—that the distance between Elise and me might be traversed. My mood shifted again.

Elise and I were through. Not really, officially, emotionally, or even sexually through. Just effectively, irreparably, and finally, through. Her voice mail said only, "Jaime, will you give me a call?" But her beaten, perhaps apologetic, definitely unwavering tone foretold the remaining sequence of events: there would be my call back, Elise's thinking-about-seeing-other-people talk, my surprisingly honest realization that it would probably be better for her to do so, several follow-up phone calls, two weeks' worth of talks in person, promises to stay in touch,

and,

eventually,

no more calls.

Ever.

That night, all of the pain of the coming weeks visited me at once. I must have picked up the phone thirty times, but I hadn't the heart, the mind, or the guts to talk. And all I could think was, if I can just win this bet, everything will be OK.

———

I entered my time with Elise when I was seventeen, clean. I left it at the age of twenty-three, just as clean. I showed up in September of 1997 for my third year of law school with one sexual partner behind me. A dubious distinction—

one of the most sexually inexperienced people at one of the most sexually barren places in the universe. But I wasn't *the* most inexperienced. That one I dated.

Rebound Girl was a 21-year-old prelaw student from Harvard undergrad. She was a nondenominational Christian with a lot of questions and too many simple answers. She was a dedicated student and a hard worker, in awe of Harvard Law School. I would tell you this was all a coincidence, but you'd argue, and I'd end up agreeing with you. She was also a virgin. Rebound Girl was a serious person, and I was trying my best not to be. But she had a weakness for expensive beer from the tap and boobs that would put Anna Nicole Smith back in a coma, so it worked. I spent my first couple dates with Rebound Girl convincing her that she was not—at least not necessarily, not yet—Rebound Girl. And she wasn't, really, or at least not necessarily. Yet. After our third date, Rebound Girl gave me The Three Choices. I forget how she put The Three Choices to me in a manner and tone that preserved the importance with which she viewed the occasion and still got the message across, but somehow she managed:

(A) Hand
(B) Tits
(C) Mouth

Apart from the glaring omission of a couple of options, it's still one of the most benevolent acts anyone has ever committed for me. It being the third date and all, and this being a linear affair, it was an easy enough choice that night: (A). Thereafter, The Choices were pure torture.

Some people are straight (C) folk all the way. Not me. (C) was nice, probably the nicest, but it guaranteed a residue of guilt, an unfortunate scar from my not-yet-distant-enough past. I also had a feeling (C) meant more to Rebound Girl than (A) and (B), probably because she once said to me "Jaime, (C) means more to me than (A) and (B)." The Kankoos was a (B) man, himself. "D'ya slap one on last night, Marquart?" was the question that greeted me every other 3:00 A.M. as I stumbled in from Rebound Girl's dorm room. And I did get my (B)s in, if for no other reason than that I had never gotten any (B)s in. But in the end, (B) too was cumbersome—messy as hell and intimately disrespectful. I usually settled for (A) and then closed my eyes and imagined it was (B) or (C). Or Elise. (A) was almost as good for me, but held all of the intimacy of a casual back rub for Rebound Girl. I liked it that way, as long as anyone can expect to like it that way.

By the middle of October, Rebound Girl and I were no more. After that I threw my line far over Harvard's walls, amassing an odd stringer of flickering interests: a flight attendant from New Jersey who spoke in a prim English accent at the most unexpected times; a soccer-groupie-gone-Harvard-groupie who hadn't yet realized she was taking an embarrassing step backward; and someone The Kankoos put in bed with me one night when he brought home one more girl than he needed from Grendel's. I kept my interest in each of them just until I'd rendered her at once mildly unattractive and nearly indispensable. Three weeks, for all three.

Then, at 9:20 P.M. on a Thursday in early November, as everyone was heading for Lincoln's Inn and from there to parts unknown, I wedged myself resolutely between the cushions of The Parlour III's couch. Everyone continued out the door, oblivious to my reticence. I intended to spend at least three or four days on that couch, and I would have, had The Kankoos not stopped short of the door.

"We'll catch up later," he shouted out the door. He reached into his humidor and pulled out the Monsignor and packed in a bowl.

"Know what's bothering you, Marquart?" he asked.

"Yep."

He handed me the Monsignor, and we smoked in silence all night. At 3:00 A.M., just as my last fragment of thought gave way to sensation, he spoke again:

"I once had a shrink tell me that addiction is a disease of perception. He claimed I had a mental defect that caused me to attribute more importance to the negative aspects of my life and less importance to the positive ones. 'But what if there really are more negatives than positives?' I asked. 'I'm talking about how you *feel*,' he said. 'If you want truth, go to a philosopher.' I went to law school instead. And I've learned that my shrink was right. We do have a disease of perception. We see everything a lot more clearly than we were ever supposed to."

"At least there's nothing left to lose," I said.

He laughed. "You're right about that. But that doesn't necessarily mean there's nothing to gain. Table games and law school are zero sum—something lost, something gained. But life is not."

"Nothing to lose, everything to gain, huh? Sounds a lot like chasing losses."

"Of course we're chasing. It's the number one sign of problem gambling."

"That's funny, I had it at number two. I always figured not quitting when you're ahead was worse."

"We've never been ahead, Marquart."

"So where to now?"

The Kankoos gazed lazily around the room, then stopped and centered his focus on the old topographical map that had decorated The Parlour's walls for the past three years.

"The Trail."

"The what?"

"The Appalachian Trail. It's a hiking path covering about two thousand miles of deep forest and mountain from Georgia to Maine. You can hike an entire day on the Trail and never come across another person. We're only a couple hours away from the New Hampshire–Maine leg—supposed to be the best part."

"Just one problem, Kankoos—it's something like zero degrees in Maine at *sea level* right now. I ain't gonna drag myself and forty pounds of supplies up a mountain in that."

"Damn, winter...well, when you lose all faith in everything and everyone around you, the world leaves you with just two roles—suicide victim or con artist."

The next morning, as all of our classmates were dragging ass to class, The Kankoos and I strolled into Cambridge Savings Bank. We opened a joint checking account with two thousand dollars in it. The Team was born. The Team's goal was as simple as any business or any scam for that matter. Take a dollar and make two. That day, we went to Foxwoods and sat down at a $25 blackjack table. It was a busy table on a busy day. Each of us cashed in $1,000 and started gambling two $25 hands simultaneously.

Blackjack is generally not a good basis for a business. The rules are stacked against the player, and it has a guaranteed negative return in the long run. But The Kankoos and I were not living in the long run. We also were not playing the same game as everyone else, though it was hard to tell the difference. No one in the casino ever noticed that The Kankoos and

I increased our bets only when there were more tens and aces in the deck than usual; or that we won a little more of our bigger bets than the smaller ones; or that we were terribly slow players with the bladders of three-year-olds that demanded frequent attention every time there were too few tens and aces left in the deck. Had they noticed, they might have figured it didn't pay to keep us as customers. Then again, in the scheme of things, we didn't matter. And we still had to be lucky. That day we were. After three hours, we reached our modest goal. The Team cashed out with $2,500, up $500, plus comps (about $300 worth of meals, hotel rooms, and merchandise).

For the next few months, the Team continued winning, every so often taking its show farther down the road, with stops in Montreal, Vegas, and Atlantic City, returning to Harvard for the occasional exam. There were also nongambling stops—Vail, Los Angeles, and New York. Days faded into months. Our travels didn't promise meaning, nor did they deliver it, but they guaranteed distraction. They also guaranteed movement, though to where was never certain. Only my direction was apparent. I was spiraling downward.

The Team, though, was experiencing a boon. At the end of our first six months of operation, around the first of May, our funds stood at $10,000. Comp was in full flow. Steak dinners, hotel suites, gallons of beer, and a potpourri of other chemicals filled our days and nights. What started out as a distraction had us thinking there could be something lasting, if not meaningful, in it all. Maybe even a postponement of our looming law jobs. There's such a thing as professional gamblers, after all. They wouldn't make movies about them if there weren't. It seemed like our streak might never end.

In three strange days, it would all be gone.

Day One, a Monday, back in Cambridge: The Kankoos and I had just returned home from another profitable tour stop in Atlantic City. The end of law school and exams were a few weeks away, but that was not the occasion for our return. Winter had finally succumbed to spring, and the next day Brian, The Dynamo, The Kankoos, and I would prepare for a four-day hike on the Appalachian Trail, our final trip together before exams, graduation, and, eventually, new lives in different cities. As we were unpacking, The Kankoos got a call on his cell phone from a friend of his who knew some guy who knew some other guy who supposedly overheard some guy at a poker game say that a publicly traded company was going to come out Wednesday with breaking news that could put its stock at somewhere around six dollars a share. The beautiful part was the current price: nineteen cents. We put half of our nest egg into the stock. If the rumor were true, we would turn $5,000 into $150,000. Real money. With our stock order placed, the Team was done gambling for the day.

Day One Closing Balance: $10,000.

Day Two, a Tuesday: I was awakened at 7:00 A.M. by the sounds of The Kankoos rummaging through his closet for hiking gear. We were still two days away from setting out for the Trail. The Appalachian Trail was the only thing I had ever seen The Kankoos prepare for with both care and anxiety. He effused a hope that day I had never seen in him, and I think I know why. In an integrated world, the Appalachian Trail promised the impossible—separation. That was the first day we didn't lay down a bet of some kind in more than a year.

The Team did make some gains, though. The Company's stock had risen to fifty cents, apparently based on the same rumor we had heard, more than doubling our $5,000 stake. We expected even better news the next day. On Thursday, The Kankoos, Brian, The Dynamo, and I would spend the night in New Hampshire. On Friday, we'd hit the Trail. Rather than wait around in Cambridge for two days, The Kankoos and I decided to head back to Atlantic City. First, we checked our student mailboxes.

Walking into Harkness Commons, where our student mailboxes were, a familiar feeling overcame me. It was the same feeling I felt in first grade, sitting behind a tree in the sandlot, knowing that I was about to confront my bully. The Kankoos, too, appeared to be confronting his bully, and he, too, looked outmatched. But he was braced for a fight and determined to go the distance. The Kankoos was no stranger to institutionalized bullying. The surface cause of our dread was simple—exposure, coming in the form of a note from a teacher demanding that we attend or fail or, worse yet, from the registrar, saying it was too late for last-minute makeups. We each avoided eye contact as we weaved in and out of people on the way to our boxes. With not-so-steady hands, we sifted quickly through the crinkled mound of flyers and advertisements, stopping only for the occasional formal-looking envelope with return address Harvard Law School. Each time, it turned out to be something from the financial aid office or registrar requesting some insignificant administrative information. This time, like the others, there were no demands. Still, ditching, like any con game, doesn't come without its drawbacks. Dread is one of them. Granted, we felt it only occasionally, on the slopes of Vail or in a complimentary suite at the top of Trump Plaza. But it was real, nonetheless. Ditching isn't for everybody.

"Hey Marquart! Kankoos!"

I turned around and saw Edgar. He was hanging out in the Commons with Tom O'Toule and Vicky Sentence, who now insisted upon being addressed as "Victoria."

"What's up, Edgar?"

"Not much. By the way, it just so happens Fed Lit is meeting right now, and, as you can see, I'm not exactly compiling a stellar attendance record this semester. Catch my drift?"

"So you're the big slacker now, huh, Edgar?" The Kankoos asked.

"Oh yeah!"

"Great! You up for another trip to A.C.?"

"Maybe maybe," he said with a quick half-smile. "I'll, uh, give you a call if I get free. If you don't hear from me, uh, don't wait up. See ya!"

Edgar returned to O'Toule and Sentence, who nodded back at us with a tacit, peaceful understanding of some sort. They wore leisurely, rested smiles that contrasted with our weary, ragged look.

Back in the comfort of The Parlour, I dissected the scene:

"What is it about coming back here?"

"What do you mean?"

"You know, that feeling."

"The fear of getting caught is part of it," he said, anticipating my best guess. "But that's not the principal drawback."

"Then what is?"

"It's so simple, it's no wonder we overlooked it. Every time we came back to check our mail, those envelopes from Harvard used to be the thing I dreaded most. But now, it's all of the flyers and announcements we skim over that give me the shakes. It's not the fear of getting caught or the dread of obligation that makes me feel so heavy. It's the fear of what I might have missed. Living fast doesn't eliminate opportunity cost."

"Are you saying we shouldn't have ditched?"

"No such thing as a choice *not* to ditch, only *what* to ditch. We're always ditching something."

I stuffed a few clean T-shirts and a three-inch stack of mail into my bag. Then The Kankoos and I loaded the car for the Appalachian Trail. Five hours later, we were asleep in Atlantic City. Edgar never called.

Day Two Closing Balance: $18,158.

Day Three, a Wednesday in Atlantic City: At 10:00 A.M., the Company came out with its news—a few paltry contracts worth less all together than The Team itself. The Company's stock price dropped down to six cents before our frantic market order to sell the stock was executed. Six cents. A penny more than a nickel. The $13,000 worth of stock we'd started the day with was now worth a little over $1,500.

After broker's fees, the Team's funds stood at $6,500. We hit the tables. Chasing like never before. We rolled up to the high-stakes blackjack pit, cashed in $6,500, and started playing hundred-dollar hands. We were the only ones in the pit. Atlantic City didn't have double-deck or single-deck games, which were easier to count. But the six-deck game drew less attention and allowed for greater bet increases when the count was good. In retrospect, we had grown far too comfortable and used a far too transparent cover strategy even for Atlantic City. Still, we continued to build small profits for the first fifteen minutes. We were up about $500 when our dealer took a break. In all my visits, I had never seen his stoic and silent replacement. She beat all our hands for the first ten deals. We had $5,000 left. We increased our bets to $200. She busted one hand, then took the next eight. We were down to $2,200. But the count was in our favor, so we bet the rest on the next deal. We each got what we hoped for—two tens, twenty. The dealer had a six showing. We waved off our hands, and she turned over what we thought she had—a ten, for a total of sixteen. The Kankoos and I looked at each other and smiled. She took another card. A five. Twenty-one. She smiled. We Comchecked. $5,000. We went back to the same table, out of principle. We lost it all inside of five minutes. In less than thirty minutes, we had blown more than $11,500. $23,000 and change for the morning.

There have been times when I was so angry at myself, the House, and everyone around that I wanted to toss the table in the air and scream. This was not one of those times. The Kankoos and I just sat there and laughed. Whatever we had been chasing for the last several months had just gotten away for good. After about fifteen minutes, the pit boss asked us to place a bet or move on. It was a kind fuck you—we left with two comps to the best steakhouse in the place, aka the Cold Comfort Buffet. At 3:00 P.M. on Day Three, The Team's balance was negative $5,000. The Kankoos was giddy.

"What are you so fucking happy for, Kankoos? We've got exams in a week, and I don't even remember what classes I'm in. I'm in constant fear of checking my mailbox. If we do graduate, we've got the Bar Exam in a couple of months, and we don't know shit about the law. If we pass the bar, our reward is a dull job with long hours, Zero Summer bosses and Cold Stover colleagues. And we have no choice but to take the job—we're each a hundred grand in the hole. We're like the executive who traps himself in his career with a new house and a wife. Except? No wife! No house! We're fucked!"

The Kankoos laughed harder.

"Well, Marquart, everybody I know who isn't dead yet has one of two things in common—something to look forward to or something to worry about. Sounds like you've got it covered. That's your problem, by the way. You've been talking a bunch of shit the last few months about your disdain for convention, and you still can't go all the way. You'll let a naked girl rub her ass over your Levi's for half an hour, but you wouldn't dare pay her to screw you. And you probably couldn't even tell me what the difference is between the two, except that someone once told you having sex for money was wrong. You're full of have-to's and can't's, all of which are in your head. There's no debtor's prison in America, Marquart."

"I never judged you . . ."

"So? I'm judging you. If you were propelled by some deep belief, I could forgive you. If you still had your Girlfriend or your God Excuse, I'd leave you alone. But you're motivated by nothing but a compulsion left over from institutions you no longer believe in. I wouldn't even bother with you if you weren't so close to figuring it out. You can do what you want, but I'm going out with a bang. I've got at least $500 of available credit left, and I plan to blow it all on hard drugs, booze, and maybe a little poon. Tomorrow, I'm heading to Nature, to sum it all up with my friends. I hope you will be with me."

Back in the hotel room, I took some financial stock:

Checking Account Balance	$50.40
Savings Account Balance	5.00
Citibank MasterCard Available Credit	22.00
Citibank Visa Available Credit	0.00
Advanta Gold Available Credit	200.00
Stashed Cash	120.00

About $400 in available cash flow from all sources. I still had three weeks before I flew to California. Things would be tight, but I would make it. I had been in worse financial straits. But man, it's hard to go backward. The Kankoos and I lit up the last of our pot and phoned room service for two bottles of Scotch. The Scotch was still free—comps from our stellar play.

By 1:00 A.M., the Scotch and pot were gone. The Kankoos called three escort services and charged the fees to one of his credit cards. "Need options," he explained. We ordered two more bottles of Scotch. At 3:00 A.M., a woman knocked at our door. She said her name was Lola. Lola had long brown hair and olive skin. She was probably twenty-five, but looked thirty-five. Lola had a broad, but fit, frame. Her voice was deep and raspy, but not the voice of a smoker, not a cigarette smoker, anyway. It was not feminine. After watching her for half an hour, I was convinced she was a man. I kept trying to whisper my suspicions to The Kankoos, who was completely unaware of what I was saying. Apparently, I was not so tactful. Lola invited me into the bathroom, pulled down her pants in front of me, and took a piss. Sitting down. Without a dick. My mistake. She got up, pulled out a small bag of white powder, and asked if I wanted "some blow." I said no thanks and stepped outside. The Kankoos stepped inside. A few minutes later, The Kankoos and Lola left together.

I was alone. Free of distraction for the first time in six months. It was 4:00 A.M. I had not slept for more than thirty hours. Yet I could not rest. For the first time in my life, I begged for ignorance. The more I remembered, the more I drank. The more I thought, the more I smoked. I've heard it said that all animals have an innate tendency to avoid pain. For me, prolonged exposure reversed the valence. I wanted more.

There was a knock. I hopped up and swung open the door, expecting to see The Kankoos. Instead, I saw myself. She was thirty years old, drug-addicted, and named Chloe. I didn't know anything about Chloe, but she knew me. I didn't care about Chloe and she didn't care about me. On the margin, I didn't harm Chloe and she didn't harm me. We were both too busy harming ourselves. Chloe would not remember me. I would not be able to forget Chloe. Sometimes I wish I could.

Chloe stood about five-feet-seven and could not have weighed more than a buck-o-five dripping wet. She had dark, straight, shoulder-length hair and light green eyes that she fought to keep open. Betty Page on heroin. She was beautiful once, just not anymore.

"Youse guys call for a girl?"

"Uh, yeah. Actually, no. My friend called. Two hours ago. He's gone."

"Of course, your friend. You want me to leave, honey?"

Since Rebound Girl and the handful of others, I had taken sex out of my life. After six months, it was apparent to me that that tack wasn't going to last. Then I had a revelation: if I couldn't take the sex out of life, I'd take the life out of sex.

I didn't want Chloe to leave. But I still hadn't learned the money talk. It was like going to the casino for the first time. The hardest part was the ritual—how to place the bet, how to take another card or stand, how to color up.

"I feel stupid asking you this. But, uh, how does this go?"

"You gimme a hundred bucks, then I suck your dick, then you fuck me."

I doubt the words *if you know what I mean* ever completed one of Chloe's sentences. *This is perfect*, I thought. Having sex with Chloe would be like having sex alone. Taking the life out of sex. Despite a bottle of Scotch, three bowls, and thirty hours of sleep deprivation, I managed a boner. Then, midway through the blow job, Chloe stopped and walked over to the corner.

"Sorry, honey. I got gas. I just had seafood with my boyfriend. Happens every time."

Somehow, she managed to cram three incredibly unappealing thoughts into one sentence: seafood, boyfriend, farts.

I think she was being polite. She walked back over and continued as though nothing had happened. I was no longer interested. By then, though, it wasn't about pleasure, it was about finishing.

As I pressed on, I fought with futility to block out all details. But her body bore the artifacts of humanity. A tattoo reading *Bobby* suggested girlfriend. A series of marks and indentations in her pelvic area suggested mother. A mole on a breast was a reminder of individuality. No one else in the world had that exact mole in that exact place. I closed my eyes. When I opened them I noticed that Chloe was taking great efforts to cover up her breasts, which were small but unusually shapely. In spite of her current job and her likely history, she was insecure about her body. Her embarrassment aroused a complementary emotion in me—the desire to comfort, to affirm. This was not my place. These things didn't go together. I couldn't go on.

"I'm sorry," I said.

"No refund, sweetheart."

She left. I laid there motionless for ten minutes. Then a thought entered my head. Something to worry about. I walked into the bathroom, filled the rubber with water, squeezed it thoroughly, and felt the outside for moisture. It was dry. Then I began to throw up. I rinsed my mouth out with Johnny Walker, and then had a couple more drinks. You know those scenes in the movie where the person hops in the shower, trying to wash off the filthiness? Never happened. Anybody who's been there knows damn well that a shower won't do any good. A clean body is the least appropriate accessory to a filthy soul.

I went back to bed and laid there, staring at the ceiling, unable to sleep. I thought I should not be alone.

I heard the sound of a key in the door. The Kankoos was back. He was bleeding.

"What happened to you?"

"We took a cab to some bar. Then I gave Lola my last hundred bean to go buy some stuff. Ten minutes later, I went into the bar to check on her and I couldn't find her anywhere. I hope she's alright."

"Uh . . . I'm sure she's fine. But what happened to you?"

"Oh, the blood? Two women beat the shit out of me. They gave me a ride home, though."

"Cool."

"What d'you do?"

"Fucked a seafood-farting whore, then hurled."

"Good one. Come on, let's get out of here. We gotta meet the crew in New Hampshire tonight. We'll need some rest before the Trail."

By 8:00 A.M., we were on our way to New Hampshire. I was silent the whole ride. The Kankoos was exhausted to the point of delirium, but euphoric. He wore a Mona Lisa smile I had seen only once, when the Dalai Lama came to Harvard. The Kankoos was rising. I had not had enough. At that moment, I understood why Foucault cut himself. Out of boredom I opened my bag and went through the pile of mail I had picked up in Cambridge two days earlier. One piece of mail stood out. It was from the Law Access Group. The Access Group offers $5,000 loans to third-year law students to help them get by during the three months of studying for and taking the state bar exam. To ensure that the funds are spent appropriately, the Access Group waits until the last month of school to dole the checks out. Exactly one month too early in my case.

"Where are we, Kankoos?"

"New York."

"You gonna take 95 through Connecticut?"

"Why?"

"I want you to drop me off somewhere."

"Goddamn, Marquart. Haven't you had enough? I thought you were out of money. What about the Trail?"

"Fuck the Trail. That's *your* pilgrimage."

The Kankoos understood. He was never one to do anything he didn't want to do, which meant that he was never one to ask the same of a friend. He was noticeably deflated, but he didn't argue.

It was noon when The Kankoos dropped me off at Foxwoods. "Remember cover strategies," he said. I nodded. He drove away, toward New Hampshire.

Inside Foxwoods, I went through the necessary bullshit to cash a third-party check for $5,000, which actually isn't that much bullshit if you're a good customer. Then I checked into a room and crashed. I woke at 11:00 P.M., my face glued to the sheets by a batterlike substance. I would have that shower now. I shaved for the first time in four days, tugging masochistically with my old razor at hairs that had grown beyond the comfortable length. After that, I brushed my teeth three or four times and yanked out twenty or thirty nose hairs. I put on my only suit, misted it with Davidoff Cool Water to cover up embedded cigar smoke, and headed down to the bar. The only other people at the bar at 11:45 on a Thursday night were a supposed flight attendant from Los Angeles and a friend of hers I recognized as a waitress at the Mohegan Sun, another casino down the road. They were looking for conversation and I was too apathetic to stay quiet. After a few minutes of unremarkable discourse, I asked them, "Wanna watch me turn $5,000 into $10,000 or lose my ass trying?"

"Sure," they said.

And that's how I got here: Foxwoods, 2:00 A.M., Friday morning, staring at a fifteen against the dealer's ten with twenty-five hundred on the line, another twenty-five hundred already gone. If the possibilities are complex, the choice isn't. If I hit, I probably lose; if I stand on fifteen, I almost certainly lose.

Before I make my move, I lean back and exhale. They'll give me as much time as I need. But I am not so much thinking about this blackjack hand as trying to figure out why it doesn't matter to me anymore. I run through the last three years, searching for a unifying theme. The only one that comes to mind: loss. Religion, Harvard, True Love. All have disappointed. Then, suddenly the most profound thought I've had in all my three years of law school enters my brain, by nothing more than impulse. The thought, a two-word question:

So what? So I admitted to myself that I never really believed in forces I never really believed in. So I no longer hear voices that aren't there or feel guilty for doing things when I can't explain why they were wrong. So Harvard isn't nearly as difficult as I thought it would be, nor does it possess any higher purpose. So I stuck with the first person I laid a lot longer than I should have, out of fear and weakness. So religion, the law, and my love for Elise were intrinsically no more valuable than anything else I might choose to dedicate my time to. So what?

There is an optimistic corollary to nothingness that I have overlooked until now: anything I choose to dedicate my time to is no *less* valuable than religion, the law, Elise. *I* decide my purpose. But what purpose is left? What could move me as those things once had?

Now, I know. In all of my zeal to raze convention, I just kept believing that your true love has to be someone you fuck. I think back to the conversation I had with The Kankoos on the ride back from Atlantic City during our first year. I was embarrassed then to assign friendship as my highest purpose. But now I understand that the only wrong answer to the Purpose Question is a dishonest one. The only honest answer for me lies with my friends, whom I have abandoned. Now I understand why The Kankoos was hopeful the night I broke up with Rebound Girl; and why he was rising just a few hours earlier on his, our, way to the Appalachian Trail; and why he was uncharacteristically deflated when I left him for Foxwoods; and why he dropped me off anyway. The Kankoos had found what moved him— unconditional acceptance and love that was freely chosen out of strength, not given or clinged to out of weakness.

My entire law school experience has come to this: learning to say "I love you" to a friend.

Suddenly $5,000, even $2,500, has meaning. It means a phone call, a cab ride, a bus ticket, and four days' worth of trail mix and dehydrated hiker's meals. It means one last weekend atop the world with my friends. But in blackjack, as in life, there are no do-overs. I still have a hand to play. With two bad choices you either go with reason or fly with passion. Even in my darkest hour, I've been one to stick with the odds. I have been in this situation enough times before, and I know what must be done. With a stoic face that would make Bob Stupak proud, I press a relaxed right hand down in front of the little circle in front of me and take my card. This one's for you, Edgar.

Six. Twenty-one. The dealer turns over what I thought he'd had all along. A ten. Not good enough tonight. I color up, gathering my winnings more deliberately than my inner tempo would dictate. I am back exactly where I started. At last, I have had enough.

As I get up to leave, I am presented with my last meaningful choice of law school. The two women who have been sharing in the suspense are offering their congratulations. The one who claims to be a flight attendant wants to know if I'd like to go smoke a little. The other is talking about hanging out for a while in my room. My thoughts gyrate with erotic images of Stanford Halloween parties and Massachusetts governor's offices. But I just miss my friends.

The first day on the Appalachian Trail has been hell. After hiking all day, The Kankoos, Brian, The Dynamo, and I realized we made a wrong turn. It's easy enough to do—the Appalachian Trail is at times hardly a trail at all, marked only by a stray splash of paint on an occasional tree or cairn. A day of fruitless exertion had landed us at the ugly edge of a highway, two miles from our original starting point. We hitchhiked back into town, defeated. Back at the motel, everyone agrees it is time to quit. Then, The Kankoos puts down the guidebook he's been studying for the last hour and smiles. He utters a one-word sentence, a name:

"Mahoosac."

The Mahoosac Notch is the Appalachian Trail's most difficult leg. It usually takes a day's hike just to reach it, but The Kankoos has found an old mill road that will take us to a trail that is three miles from the foot of the Mahoosac. We will make up the lost day and reach camp by nightfall. There is a collective "No fucking way."

Two dissent. Tomorrow, The Kankoos and I will hike the Mahoosac. The others will take a less dangerous route and try to meet us at the top of the mountain.

The Mahoosac is as perilous and draining as its reputation. People have died here. The Mahoosac delivers pain, but to survivors it also grants peace. To the fortunate it inspires revelation. We step on a clear peak. It occurs to me vividly, explicitly: I don't want to die. This is law school's endpoint, with feeling. Free and clean, atop the beauty, physically spent and mentally liberated, I am at last separate.

The Kankoos picks up a book and begins to read. The book is *Human, All Too Human*. Nietzsche. The same book The Kankoos tried to give me two years ago. The Kankoos continues: "The decisive event for a free spirit is a great separation, and before it, he was probably all the more a bound spirit and seemed to be chained forever to his post . . . "9

As The Kankoos reads, I know now that I have finally had my great separation. I razed every last wall that contained me, and Nietzsche will

---

9. He continued: "What binds most firmly? . . . With men of a high and select type, it will be their obligations: that awe which befits the young, their diffidence and delicacy before all that is time-honored and dignified . . . for the shrine where they learned to worship. . . . For such bound people, the great separation [Löslosung] comes suddenly, like the shock of an earthquake . . . a violent, dangerous curiosity for an undiscovered world flames up and flickers in all the senses. . . .

"A sudden horror and suspicion of that which it loved; a lightning flash of contempt toward that which was its "obligation" . . . perhaps a blush of shame at its most recent act, and at the same time, jubilation that it was done . . . such bad and painful things are part of the history of the great separation. . . . Loneliness surrounds him . . . but who today knows what loneliness is?"

please forgive me if I had a hell of a lot of fun along the way. I went to Harvard fearful of its scorning faces and unseen forces, limping through it, for a time, on unseen crutches. I begin to open my mouth to speak the words *I am happy* when The Kankoos chides me into silence. He is not finished.

He goes on reading: "It is still a long way from this morbid isolation, from the desert of these experimental years, to that enormous, overflowing certainty and health which cannot do without even illness itself."

True enough, but I am moving.

As The Kankoos and I descend the summit and take the two-mile stroll to our campsite on Spec Lake, he shakes his head and says:

"There is no way Brian and The Dynamo are ever going to make it this far."

I nod.

But as we're approaching the campsite, the sound of familiar voices quickens our pace. Brian and The Dynamo have not only made it, they've beaten us there. At night, we sit around the campfire listening to the tunes that have become the soundtrack of our lives and wishing it will never end. There are no law books, no alcohol, no drugs, no parlays, no prostitutes, no dice, no cards. Just macaroni, beef jerky, and shared laughter. I tap The Kankoos on the shoulder and say:

"You know, Nietzsche was wrong about one thing. We are not alone."

POSTSCRIPT | **OH YEAH . . .**

Third year, Dawn and I lived in Los Angeles with our three dogs, Tundra, Glacier, and Caille. I worked at Young & Mathers and biked some with Bob Young, a pretty good trial lawyer and a kick-ass rider, especially on the uphill.

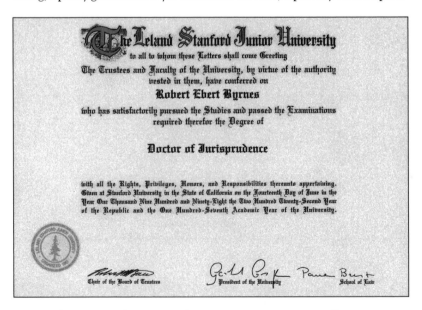

The Leland Stanford Junior University
to all to whom these Letters shall come Greeting
The Trustees and Faculty of the University, by virtue of the authority
vested in them, have conferred on
Robert Ebert Byrnes
who has satisfactorily pursued the Studies and passed the Examinations
required therefor the Degree of

Doctor of Jurisprudence

with all the Rights, Privileges, Honors, and Responsibilities thereunto appertaining.
Given at Stanford University in the State of California on the Fourteenth Day of June in the
Year One Thousand Nine Hundred and Ninety-Eight the Two Hundred Twenty-Second Year
of the Republic and the One Hundred-Seventh Academic Year of the University.

Chair of the Board of Trustees   President of the University   School of Law

330

Dawn did get into the movie business. I graduated. Not long after Stanford mailed me my diploma, I ran into Jaime Marquart in Long Beach, where we'd both just finished taking the California Bar Exam. He was heading for Vegas. A few months later, we started working at Young & Mathers full-time. We cut out one afternoon to Hank's American Bar and Grill and decided to write a book together. After we finished the book, I came out of bike messenger retirement. My job today: doing bike deliveries for Young & Mathers; some law on the side, too. Best job I've ever had.

—reb

The hard hand I feared never came upon me in my last days at Harvard. In fact, I graduated with honors. Cum laude, they called it. It sounds cooler than it is—I was only in the top half of my class. A few months after that, while ditching work with Byrnes, he and I started talking about loves past and people we were surprised we both knew. It sounded like a good story, so we wrote it all down.

—jm

VNIVERSITAS HARVARDIANA

CANTABRIGIAE IN REPVBLICA MASSACHVSETTENSIVM

P RAESES et Socii Collegii Harvardiani consentientibus honorandis ac reverendis Inspectoribus in comitiis sollemnibus

JAIME WAYNE MARQUART

ad gradum Juris Doctoris cum laude

admiserunt eique dederunt et concesserunt omnia insignia et iura quae ad hunc gradum spectant.

In cuius rei testimonium litteris Academiae sigillo munitis die IIII Iunii anno Domini MDCCCCLXXXXVIII Collegiique Harvardiani CCCLXII auctoritate rite commissa nomina subscripserunt.

Neil L. Rudenstine
PRAESES

Robert Charles Clark
DECANVS ORDINIS IVRISCONSVLTORVM

ACKNOWLEDGMENTS

de-b
Erik Feig
Jimmy Vines
The Kankoos and Tim Apparel

Shelley Holt

Renaissance Books:
Richard F. X. O'Connor, Amanda Pisani, Arthur Morey, Lisa-Theresa Lenthall, Kimbria Hays, Michael Dougherty, Kathryn Mills, Jens Hussey, Jennifer Yuan, and Bill Hartley

RAS, AWU, and JBQ

Special thanks to: Matt Krupnick, Marc Nemer, Mike Hazen, Dan Mendelsohn, Ted Weesner, Jose Juves, Eric Bjorgum, Anne Kriel, Julie Mehegan, Mike Webb, Bruce Bogle, Chris Dingman, Shon Morgan, Chris Grant, Vince Grant, John Purcell, Jon Corey, Ru, Bethany LaFlam, Ozzie, Jay D'elia, and L.A.'s bike messengers—Jimmy, Douglas, Melissa, Joe, Gonzo, David, Scott, Randy, and everyone under the bridge; 10-4

ABOUT THE AUTHORS

JAIME MARQUART grew up in Eagle Lake, Texas, with very little to do. When asked to describe his childhood, his mother said, "The boy just kinda stared out the window a whole lot. We figured him for slow." When he was sixteen, Jaime looked up from the window and went off to college, where he eventually graduated first in his class at the University of Texas at Austin. He then went to Harvard Law School, where he became bad with money and stopped believing in things. He wrote this bio, then changed all of the I's to he's, except for the ones he changed to Jaime because the editor said too many pronouns are confusing.

ROBERT EBERT BYRNES grew up in New Hampshire and attended Dartmouth, Brown, and Harvard before becoming a Boston bike messenger. For three years he wrote speeches for former Massachusetts Governor Bill Weld and then attended Stanford Law School. Byrnes currently lives in Los Angeles where he works as a bike messenger and lawyer.